Top Co ║█║██║█║███║██║║█ ʼes Praise
Your Surv D0958935 *Killing You!*

"Compelling and highly engaging reading, this remarkable book is for everyone who is willing to rethink their most basic assumptions about what works in business and life. It is a *"must read"* for all leaders and individuals who want to thrive with abundant, enduring success in our rapidly changing world."

Rick S. Braddock
Chairman, MidOcean Partners
Former Chairman/CEO, Priceline.com and
former President, Citibank

"*Extraordinary.* I loved this book! I defy anyone who has worked in the corporate world to not identify with one or all of the players. In fact, it is impossible to read this without reflecting on "What does this mean to me?" Unlike the typical dry business book that gives you lists of things to do, theorems and rules, this is an absorbing story that actually gets to the root of the problems you face. The solutions are not likely what you think they are. The concrete and practical principles presented are natural and memorable and penetrate your mind and emotions. They hold true in life as well as work. There is exceptional value here for *everyone.*"

Bill White
Professor, Northwestern University
Former Chairman/CEO, Bell and Howell Company

"*Outstanding!* This exceptional book provides eight simple yet profound tools for elevating your performance at work and your experience of life. If you read only one book this year, make it this one. What you discover about yourself within these pages, will surprise you and change your life forever."

Rob Davidson
Vice President, Sales and Marketing, Quixtar, Inc.

"*Your Survival Strategies are Killing You!* masterfully connects readers with their own potential by skillfully including them as participants in a compelling human tale. Author, facilitator, and coach, Martha Borst, captivates from the outset by inviting her readers along for the ride as her four protagonists experience their own journey of self mastery. It isn't long before you realize she is talking directly to *you*! As the drama unfolds, the power of these principles to clear up many of one's problems and the wisdom to create an exceptionally successful life become impossible to ignore. I can't think of one person who wouldn't benefit from reading this book."

Janice Jackson
Executive Director, Innovations
AstraZeneca Pharmaceuticals LP

"Your Survival Strategies are Killing You! is a fast and fascinating read full of great lessons. The story will teach you what you need to know **today** to help you and your team be more successful. Martha brings clarity to issues that we struggle with in business but should not. Her approach has changed the way I deal with people everyday. This is a book you will want to share with everyone you know. I guarantee you, one copy won't be enough!"

John Parker
President, Amway Japan

"Your Survival Strategies are Killing You! will be required reading for anyone I work with. In these pages, Martha captures and demystifies the beliefs that you *think* will drive your success and ultimate happiness, but she shows you that in order to grow into your potential, you have to first look at yourself; your self-perception and your self-seeking behaviors. Can a single book fix all of your company's problems? Probably not. But can you fix all of your company's problems without the principles in *this book*? Definitely not!"

Beto Guajardo
Vice President, Strategy Planning and New Business Development
Avon Products, Inc.

"Martha Borst's practical and profound voice is calling in a wilderness of high achievers stymied in their search for fulfillment and effectiveness. She's urging us to pay attention to our own lives in a way few people do. *Your Survival Strategies Are Killing You!* is a simple, straightforward story that opens the door of self-awareness behind which personal freedom and professional success are found. *A rare "must" read*; accessible across the organizational chart, this remarkable book invites everyone to take ownership of their individual and collective destinies!"

David Luckes
President/CEO, Greater Saint Louis Community Foundation

"The message of *Your Survival Strategies are Killing You!* works universally. I put the teachings at the heart of three different companies, across four cities and two continents. It's been the difference between success and mediocrity of my teams, and it's brought personal fulfillment and joy to my own daily life. Living the book is a must for any entrepreneur eager to compete in the fast-changing global economy."

Dr. Elvir Causevic
Founder and President, Everest Biomedical Instruments, BrainScope
Company, Inc. and Inspire LLC
J.W. Gibbs Assistant Professor, Yale University

"I have had the privilege of actually attending a Martha Borst course similar to the one described in this book. I can unequivocally say that every leader who wants an empowered, accountable, aligned, excited, productive team should read this immediately – and then give copies to everyone. Like her course, the experience delivered in the reading of this book is both enlightening and entertaining – and ultimately a springboard for effecting powerful organizational change."

Mark Frost
Chief Operating Officer, SABA

"Martha provided me a much needed "life-jacket" as I was "drowning" in my personal and professional life. Through her mentoring style and friendship she had me understand who I am and how I could gain control of my life. Thanks to Martha I have gained balance in my life..... I am again excited about work and the interactions with my colleagues, and more importantly I have reconnected with my family. I strongly recommend you embrace and commit to Martha's principles; they will help you understand the world around you and will show you how you can be in control of your destiny."

Michael Norris
Chief Marketing Officer, Gold Canyon Candles, L.L.C.

"Martha Borst knows how to achieve SUCCESS! As her personal physician for several years, I observed her doing so in spite of her formidable health problems with rheumatoid arthritis which she faced with a positive attitude, grace, and courage. Reading and studying *Your Survival Strategies are Killing You!* will help you develop new and important strategies for overcoming your own obstacles while achieving your goals. I wish that I had read it twenty years ago!"

Richard Brasington, MD
Associate Professor of Medicine
Washington University School of Medicine

"*Your Survival Strategies Are Killing You!* is the single best approach to effective team building and personal empowerment that I have ever observed. As an HR professional, I enthusiastically endorse this book as a valued resource tool. Martha Borst masterfully makes the learning process easy by using an entertaining and engrossing story to reveal a set of guidelines that can transform not only your corporate culture but your life as well."

Rodney Gee
Principal, Human Resources, Edward Jones Investments

"Operating effectively in large, matrixed organizations -- particularly in competitive and rapidly-changing markets -- requires a level of teamwork and positive discipline that don't evolve by themselves. The frameworks Martha Borst delivers in these pages create a cultural context for empowered, accountable teams. As she says, in every encounter and with every decision you make, you either choose to generate reasons, or results. This book generates results."

Mark Lange
National Vice President, Human Capital Management Solutions
SAP Americas

"*Your Survival Strategies Are Killing You!* is a great read. Its fictional style hammers home perspectives and lessons that we need. It teaches people how to collaborate more effectively and how to use wisdom to become more productive, impactful, and happy. What a book! Not only is it entertaining but it provides valuable tools that create the kind of behavior and thinking that we need in our fast changing global innovation economy."

Ken Harrington
Managing Director, Senior Lecturer
Washington University Center for Entrepreneurial Studies

"Having sponsored a team who participated in one of Martha's courses, similar to the one depicted in this book, I was able to actually see the personal growth experienced by my colleagues, as well as myself, over our three days with her as our coach. The valuable insights she shares in *Your Survival Strategies are Killing You!* opened our eyes and helped each of us to take a fresh look at our attitudes and behaviors. Everyone would benefit from reading this book closely and then refreshing themselves with it every six months!"

Craig Witcher
Vice President/Corporate Controller/General Tax Counsel
Alticor, Inc

Your Survival Strategies
Are Killing You!

The Eight Principles You *Must* Follow
To Thrive in Life and Work

STEPS TO SUCCESS

by

MARTHA BORST

Avista Press

Healdsburg, California

Published by:

Avista Press

1083 Vine Street

Suite 515

Healdsburg, California 95448

www.avistapress.com

email: info@avistapress.com

Phone: 888-433-1083

ISBN - 13: 978-0-9791561-0-6
ISBN - 10: 0-9791561-0-6

Library of Congress Control Number: 2007924376

Printed in the United States of America

10 9 8 7 6 5 4 3 2

*This book is dedicated to
my two greatest teachers...*

*my mother, Mary, and
my daughter, Gabi*

I give you both my boundless love and appreciation

In Acknowledgment...

*"Adam had the best of it all. When he said something, he knew
no one had said it before."*
Mark Twain

As I review this book and think of all the people I want to acknowledge for the support and guidance they have shown me
throughout my life, I am overwhelmed with gratitude. I truly believe no book, or in fact anything of significance, is accomplished
alone. We are all a product of each other. So it is with this book.

Over the years many, many people have influenced me. I have
read books; taken courses; listened to great teachers; and watched
and learned from my friends, family, neighbors, co-workers, clients,
loved ones, students, and strangers. With each encounter I have tak-
en away something precious that has become "mine." Although all
my thoughts may not have originated with me, they have become
a part of me and been a seed for further thought. In the process of
acknowledging the sources and resources of the thinking that are
contained on the following pages, I am fully aware that none of it is
truly original, nor do I claim it to be. I humbly realize that some of
what I have stumbled upon "on my own" and present to you here
has in fact been a part of many ancient philosophies and religions
for thousands of years. Whenever possible, I have recognized the
source of an original story, a quote, or other forms of contribution
that are a part of this tale.

I am sure that I will never be able to identify all those who have
made a difference in forming my thinking, thereby making it possible for me to write this book. I wouldn't even dare to try to list

them for fear that I would leave several out who were most deserving. Please just know in your hearts that, because of you, I am able to write this today and I am deeply indebted to you.

Some people have had a particular influence toward the writing of this book, however; and I experience them all as people who continuously strive to be examples of the eight principles. Without a doubt one of the most profound contributors has been my dear friend, Tricia Crisafulli, who walked by my side through every page many, many times over. Her encouragement, positive attitude, writing skills, guidance, and suggestions have been extraordinary, and it is impossible to calculate the significance and value of her support and influence. Another is my good friend, Mike McKeon, who walked by my side as I discovered each of these principles and never stopped believing in me. To him I say "Namaste." Although he is now gone, he is never far from my thoughts when I do this work. I miss him and wish he was here.

I am grateful to Ron Baechle of Baechle Design, Inc. who designed the marvelous graphics. He is not only creative, fun, and easy to work with, he has the biggest heart I have ever seen. I also thank the talented Jessica Baechle for her pleasant, reliable and steady support. I am grateful to Mike Freeland, the Senior Art Director of John Wiley and Sons for capturing the essence of survival with the remarkable cover design. I thank him also for his patient professionalism while attending to my many novice requests. I thank Mike Vezo of Westcom Associates for the back cover and internal book design and help with so many aspects of printing and publishing while calmly answering a plethora of questions. I thank Joy Dean Lee for her copy editing and also Marsha Meyer.

I thank Mary Baechle, Pat Chiappa, Debbie Haferkamp, and Karen Theissen, my past and present assistants, all of whom continuously maintained a positive attitude and demonstrated the most remarkable patience when working with me on my many simultaneous projects and handling a multitude of requests. I especially appreciate Mary and Pat for their research, ideas, suggestions, and honest feedback, especially when I didn't want to hear them. There never will be words or time enough to thank my buddies and huge supporters, Kim Ramsey and Dan Harr, whose unconditional devoted service to me and this work has transcended all limits. Your selflessness and dedication inspired me every day. Marie Elser and Rylla Resler were extraordinary City Managers of my company and managed the daily details with commitment, accountability, and impeccable integrity, allowing me time to create. I am grateful to Randy Hunt and Jack Zwissig, fellow facilitators and professional partners who brought forth many ideas and passionate perspectives that opened my mind, and to John Webb whom I shall always revere as my teacher.

I am grateful to the numbers of people who reviewed various aspects of my manuscript and gave me invaluable feedback, publishing, and marketing guidance. I thank Jeff Cook for introducing me to Jut Meininger, the first professional to point out to my naive self that a manuscript needs to be read, re-read, reviewed, and rewritten a gazillion times and who contributed an exceptional amount of his valuable time to give me extremely helpful suggestions. Also, thanks to Molly Fumia who gave me warm encouragement and advice. I am grateful for the continuing support and collaboration of my business partners, Keith Merron, Marty Kaplan, and Bill Stevens whose insights are always enlightening.

I will be forever grateful to those who so graciously wrote endorsements for this book. They all have many demands on their time, and I am truly honored that they chose to spend some of it reviewing the manuscript and writing such complimentary comments.

I acknowledge my many friends who gave in many ways. Your contribution can never be measured. You generously responded to my frequent requests for feedback and kindly listened to me as I endlessly talked about "the book" and never rolled your eyes, (not even once): Heidi and Paul Cavagnolo, Cindy and George Drew, Sue Drusch, Sarah and Dan Fuhrmann, Sophia Garcia, Howard Goldman, Janet and Peter Jackson, Martha Jewett, Debbie and Jim Kiske, Suzanne Knecht, Cindy Kohlbry, Mark Lange, Vicki Levinson, Matt Livingston, David Luckes, Bob Morley, Deborah Morley, Lynn Morley, Jerry and Mert Parsons and Dick Stieglitz. I thank Fred and Donna Resler who loaned me their summer home "to gather my thoughts" and Olive Erickson for reminding me to live Principle #6 "What's For Lunch?" when I was ready to commit hari-kari after losing at least 40 pages of text to the irretrievable, invisible innards of my computer.

I thank the thousands of people who participate in my programs and my many clients from whom I learn so much. Your transformation sustains my spirit. Working with them is not a job; it's a privilege—a journey of continuous enlightenment. They will always have my undying respect for their unwillingness to settle for mediocrity and for the courageous self-reflection that has led them to continuously raise the bar of excellence. The world is a healthier place because of their commitment to conscious leadership.

Finally, I give generous thanks to my closest friends who know me better than anyone and yet still remain my friends: Scottie and Rob Held, Glenda Martin, Dorothy Largay, Wayne Rosing, and Karen Aiken. Never could there be a more fortunate person than I to know the depth of such loyalty, support, and genuine love. May we continue to accept life's lessons together as we laugh, cry, and create treasured memories for years to come.

TABLE OF CONTENTS

❖ Introduction

Most people will survive but only the wise can thrive.

Most people know how to survive. They know how to get through the day. They know how to get up and go to work, and they know how to pay bills, put food on the table, drive to soccer games, entertain, fit in a vacation when they find time, and somehow get to bed at night in spite of life going in a thousand different directions. But when they put their heads down on the pillow, most people know that something is missing. They long for joy, personal fulfillment, freedom, and internal peace.

At work, they unconsciously slip into patterns of discontent, complaining about the company, customers, management, coworkers, and direct reports. They find themselves overwhelmed with commitments they can't keep, stressed and anxious about deadlines, and uneasy about the future. They fear making a mistake, looking foolish, losing control, and failing. Unable to convince others to do what they want, they let their emotions get the best of them, and frequently they feel as if they're swimming upstream, exerting a lot of energy, and not getting anywhere. They long for a sense of control, clarity, security, and direction.

These are not stupid people. They are smart, intellectually bright, and capable people. But they are missing one ingredient. They are not accessing their inner wisdom.

Wise people don't just survive. Wise people thrive. They are able to see the big picture. They can step back from all the confusion and make sense of everything before them. Self-sufficient and complete within themselves, they walk with a sense of calm and inner confidence and can be relied upon to act appropriately in any given situation. Firmly grounded in strong ethical standards, they are profoundly aware of the world around them. They generously contribute to others but never at their own personal cost. They feel complete because they have found meaning, purpose, and significance, and they are at peace with who they are. Guided by this solid natural knowing, people who access their inner wisdom make sound decisions and good choices. They are effective in all aspects of business and life because they are in the driver's seat and trust where they're going.

Throughout history wise people known as sages have been sought out for their insightful knowledge and intuitive understanding. In today's world, we frequently think that wisdom belongs to philosophers and great teachers, or to someone of significant achievement or learning, or to a respected person who has reached a venerable age. Wisdom, however, doesn't belong to an occupation, school of thought, age, or gender. Natural knowing, which leads to wisdom, is inborn and can be accessed at any time. Yet, for many of us, this internal knowing lies dormant like a seed until it is brought forth and nurtured. In this book we also seek the Sage, not by looking atop mountains or in faraway deserts but by going within where it waits for us to discover it anew.

The antithesis of the Sage is the self-centric, overly protective ego which is driven by fear and sees the world as a place of scarcity and want. It fights to survive. The sage, on the other hand, has a healthy detachment from self-absorption, possesses a deep understanding of natural laws, and is guided by a set of truths. These truths show us how to thrive, and when we follow them, we walk powerfully in alignment with the universal order.

Even saying the word "wisdom," creates a shift of possibility and may well be the greatest need we have in our individual, cultural, societal, and business worlds. It calls us to a higher way of being which in turn allows us to be more effective. When we are engaged with wisdom, we communicate more clearly, interact more openly, and release our need to judge. No longer afraid that there's not enough, we expose scarcity for the lie that it is and instead live with the certainty of life's abundance for others and for ourselves. Wisdom leads to a win/win way of operating, especially in business, which honors a kind of healthy competition calling forth the best in all of us and countering the fear-driven competition that wants to wipe out and annihilate.

Wisdom works. This book shows you how to find it.

This story is about connecting with your personal power so you can create an exceptionally successful life—personally and professionally. On this journey of discovering how *Your Survival Strategies are Killing You!*, you will rediscover the eight principles you must follow to thrive in business and life. The eight principles are the foundation of attitudes and behaviors that, when adopted and used repeatedly, allow you to thrive. These principles are also an expression of a natural knowing you already possess but may have lost sight of, forgotten, or perhaps never taken the time to fully comprehend.

The eight principles are not the property of any one person, group, religion, or nationality. They contain and reflect the laws of physical nature and universal order, which, when followed, allow everything to relate effectively and work smoothly. When there is alignment and unity, people, relationships, and businesses thrive.

Perhaps you think you already know these principles, and on one level, maybe you do. But you are about to embark on a journey with four other highly intelligent people—Sarah, Dan, Paula, and Alex—a journey which will take you to a deeper, more profound understanding of what the principles really mean, the realization of which can transform your life. The three September days you spend with these four characters at a remote lodge on the Illinois/ Wisconsin border will free your spirit and empower you in ways you have likely not yet fully experienced or understood.

You can expect to emerge from this awakening and challenging adventure with the wisdom and tools that will enable you to be more effective in the areas of your life that are most meaningful to you. You will have ready access to the natural knowing you have within you. This knowing will allow you to attain greater personal and professional power, success, and fulfillment. You will become one of those enlightened people who are alive and thriving!

❖ Preview

The Players are Chosen

Martha looked up as Jack approached the table where she was seated. She could tell by the look on his face that there was more to their lunch than just a welcome opportunity to meet in person. After some small talk to catch up, Jack proposed an intriguing idea: He wanted Martha, his long-time executive coach, to teach his senior management team at Stellar Point Financial how to thrive, not just survive, using the eight principles. His ultimate goal, he explained, was to integrate the principles throughout the company. But first he wanted to show his team the power of the principles in action.

"I thought it would be a good idea to pick a few high-potential individuals—people with obvious talents in their areas—who would benefit the most," Jack explained. "Once the executive team sees what these few people gain from the program, I feel confident they will eagerly participate themselves, and then we'll be ready to roll this out to everyone."

Martha nodded as she listened. "It's a little different way of going about it, nonetheless, I like the reason you're putting it together this way. You want to enroll your executive team, not sell them. I also like the idea that these people will come from different ranks in the company."

Jack grinned. "So you'll do it?"

"For you, Jack?" Martha smiled back. "You bet I will!"

The program, titled *Your Survival Strategies are Killing You!*, was set for the second week of September. It would be held off-site at a small lodge on the Illinois-Wisconsin border. This beautiful, natural setting was far enough away from the company's headquarters in downtown Chicago that the participants would have the necessary emotional and physical distance from their day-to-day lives.

When Jack Williams laid out the idea to his executive team, he could read on their faces who accepted it, who was ambivalent, and who was outright skeptical and resistant. His Senior VP of Sales was enthusiastic. He quickly identified one of his top performers, Dan Delgado, as the one he would send to the course. Although a wiz at bringing in clients, Dan's interpersonal skills within the company were sorely lacking. A real controller, he was not very popular with his direct reports, and he needed some serious leadership development.

The Senior VP of Information Technology was skeptical. She couldn't imagine how a simple course could make the difference that Jack said it would. She needed proof. If she had to send someone, then the perfect test would be Alex Madison. He was brilliant when it came to programming, which was critical for developing investment models and managing intricate databases of client accounts and returns. However, his people skills needed awakening, to say the least. Lately, a conflict with one of his direct reports had escalated to the point that it was hurting the department's morale and productivity. She chose him on the off chance that he might learn something to help him advance as a manager, but she didn't expect much.

Jack's Senior VP of Marketing wasn't sure that a three-day course could completely turn someone around—especially in her department. Her staff was comprised of creative people with high energy and high emotions. She believed that putting up with their idiosyncrasies was part of the territory, as long as their creativity wasn't stifled, and she certainly didn't want some brainwashing exercise to mess with that! Still, she trusted Jack's judgment. If he wanted to try this, then she would support him.

The CFO didn't see how the company could reap any positive

return from this. Maybe people would feel good for a few days, get in touch with their inner child or whatever the heck they did at these things, but the reality was he had a department to run. He worried that maybe Jack had forgotten that they were now a publicly traded company and that quarterly financial statements were a huge responsibility. He did not want to ship off one of his people to a kumbaya-fest in the woods.

In a few days, the participants were chosen: one each from client sales, marketing, finance, and technology. At the last minute, there was a substitution from finance. The CFO refused to let one of his managers go. The second week of September was too close to the end of the third quarter to have a key member of his staff out of the office. Instead, he was sending his executive assistant. He hated to have her go, but she was the only one he could spare for a few days. Her presence would satisfy Jack's requirement for one person from his department. Besides, he could trust her to give him the inside scoop on what went on in this course.

The course would begin with check-in on a Wednesday evening and continue through Saturday afternoon. The program materials were distributed to the participants who were purposefully told only the name of the course, the objective, and the schedule. They knew that their managers had personally recommended them, but that was all. Little did the four participants know that they were about to embark on an extraordinary three-day journey that would change their lives forever.

❖ Part I:

How to Play the Game

❖ Chapter One

Dan Delgado

Dan Delgado was a workaholic. He prided himself on being one of the first people in the office each morning and one of the last to leave. In addition, he traveled for business three days out of five, and sometimes over the weekend, meeting with both established and prospective clients.

At 39 and a vice president of Stellar Point Financial on LaSalle Street in the heart of Chicago's banking district, he knew what he had to do to get to the next level. In his five years with Stellar Point, he had grown right along with the company, promoted from an account rep to a client services manager and then to vice president. But that was two years ago, and now he seemed stuck; he was losing momentum.

He grumbled aloud as he looked at his watch. It was quarter after five and he would have to leave soon. It seemed completely unreasonable that he had to arrive at "the lodge" – what kind of a place was that for business training? – precisely at eight o'clock for check-in. Couldn't he just show up for the first session on Thursday morning? Wasn't it bad enough that he had to miss two days of work because of this course without having to leave early?

When his boss, Peter, had told him he was one of four people selected to attend the program, Dan believed at first that this was his ticket to a promotion. Then he heard the rest. "I think this training will really help you with your interpersonal skills," Peter had told him.

Dan still bristled at the memory of Peter's comment. There was nothing wrong with his interpersonal skills, he thought, as he walked briskly down the corridor, his footsteps sounding heavy even on the thick carpeting. He communicated just fine, and, hell, he was a leader. Just then an attractive young woman rounded the corner and walked toward Dan. His scowl changed instantly into a winning smile. When it came to women, he thought smugly, he certainly didn't have any problems with his "interpersonal skills."

That thought brought up the memory of Christine and the six-month affair that nearly ended his marriage to Donna, his wife of eleven years and mother of their two children. There had been no pressures with Christine; everything was easy. Then Donna found out. While Donna went to a counselor for three months, Dan had agreed to be "more sensitive" to her needs. To him, that meant giving her more spending money and letting her do whatever she wanted with the house and the kids.

Donna never seemed satisfied. They lived in Wilmette, one of the most exclusive suburbs on the North Shore, with a monthly mortgage payment that would choke a horse, but she still wasn't happy. The woman was impossible, but he had to keep it together for the sake of the kids. Being divorced wouldn't do any favors for his career, either.

Dan arrived at his office, which was small but had a coveted window overlooking LaSalle Street. He was prouder of that stupid window than any achievement award he had ever received. He remembered the day that he was promoted to vice president and moved into that space. He had called his parents in Arizona. His mother had answered the phone in a breezy way that let him know it was already cocktail hour. Dan asked to speak with his father.

"You got an office with a window?" his father had laughed sarcastically. "Where the hell have they been keeping you all this time? The broom closet?"

He had laughed right along with his father, kicking himself for saying anything about the promotion. Nothing would be good enough for his old man.

Riled up by memories of his father, Dan abruptly issued orders to his assistant as he prepared to leave the office. "I'm going to be gone from work for two days, but I've taken care of everything. Nobody needs to touch anything, okay? The only thing left is the Johnson account. They are expecting a call from us on Friday, which I'll make myself. The Johnson account will mean a significant amount of money under management, and I don't want anyone else making that call. Tim has been working with me on this, but I don't want him doing anything. I've already told him that."

Dan clenched his jaw. This stupid course would come up just as he was bringing in one of the largest clients he'd ever landed. He had it all set with Johnson's guy for a trip to Vegas compliments of Stellar Point. Dan already knew how to hide it on his expense report, but if that's what it took, he'd do it. He seethed inside when he thought of the timing. He should be living it up at the Bellagio, not going to some retreat out in the woods.

"You can reach me by cell phone. If anything comes up, get in touch with me right away," he continued. "Don't think twice about it. If there's anything you think I should know, call me."

From the moment he merged onto Lake Shore Drive and drove up Sheridan Road to Wilmette, Dan was on his cell phone. Pulling his midnight blue BMW into the driveway of the stately, but overpriced, brick colonial, he knew that no one was home. Donna must have taken the kids somewhere. Probably shopping, he grumbled to himself.

Upstairs, Dan found his empty suitcase right where he had left it after asking Donna if she would pack for him. Inside was a note: "Pack your own suitcase. I have enough to take care of around here without doing that. PS: I hope this course helps you figure yourself out. Nobody else can, and I'm tired of trying."

Dan crumpled the note, stuffed it into his pocket, and then started to pack for a trip he definitely did not want to make. Before going he made himself a quick sandwich, left the crumbs, empty milk glass, and a bread knife covered with mustard in the middle of the counter. He threw his suitcase in the car and left.

*   *   *   *

Paula Jensen

Paula Jensen was in a race against the clock. A graphics designer in the marketing department at Stellar Point Financial, she had been working on the layout for the redesigned web site. She had promised her boss, Sylvia, she'd have it done by Friday, then Monday, and now it was Wednesday, and she was trying to finish before she had to leave for this course that Sylvia had signed her up for.

She ignored her cell phone ringing in her purse. The voicemail chime went off, but she didn't have time to think about it now. But when it rang again, Paula couldn't resist answering. It was her friend, Kelly.

"We're going out after work tonight," Kelly coaxed.

"Count me out," Paula told her. "If I don't finish this project, I'm screwed. I'm already late as it is."

"Come on. Just for one drink before you have to go get your head shrunk, or whatever it is you're doing."

Paula gave in. "Okay, okay. I'll try to stop by, but I can't stay long because I've got to be somewhere up north by eight o'clock."

"Or what, they'll lock you out? Good, then you can come back here and play with us on the weekend."

Paula laughed. "Let me go so I can finish this and meet you guys later."

Switching off her phone, Paula kicked herself for agreeing to meet with them. She would be lucky to finish this design by six, and then she had to go home and pack, and…her key! She had to give her extra key to Kelly, who was going to take care of the cat while she was gone. She had nearly forgotten. Now she would have to meet with them, but one drink and that was it.

Just before five-thirty, Paula finished the design, saved it into the shared files where the team could access it, and sent an email to her boss. Logging off her computer, Paula knew Sylvia would love what she created; Sylvia was always pleased with her work and never gave her much grief about missing deadlines. Maybe she really did do her best work under pressure.

But if that were true, would Sylvia be sending her to this course? At first Paula had been pleasantly surprised when she had been approached to take a special program that the company was offering to just a few attendees. It had all sounded fine to her, until Sylvia made the comment: "I think this could be good for you, Paula. You have a lot of potential—a lot more than you realize."

If that didn't sound painfully familiar.

At twent-eight, Paula knew she was a lot like her dad. He never made much money but always had a scheme that would make him rich some day. None of his ideas ever panned out, of course, but he knew how to have a good time. In the middle of it all was her mother, always looking at how much things cost, always complaining about the mess she had to clean up. Her mother wouldn't know a good time if it kicked her in the butt. How her parents ended up together was a mystery to her. Wasn't it that way with most people's parents? Her mother had a look of constant strain and disappointment on her face. When she finally gave up trying to bully her husband into shape, she started on her kids. The more her mother nagged, the more Paula tuned her out. In her last birthday card, her mother wrote, "I hope your twenty-eighth year brings you a sense of direction." What kind of person would write that in a birthday card?

Her phone rang again; it was Kelly, wondering what was taking her so long.

Paula caught up with Kelly and three other girlfriends, Meagan, Rachel, and Loreen, at a noisy bar/restaurant nearby. She knew she had to get going soon, but she promised to stay for one drink. They sat around the table, laughing and gossiping about their friends, their friends' relationships, and guys they used to date. At the time Paula was not in a relationship, but that was fine with her.

"So where is it you're going again?" Meagan asked.

"I'm going to this course to become enlightened." Paula faked a meditative posture, her eyes closed. "Don't you think everybody should be enlightened? Besides, it's three days in the country at a lodge with all expenses paid. What's not to like? I wish you were all coming with me." There was more truth in that statement than she wanted to admit.

"This isn't some kind of religious thing is it?" Rachel raised her eyebrows, as if in shock.

Paula contemplated her beer glass. "What do you think? Do you think I'll have to take some sort of vows there?"

"Poverty would be easy; you're broke half the time," Kelly joked. Paula slapped her hand playfully.

Loreen smiled sweetly at her friend. "What about obedience?"

"Oh, let's not forget chastity," Meagan added.

Paula laughed it all off. "It's not like that at all," she said, rolling her eyes. "It's something for work."

Kelly persisted. "So are you going to come back all different?"

Paula shook her head and chuckled. "Not me!" She didn't have to change. She didn't have any "strategies that were killing her." She liked her life, she thought. She had great friends, a really good job, and while she was low on cash most of the time, she didn't have much to worry about. It's not that she didn't have ambition; she had a zillion ideas in her head although putting them into action was another thing.

Finishing her beer, Paula begged off having another, saying she had to go. Remembering her key at the last minute, she gave it to Kelly, who promised to feed the cat, and left before they convinced her to stay any longer. It was 6:25 when she hailed a cab at the corner; twenty minutes later she was at her apartment. Throwing things into a duffel bag, Paula looked around for her cat and found him asleep in the middle of her unmade bed. Grabbing her car keys and a bottle of water, she dashed downstairs to where her car was parked, pulled off the latest parking ticket from the windshield, and stuffed it into the glove compartment with the rest of her collection.

She thought about putting the top down on her bright red VW Beetle convertible but decided it was too cold. She hated the thought that summer was over or officially would be in a few days. As far as Paula was concerned, autumn sucked and winter was worse. Lake Shore Drive was a sea of brake lights as Paula guided her Beetle from lane to lane, jockeying for the best position. When she finally hit the highway, she floored it. She had a little less than an hour to get to the lodge, and she just might make it.

* * * *

Alex Madison

Alex Madison was ready to log off his computer at 5:30 when the email icon popped up. Clicking on the inbox, he scanned the latest missive from Frank, complaining about how the new database project was being handled. Without replying, Alex hit "forward" and sent the email to his boss, Maureen, along with a one-line note: "Another example of Frank's attempt to undermine this project."

Logging off, Alex reached for his laptop and double-checked that he had both his cell phone and Blackberry with him.

Frank looked up from his cubicle as Alex walked by; neither man acknowledged the other.

Alex had informed the team that he would be out Thursday and Friday at a course being held at a lodge approximately an hour north of Chicago. Although he had been concerned initially about being out of the office for two days, Maureen had never wavered about him going. He had met with his staff earlier in the day, received an update on their projects, and ignored most of Frank's tirade on everything taking too long. The rest of the day his eyes had barely left his computer screen.

In the parking garage next door, Alex opened the back of his black Lexus RX 330 SUV, making sure his suitcase was there. Then sliding into the driver's seat, he put his briefcase next to him on top of the latest issue of *Consumer Reports*, which he enjoyed reading in his spare time. As he pulled out onto the street, he was able to get a clear signal on his cell phone and called his wife, Ann, leaving her a voicemail message.

At the red light Alex changed from his regular glasses to his prescription sunglasses. He would have plenty of time to get to the lodge, which suited him just fine. He never liked rushing around or being late. There was really no need for it, not if people planned ahead of time. That's one of the reasons he and Ann had decided not to have children. People they knew who had children were always frantically running from one place to another. Their lives were messy and disorganized.

Of course, his own childhood hadn't been anything like that. The middle of three children, with an older sister and a younger brother, he had grown up in a quiet and orderly house. His parents had raised him and his siblings to be disciplined, self-reliant, and responsible, which they saw as the keys to success for African-Americans today. He didn't remember being unhappy. No, he didn't remember anything like that at all. It was a smooth and quiet childhood, and he grew up just fine.

He was a good student, taking advanced classes through high school. Some kids called him "The Brain," which was to be expected since he did have the highest grade point average of the class, while others called him "The Robot." He never fully understood why he was tagged with that nickname. It still hurt a little when he thought about it, even these many years later. Otherwise people had not paid much attention to him one way or the other. Accepted to Northwestern University's School of Engineering, he spent four years among peers who had similar interests. After graduation he evaluated numerous job offers and decided to stay in Chicago to take his first job as a computer programmer. Later, fascinated by the field of data management, he joined Stellar Point Financial when it was just starting up. Now at age thirty-eight he was a project manager and, his irritation with Frank aside, it was a pretty good job. He would probably stay with the company for a while.

About five years ago, he had met Ann through a friend. He had dated off and on but did not have many serious relationships. Dating had always seemed superficial to him, but with Ann it was different. Spending time with her was like spending time with himself. They decided to get married about two years ago. Considering the divorce rate, he and Ann were fortunate that they were so compatible.

Deciding that Lake Shore Drive would be too crowded, Alex headed out on I-90/94 toward O'Hare and then took the exit for the Edens Expressway, heading north. It was only six o'clock, two hours before he had to get there, and he didn't want to be too early. Being born and brought up in the city, he always felt uncomfortable when driving away from it. The directions indicated that they would be in a fairly remote area and that also made him nervous. He wouldn't know anyone there, and he didn't want to sit around with a bunch of strangers waiting for the course to begin. He'd get off the highway soon, look at the map again, and grab something to eat. That would kill some time; besides, he was getting a little hungry.

He drove in silence. He'd been thinking about the title of the course ever since he first heard it. He didn't like not being able to figure out what survival strategies he had that were killing him. He didn't like surprises or being caught off guard. And there was another thing that made him uneasy. It was the fact that Maureen had indicated only a few people from the company would be attending. Perhaps there would be people from other companies as well, which would fill up the room. He sure didn't like the idea of being only one of a few people in a class that was designed to be participatory.

Maureen had told him she thought the course would help him. Alex recalled her exact words: "I believe this may help you open up, develop your people skills, and be a better manager."

Alex certainly knew he was quiet, but he didn't understand her comment about "opening up." He managed his data projects very well. He communicated clearly with his colleagues and direct reports, with the exception of Frank who was getting to be such a problem he should be fired. But as far as he knew, no one complained that they didn't understand him. There was something about this course that just wasn't sitting right with him, but as usual, he kept his thoughts to himself.

* * * *

Sarah Albrecht

Sarah Albrecht fretted as she looked at the clock and hustled for the express train from Northwestern Station to Mount Prospect, where she lived. It was the same train she always took, but this time it was different: She would be gone for three whole days, and it might as well be a month for all the preparation she had to do. She couldn't believe Bernie had asked her to go to this course—never mind at the last minute.

Of course she had said yes because Bernie was her boss and it was her job to handle things for him. Bernie was the CFO and the head of the entire finance group at Stellar Point. If going to this course was going to help him, then she'd do it. She just wished he had told her sooner.

At forty-one Sarah had been Bernie's administrative assistant for four years. She took pride in how responsible she was. She knew

Bernie counted on her for everything from his schedule and his correspondence to reminders about his doctors' appointments and his children's birthdays. She doubted Bernie had any clue how much she really did for him. And, of course, there was Charlotte, Bernie's wife, who figured she could call with anything she needed—dinner reservations, flights for the family vacation, you name it.

Sarah sighed. It was all part of her job. She was worried about being out of the office on Thursday and Friday. Something could come up she hadn't anticipated. Bernie had told her not to fret so much, that they'd get along fine without her. Well, she hoped that was true, but she doubted it.

As the train pulled out of the station, Sarah's thoughts shifted to home. Tonight's meal was in the refrigerator. Beth, her twelve-year-old, had been told to pop it in the oven. Even Kyle could do it although she didn't like the idea of a ten-year-old near the stove. Little Stevie was only eight, and he couldn't pour himself a glass of milk without help. Sarah felt a stab of guilt so deep she winced. She had never been away from her children, especially not overnight. Her husband, Stephen, sometimes traveled for his job, but it was different for men. Women were the ones who kept things together.

Sarah reeled in her wandering thoughts. For Thursday night's dinner, she had made beef stew and had frozen it in a container marked "Thursday." She should have made biscuits, too. Maybe she could do that before she left. Friday's planned meal was spaghetti and meatballs, which was Kyle's favorite. She had plenty of fruit and vegetables in the refrigerator and homemade cookies in the jar. She had made sure they wouldn't lack for anything. They'd hardly know she was gone.

Sarah glanced at her watch. The train would get to her stop about 5:30. She could run home, grab her suitcase, make the biscuits for tomorrow, and hit the road by 6:30 at the latest. She probably wouldn't have any time to eat dinner before she left. Sarah felt in her coat pocket for a Snickers bar. She took a bite and then stuffed it away.

Stephen met her at the door with a big smile, which was a surprise. He must have come home early. Stevie ducked under his father's arm. Anticipating a hug, Sarah opened her arms. Instead, Stevie leaped about a foot in the air in excitement. "Dad's taking us out for pizza!" he yelled out.

"What? But I made the casserole," Sarah said, stunned. They were treating her absence like some kind of holiday, and she wasn't even gone yet.

"Honey, don't you worry about a thing," Stephen assured her. "You just concentrate on yourself right now. We'll be fine."

Sarah opened the freezer, took out Thursday's meal, and set it in the refrigerator next to the casserole that wasn't in the oven like it was supposed to be. She opened her cookbook to her "quick biscuit" recipe, reading the list of ingredients through tear-blurred eyes. She felt Stephen's firm hands on her shoulders.

"Honey, we're going to do great. Please get your things together. I don't want you rushing on the road, and there's bound to be traffic."

"Fine," Sarah said, slamming the recipe book shut. She ran upstairs.

Her suitcase was packed. She had done that early in the morning while everyone else slept. Now, with nothing to do, she changed out of her clothes into a loose top and pants that were a little too tight around the waist. Resigned, she descended the stairs to the living room where her family waited. Sarah plowed ahead with instructions for homework, showers, brushing teeth, and taking care of the dog.

"Honey, it's time for you to be hitting the road," Stephen said gently but firmly. He kissed her on the cheek.

Despite his impatience to begin the pizza run, Stevie wrapped his arms around her in a long, clingy hug, which she found satisfying. Beth simply returned her embrace, and Kyle barely leaned forward as she tried to hug him. Stephen held the door open as Sarah rushed out and got into her old green Toyota Corolla before the kids could see her crying.

* * * *

The small lodge nestled against a high hill. The property had miles of trails for cross-country skiing or, in the other three seasons, hiking or jogging. The building was a classic A-frame with a steeply pitched roof that nearly touched the ground. Tall pine trees ringed the lodge. In the cleared meadow beside it stood two oak trees, long since grown together into one massive network of bark and boughs. Behind the lodge was a spring-fed pond, and down the path beyond the pond were two guest cottages.

Lining the stone steps of the entrance were pots of yellow and rust-colored chrysanthemums. In mid-September they were the first dramatic colors in a landscape that would soon turn into an autumn panorama. In spite of the warmth of the day, the air was quickly cooling off as the sun set behind the hill.

Pulling up the long driveway, Sarah was the first to arrive. Parking her car, she called home on her cell phone, careful not to waste the minutes but wanting them to know she had arrived safe and sound. Beth hung up before she had a chance to talk to Stephen.

His tires spun over the gravel as Dan turned his BMW into an empty space. Seeing the woman in the car talking on her cell phone, he thought about calling home but decided against it. He didn't have anything to say to Donna, and he was sure she didn't have anything to say to him. The woman in the car caught his eye and waved. Dan glanced back at her, the corners of his mouth barely curving upward. It was going to be a long three days.

Alex arrived five minutes later. Along the way he had stopped at Burger King for a hamburger and a Coke, but now seeing only two other cars in the lodge parking lot, he wondered if it was still too early. He glanced at his watch again. It was 7:50 P.M. and check-in time was 8:00 p.m. He looked around but saw no one. Retrieving his suitcase and briefcase, he walked with even, measured steps toward the front entrance.

The others were already inside the lodge when, at five after eight,

Paula roared up the driveway. Her gas tank warning light had come on fifteen minutes ago, and she knew she probably had just a couple of gallons left, plus some fumes. Grabbing her stuff out of the back seat, she sprinted for the front door.

A fire crackled in a stone fireplace along one wall of the Great Room. Comfortable chairs and sofas were angled toward the fireplace, clustered in intimate groups of twos and threes, inviting quiet conversation. At the other side of the room stood a long table. The caramel coloring of the wood glistened in the firelight. On the table stood a large fall arrangement of red, orange, and yellow flowers and four individual envelopes. On each envelope was a person's name.

Dan snatched his envelope from the table and tore it open.

"Oh, are we supposed to open those?" Sarah asked hesitantly. "I'm Sarah by the way. I'm the executive assistant to our CFO." She held her envelope up like a small placard. "See?"

He was in a course with an admin? Dan scowled. What was his boss thinking? A chill crept over him. Maybe they were trying to get rid of him; he'd have to get to the bottom of this! Dan ignored her.

"You must be Paula," Sarah smiled, handing an envelope to the other woman in the group.

"And Alex." She handed him his envelope. "What departments are the two of you in?"

"Marketing. I'm a graphics designer," Paula said, looking around the room.

"Tech," Alex said.

"We're the only ones here from the looks of it," Dan said. "I busted my ass getting here, and there's no one here for check-in."

Paula stretched her arms over her head, showing an inch of trim waistline between her slacks and her top. A tattoo was etched around her navel. Sarah pursed her lips primly but stood a little straighter and tried to suck in her stomach. "Well, perhaps someone will be here shortly," Sarah offered.

The welcoming notes were brief, giving each person his or her room number and a key. For those who had not eaten, a cold buffet would be available in the kitchen. Otherwise, they were free to go to their rooms where they would find further instructions.

Dan wadded up the welcome note and stuffed it in his pocket next to Donna's and left to look for his room. Sarah watched him nervously.

"I'm hungry," Paula grinned at the others. "Wanna raid the kitchen?" Sarah had decided it might be easier to start her diet while she was away from home and her well-stocked refrigerator. Still, she couldn't let Paula eat by herself. "I'll come with you."

"Alex?" Sarah smiled at him.

He shook his head and looked down at the note in his hand, reading it again as if he had missed something the first two times.

In the kitchen Paula and Sarah found trays of cold meats and cheeses and baskets of rolls. Bottled water and juice were arranged in a decorative metal tub of ice. Paula babbled about nothing much as she made a sandwich. Sarah listened, marveling at how someone so thin could eat so much. She was happy that she had made a friend right at the start.

"I'm not sure what this is all about, but my boss wanted me to come, so here I am," Paula said, spreading mustard on her French roll.

"Well, I for one am very glad you're here." Sarah slipped another slice of cheese into her sandwich. "My boss wanted me to attend, too, of course." She didn't add the part about Bernie asking her as a last-minute substitute because everyone else was too valuable to be away from the office.

Upstairs on the second level, where the guest rooms were, Dan turned on all the lights in his room, threw his suitcase on one of the twin beds, and looked around. It was modest and clean, and thank God, he was by himself. He hadn't even thought of the possibility that he might be staying in some dormitory with a roommate. On a small desk was another envelope with his name on it. Tearing it open, Dan scanned the short note. "Welcome to *Your Survival Strategies are*

Killing You! – The Eight Principles You Must Follow to Thrive in Life and Work. Your assignment for tonight is to DO nothing. Just BE. In the morning, come to the Great Room. The first session will start promptly at 8:00 A.M."

Peter had to be out of his mind for suggesting this! Dan paced around the room. Sitting down at the little desk, which was about the size of the one in his son's room, Dan took out his laptop and a stack of papers. He had a proposal to work on, and if he had a free night, he was going to make the best of it.

In his room next door, Alex read the same note: "Your assignment for tonight is to DO nothing. Just BE." That was puzzling. Just be what? He would have liked more instructions and some idea of what was happening the next day, other than that the session would start at 8:00 A.M. He called Ann at home, told her he had arrived, and then after a brief conversation, he hung up. Taking his laptop out of his briefcase, Alex opened a file he had been reviewing earlier: a technical manual written by one of his direct reports.

No longer hungry, Paula excused herself from the table in the kitchen. She had her cell phone out even before she got to her room. Without even reading the note on the desk, she collapsed across the bed and talked.

After Paula left, Sarah rinsed both of their plates in the sink, dried them with paper towels she found on the counter, and after opening a few cupboards, put them back in the right place. She looked longingly at a basket of big cookies, took one, and then reached for a second. In her room she read the note assigning her "to DO nothing. Just BE" and wondered what that could mean. Sitting by herself, she noticed how fat her thighs looked in her slacks. She looked around the room for something to occupy her time, and then got an idea. She took a little notepad out of her purse and wrote a brief welcome note to the other three.

She slipped the note under Dan's door. He noticed it a half hour later on his way to the bathroom. After reading the first line, he threw it in the trash, where he had already deposited Donna's note and the welcome letter.

Paula was still gabbing on the phone when Sarah approached her door and wouldn't find her note until the next morning. Alex saw the note, read it, and put it on the desk, next to the one telling him to "DO nothing." He continued working on his laptop until he had finished reviewing the document. Then he opened his copy of *Consumer Reports* and read until he felt drowsy.

By quarter to eight on Thursday morning, Sarah, Dan, and Alex were in the Great Room. Sarah attempted to make light conversation with the two men, but neither seemed very interested. Silently, they filled their plates with muffins and fruit and helped themselves to coffee. A sign in the Great Room told them that at five minutes to eight, they could enter the session room. At 7:55 A.M., the door on the right was opened.

❖ Chapter Two

Agreements Made and Broken

The meeting room was small, able to hold ten chairs comfortably, although at the moment there were only four arranged in a row about a foot-and-a-half apart. Each chair had a single arm that widened out in front to form a small writing surface. Along the wall were three windows covered by vertical blinds, angled to let in slivers of morning light. In the front of the room stood a flip chart on a tripod; beside it was a chair.

Dan entered the room first and took the seat nearest the door. He would turn his cell phone off for now, he decided, but as soon as they took a break he needed to be out that door, checking voicemails and, if there was time, his emails on his laptop in his room.

Sarah walked in behind him and glanced at the chairs. She wasn't going to sit next to Dan who hadn't spoken a word to her, unless you count whatever he grunted after she said "Good morning" to him. Sarah took the third seat, leaving a space between Dan and her and an empty place by the window.

Alex finished his coffee and muffin in the Great Room and walked into the meeting room. Looking at the two remaining seats, he chose the one by the window; that way he would only have one person—even though it was that talkative woman—beside him. He took note of the clock on the wall above the door, the kind that would be in a classroom with a plain, easy-to-read face. At exactly 8:00 A.M., the instructor entered the room. Alex noticed that the second hand on the clock was just reaching the number twelve.

The fourth seat in the room, the one that was supposed to be occupied by Paula, was empty.

The instructor was tall, or rather she had been once, and slender, but now her back was slightly stooped. Dressed in stylish black slacks and a pewter-colored sweater, she walked with a slight limp and entered the room slowly.

"Good morning," she said with a welcoming smile. "My name is Martha, and I'll be leading you in this course to learn how your survival strategies are killing you and even more important, how to thrive through the eight principles. These principles contain the essential, universal wisdom and knowledge needed to make your life work. They teach you how to thrive, not just survive."

"Each of you has been specifically chosen to participate in this course," Martha continued as she stood before them. "Whatever the circumstances or the reason, know that being here—right now in this moment—is the result of many factors coming together, a summation of your life choices, both conscious and unconscious. I am so very glad that you have chosen to be here."

Noticing Martha's nicely styled auburn hair and attractive makeup, Sarah wondered if she should have dressed up a little, instead of the casual drawstring pants and sweatshirt she wore. Her eyes moved to Martha's hands and feet, twisted and gnarled from what Sarah guessed to be rheumatoid arthritis. Her sister-in-law suffered from it and had difficulty getting around at times. She wondered if Martha was going to need help getting in and out of her chair.

Around her neck, Martha wore a necklace of small zebra-striped wooden beads with a simple pendant of a gazelle, its horns tipped in gold. It looked African, Alex noted, and wondered if she had traveled there. Small gold hoops at her ears caught the light.

Martha continued, "Inside each of us are a number of different voices which represent different aspects of ourselves. Some of the common ones are the Self-Critic, the Procrastinator, the Controller, the Judge, the Analyzer, the Martyr, the Pleaser, the Parent, the Helpless Child, the Rebel, the Protector…It's a very long list. Frequently they drown out another very important voice, and one that we don't listen to often enough: the Sage. The Sage, which is the source of inner wisdom, knows how to effectively guide you not only in this workshop but also in all areas of your life—that is, if you're willing to listen to it."

Dan groaned inwardly as he watched the instructor settle into her chair. The way Peter talked about this course, he was expecting some high-powered consultant. How could he learn anything from this woman? She could barely get herself around.

Seeing the look on Dan's face, Martha posed a question to all of them: "If you are wondering right now if there is any value for you being here, then ask yourself, 'How's life working for me right now?' If you can honestly answer that everything is exactly the way you want it, then there's probably nothing for you here. But if you're like most humans, I imagine that you can see areas in which you can be more effective—situations and relationships in which you want to get your power back."

Dan frowned and crossed his arms tightly. My power isn't missing, Martha, he argued silently. Just ask any of my direct reports.

Martha continued, "To succeed in this course, it will be important to remember that participation is the key. The way you participate determines how you experience the course and the value you create for yourself. Just as in life, what you put into this course is what you're going to get out of it. It is completely your choice as to whether you walk out of here as a more effective person—or not. For some people who have taken the course, it has been the most valuable three days of their lives. That's what's possible. I don't know what it will be for you. We shall see."

Alex swallowed hard. This was not the crowded lecture room he had envisioned.

"In this course," Martha continued, "when you fully understand and apply the eight principles, you will automatically reconnect with the extraordinary power you already have within you."

Sarah hoped this wasn't going to be one of those courses that taught you how to be more aggressive. And as for "power," that was half the trouble in this world! Power manipulated and hurt people.

Martha paused for a moment. "I notice that one of our group is missing. Does anyone know where she is?"

"Paula," Sarah piped up helpfully. "Her name is Paula. But I'm not sure where she is."

"Thank you, Sarah." Martha replied and then continued, "In my view everything in life is just a big game. Work is a game. Relationships are a game. This course is a game."

And games were meant to be won, Dan thought as he continued to size up Martha.

What was this talk about games? Sarah asked herself. Life and work and family weren't that frivolous.

Alex shifted in his chair. Why weren't there more people in this course? He had never heard of a corporate course for only four people—or three, at the moment.

"If you looked outside right now and saw a group of people playing a game and you wanted to join in, what would you need to know to be successful in that game?"

"The rules," Dan said flatly.

"Yes, Dan." Martha paused, looking at him to acknowledge his name. "But what do you need to know even before the rules?"

"How to play?" Sarah said meekly.

"That's the same as the rules," Dan declared.

Sarah sighed loudly. Alex stared straight ahead.

"What you need to know," Martha offered, "is the purpose of the game. You can't play a game and win unless you know the purpose. For example, let's say that you and another person agree to play ball. But as you kick the ball across the field, the other person is trying to hit it with a club. You each become upset because you think the other person isn't playing correctly. You complain about what the other one is doing; you end up arguing and fighting. The problem, however, is not the way you each are playing the game; the problem is that you're not playing the same game! One person is playing soccer and the other is playing golf. You set yourselves up to have failed interactions from the very beginning because you didn't first determine the purpose of the game. Maybe this is why some of your relationships aren't working and why you aren't producing the results that you're looking for together. The same thing applies to your personal life. Right now how many of you could tell me the purpose of your life?"

Sarah looked nervously at the closed door and raised her hand. "Excuse me, I'm worried about Paula. Should I go look for her?"

"Sarah," Martha replied evenly, "we are talking about the purpose of your life."

Sarah protested, saying she was worried that Paula might be sick, but Martha steered her back to the subject at hand. "Sarah, let me ask you, if you leave the room now, what discussion will you be missing? What will you be avoiding or running away from?"

"You mean this discussion? About the purpose of my life?"

"Exactly. So what is it that you don't want to look at? Why would you want to avoid talking about the purpose of your life? I imagine that this isn't the first time that you've avoided your own life because you're so busy looking out for someone else. So I ask you, Sarah, how's that working for you?"

Stung by the question, Sarah sat quietly.

This was going to take the whole damn day, Dan grumbled. He piped up, a touch of arrogance in his voice: "I already know the purpose of my life. I'm a vice president of my firm, and I produce results."

"Wow. That sounds like a machine. Let me ask you a question, Dan. Are you your results? In other words, when your results are good, do you think of yourself as good? When your results are bad, are you bad? When your results are nothing, are you nothing? And what if you lose your position of vice president, does that mean you've lost yourself? Is that what you are saying to me, Dan?"

His jaw clenched, and he said nothing.

"Maybe, just maybe, you are not your results or your position, Dan. And what if you're not? What if you're a lot bigger than any of that?" She paused and looked straight at him. "Even more important, what if the truth is, you really don't know who you are or what your purpose is?"

Martha held Dan's gaze until he broke it off. Turning back to the group she continued: "If you don't know the purpose of the game you're playing, how can you be successful in the work game or any game you play in life? Let's look at relationships, for example. Do you and your partner have a clear succinct statement of your purpose for being together? Can you tell me right now what it is? Is your spouse's idea of the purpose of your relationship the same as yours? Do you even know?" Sarah felt the pinch of those words deep inside.

"And in the work game, what is your purpose there?" Martha asked.

"To make money," Dan said, regaining his tone of authority and stating what to him was the obvious.

"Sure, money is part of it," Martha went on. "But is that really giving you what you're looking for? Does money satisfy a deep internal need? What else would make work a worthwhile experience? What do wise people have in the work situation that others do not?"

Alex leaned forward slightly in his seat. Where was she going with this?

"If you want to win whatever game you're playing, you must first fully understand what the purpose is, and then you must realize what winning really means," Martha explained.

The door opened and Paula walked in the room; it was 8:23 a.m. "Hi," she said simply, taking her seat.

"Good morning, Paula. Did you know that we started at eight o'clock this morning?" Martha asked.

"My alarm clock didn't go off." Paula smiled and shrugged. "Sorry."

"Okay, but that's just an excuse, and I didn't ask that question. The question I asked was did you know that we started at eight o'clock?"

"I got up late and I didn't know where the room was," she said defensively. "Nobody was around and…"

"Paula, the question is did you know that we started at eight o'clock? It's a very simple question, and all it requires is a simple yes or no."

"I don't know, eight, eight-thirty, something like that."

"Are you being honest when you say that, or are you just pretending not to know?" Martha paused. "These sound like excuses to me and excuses do nothing but keep you from being the exceptional woman you are. A more powerful response might be, 'The details of this course were unimportant to me, and I chose to ignore them.'"

Paula's eyes widened. Oh, God, this was going to be worse than she thought. She tightened her lips and glared at Martha.

"Do you know why that would have been more powerful?" Martha looked directly back at her and waited. The silence in the room was palpable.

"Because it's the truth, Paula, and people who thrive have an honest relationship with reality. They tell the truth."

Paula shrugged and turned her head. "I thank you for being our teacher right now, because you have just brought to the surface the first principle for thriving." Martha approached the flip chart and wrote:

Principle #1
Tell the Truth. Period.

"This principle is grounded in having an honest relationship with reality. In fact, you will soon discover that all of the next seven principles are rooted in the first principle: 'Tell the Truth. Period.' It means digging deeper to discover what the truth really is, and often it requires you to tell on yourself—like admitting that you overslept, you didn't pay attention to when the course started, and you didn't have a firm commitment to be on time." She looked directly at Paula.

"In addition, by being late, you missed the first discussion which was on the purpose of your life. I wonder why you missed that part. Now we're coming to the second part—the rules," Martha smiled. "Probably not your favorite topic."

Paula rolled her eyes. Who the hell does this broad think she is? My mother? She looked away.

Sarah's eyes darted nervously between Paula and Martha.

Her demeanor calm and her voice neutral, Martha emphasized her request that each of them be on time for all sessions. Then she picked up the thread of the discussion, again emphasizing that to play successfully and win at any game, you must first know the purpose. "Second, you have to know the roles and responsibilities of the participants in the game," she continued. "Third, you need to know the rules that you're going to follow. Fourth, you must understand what winning means. Fifth, you need to have an effective strategy. Sixth, you need the necessary skills and tools and seventh, and perhaps most important, players need to be engaged with passion, energy and spirit."

Getting up from her chair in the front of the room, Martha turned toward the flip chart and turned to the next page.

"We are about to begin a game, which is this course. In this game, there are two basic choices: to keep doing what you've been doing or to reclaim your power and live a life that really works for you. The choice you make will determine your outcome. If you choose the status quo, then that's what you'll get. If you choose to have a life that really works, then that's also what you will get: a vibrant, full, rewarding, and purposeful life with all the challenges and adventures that entails. As you weigh your choices, you will need to ask yourself continuously, 'What is my inner wisdom telling me?'"

"Therefore, the purpose of this course is twofold: First, to become aware of your survival strategies that are sabotaging your success; and second, to understand the eight principles that will reconnect you with your Sage so you can thrive in business and life.

"The next thing we need to do when playing a game is to identify the roles and responsibilities of those involved in the game. My role is the coach and guide. Imagine that we're all on a raft going down a river that you've never traveled. I'm your guide, and I've been down this river many, many, many times. I know this river. My responsibility is to get us to the end successfully. You are the paddlers. That is your responsibility, and I expect you to participate fully by keeping your oars in the water. As the guide I may give you assignments during the course of the journey that require different things of you, and I expect you to accept them. I also encourage you to share your ideas and views. If you disagree with me, say so. If you see something in the river that I don't, say something. Your input is valuable, and I will listen carefully. However, if a final decision needs to be made, then I am the one who will make it. Okay?"

"Yes," Sarah said aloud. Dan and Alex nodded. Paula moved her head almost imperceptibly.

"The third necessary element for playing a successful game is the rules, which are the agreements that we will follow. The agreements give us guidelines and boundaries so we can effectively interact while playing the game."

Agreements

Turning to the next page, she wrote the word:

"Agreements are the cornerstones of all relationships. The implied or expressed agreements between us determine the form of the relationship. The rules change when the form changes. We don't expect much of strangers. With friends, however, we have certain implied agreements, and if we don't keep them, we will no longer be friends. If you marry, the rules change yet again. Therefore, how well you give and keep your word determines the quality of your interactions with others," Martha explained, "while the type of relationship determines what your obligations and responsibilities will be."

She gave them a handout and began reviewing the agreements that would support an environment for maximum learning in the course. It read:

Agreements
- Confidentiality
- Take care of yourself
- Be respectful—No side talking
- Participate fully—Be open honest and direct
- Be on time
- Be fully present—Turn off cell phones and pagers. Remain in the workshop except for a personal health need that cannot be taken care of on the break.

Martha explained what each of the agreements meant in detail: from confidentiality (meaning never discussing what is said in the course with anyone else ever) to being on time (meaning sitting down in your seat ready to go, not just in the room or in the lodge).

"Before I ask if you will keep these agreements, I want you to understand one more thing," Martha added. "When you give your word and keep it, you begin to control your life. You are exhibiting integrity. When you break your word, you allow the outside world to control your life. Integrity is who you are with yourself when you know that no one is looking as well as who you are when you are with others. Integrity demands that your actions be consistent with your words, and keeping your word means doing what you say you're going to do. She paused only a moment, then said, "If you agree that you will keep these agreements no matter what, then please stand up."

Sarah and Alex stood up promptly. Paula put both feet on the floor and hauled herself upright. Dan remained seated.

"Thank you. Please sit down. You have just given your word, and I expect that you will have the self-respect to keep it." She turned to Dan. "So, what's going on?" she asked him.

His eyes never wavering from her, he replied, "I have a very important phone call that I must make on Friday morning. So I will not be in the room during that time. As soon as I'm done, I'll be here."

"That would not be keeping the agreements of the game we're playing here," Martha told him calmly. "To play this game, your commitment must be to be here. Can you imagine playing a football game and saying that everyone has to play by the rules except for you, Dan, and that you can run outside the boundary lines in the third quarter? It's unworkable."

"Well, I'm sorry, but I have to make that call. It's extremely urgent."

"Okay, but unless you have mastered the art of being in two places at one time, you can't personally make that call and be in this course. Participation is the key, and either you are committed to fully participate in the course and your evolvement and growth here, or you are committed to personally making the phone call."

Dan wasn't giving in to her just like that and after debating the point back and forth several times, he heatedly declared that he was committed to making the phone call—this was a key client after all. "I'm not asking you to ignore the client, Dan, nor am I asking you to violate a commitment to your work." Martha replied, keeping her voice neutral. "All I said was: if you are committed to gaining value from this course, then you need to remain in the classroom."

Exasperated, Dan threw his hands up in the air. "How can I remain in the classroom and make the phone call? I'm the only one who can make this call—and I can't use a cell phone, remember?"

Sarah looked tensely from Dan to Martha and back to Dan, wishing that Martha would just let the poor man make his phone call. Paula crossed her legs, grinned, and started jiggling her foot. Alex wondered how much time they were going to spend on this when there were probably a lot of things to be covered—or at least, he hoped there were.

"You have an agreement with your employer to be responsive to the clients," Martha said. "And you have an agreement to be here, in this room. In order to participate in the program, you must remain in the room. You have a problem. You have two conflicting agreements. So how are you going to solve it?"

"I told you how it could be resolved. I've got to call this person."

"Then you'll need to leave the workshop."

The discussion went back and forth several more times, as Dan's frustration escalated. Finally, Martha broke through his angry defense with a question: "Dan, are you committed to retrieving your power? Because right now, you are smack dab in the middle of the survival strategy to play it safe by not challenging yourself to commit to a bigger game. Can you see that you are giving your power away to a phone call? Is that what you want, to just be a stimulus-response machine to a phone call?"

"Fine." Dan stood up. "I've got plenty of power. I'm a respected VP. I make a helluva lot of money, and if I have to leave this course, then I'm gone." He started heading toward the door.

"How many times have you let your belief—that you, and only you, can do the important things in your job—run your life, Dan?" Martha continued. "How many times has it kept you working late and long hours, interfering with your family, with your personal commitments, and with your commitment to yourself to be healthy? How many times has your response to the belief that you're more capable than others kept you from being fully effective? How's it working for you, Dan? I mean, really, deep down inside, what's it like to let a belief like that be so powerful?"

Dan stopped and turned around.

"Your belief is driven by your fear of losing, Dan, and it launches you into your survival strategy of doing everything yourself."

"I'm going to ask you to trust the process," Martha told him. "I want you to ask yourself: if it were impossible for you to make that phone call on Friday, but the call had to be made responsibly, how would you handle it? What are some possibilities you haven't thought of yet? What does your Sage—your inner wisdom—tell you?"

"The only thing would be to have someone else to do it," Dan said crisply.

"Exactly," Martha said, nodding. "As a leader in your company, one of your jobs is to develop the people who report to you. By supporting someone else to make that phone call, you can empower that person, keep your agreement with the client, and keep the agreement to be here. That's what you couldn't see before. You were so locked into being right—that it had to be just one way—you couldn't see any alternatives. Once you let go of being right, Dan, you could see there was another way to do this. So who else could effectively make that phone call, Dan?"

Unwilling to concede the point, Dan said there was no one else. After what felt to him like a grilling session from Martha—who repeatedly asked, "If there were someone else, who would it be?"—he admitted that maybe Tim could do it.

"So are you willing, Dan, to trust Tim and his ability to pull this off so that you can remain in the room and keep your agreement with us?" Martha asked.

Reluctantly he agreed but issued a parting shot as he sat down that he didn't like the idea of handing over the client contact to Tim. Martha thanked him for sharing his view and turned to the chart, writing down the second of the eight principles.

Principle #2
Do what you said you would do.

"This principle means exactly what it says: You do what you said you would do. There's no ambiguity in the wording or potential for interpreting it some other way. Call it whatever you like: your word, your agreements, or your commitments. Keep them—whether you make them to yourself or to others," Martha told them. "When you focus on your commitment to achieve the desired result and you don't allow room for excuses, then you will automatically move through the fears and survival strategies that keep you playing small. When you have two conflicting agreements, you need to play a bigger game. Get creative and find a way to keep your internal agreement to do both well."

Only half-listening to what Martha said, Sarah frowned as she mentally picked apart Martha's whole approach. She hated confrontation, and she was worried about how all this was going to turn out. She glanced at Dan, wondering if he would really stay. The poor man was just trying to do his job.

Alex was intrigued by the exchange between Martha and Dan. He always enjoyed mental bantering and thought people didn't do enough of that these days.

Just like my mother, making a federal case out of everything, Paula thought. This woman needs to loosen up! But at least they got two of these principle things out of the way, she thought sarcastically.

Dan watched as Martha settled back in her chair. Still fuming inside, he reminded himself he had two damn good reasons for wanting to make that call himself on Friday that had nothing to do with his ego. First of all, he had to set up the trip to Vegas, and he didn't want anyone else to know about it. And second, he had learned a long time ago that if you wanted something done right, you'd better do it yourself. His father had drummed that one into his head from the start.

Dan remembered the junior high science fair when he and a friend had set up a complicated experiment to demonstrate radioactivity. He'd built the models himself and done most of the research, and his friend said he could get a Geiger counter from his uncle and some samples to test. On the day of the science fair, however, no Geiger counter or samples appeared. All they had was a booth that explained radioactivity but no demonstration. They had won an honorable mention.

"You know what an honorable mention is?" his father had berated him all the way home in the car. "It's the prize they give to people like you who are too stupid to do their projects right. I don't want to hear any excuses. You dropped the ball, and now look what you have to show for it."

From that day on, Dan had learned to take charge, to take command and control of everything he put his hands on. At work, he delegated as little authority as he could and kept a watchful eye over everything his team did. Peter said he shouldn't micromanage, but what was he supposed to do? If somebody on his team slipped up—if they neglected to contact a client or if they failed to send the proper account forms on time—it could jeopardize millions of dollars in client accounts. And if that happened, who would be called on the carpet? He would, and he wasn't about to go there. If Tim had to make the call, fine. But he was going to coach him every step of the way, even if he had to be on the phone all night with the guy!

"What we just experienced with Dan is someone taking the first step on the Knowing Ladder." Martha turned the flip chart to the next page, revealing an illustration of a ladder.

"The bottom rung is 'I Think I Know.' That's the ego. You really thought you knew the solution to the problem, Dan," she said, glancing at him with a pleasant and warm smile. "You stubbornly locked on to it. However, as long as you thought you knew the answer, you couldn't see any other possibilities. As a coach, committed to support you to win, I'm here to tell you that one of your biggest life lessons, Dan, will be humility. Your first step to enlightenment will require you to realize that your ego doesn't know squat!" She raised her eyebrows and broadened her smile.

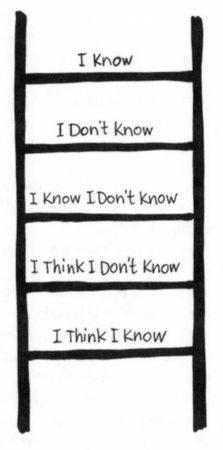

Knowing Ladder

I Know

I Don't Know

I Know I Don't Know

I Think I Don't Know

I Think I Know

She made her point, Dan thought, but I'm not going to let her shove my face in it.

"If you 'think you know,' you're stuck, Dan. You can't move. It is only by letting go of what you already think you know that you can access your inner wisdom and be open to new possibilities. At the moment of that realization, you move here to the second rung, 'I Think I Don't Know.'"

Martha pointed to the next rung above that. "The third rung is 'I Know I Don't Know.' It is here that you fully realize that there are probably alternative solutions that you haven't thought of yet. Once you understand and accept that, you can move to the fourth rung, which is 'I Don't Know.' It is the rung of humility. This is the point where you realize that you don't know squat. Right, Dan?"

Dan glared at her. Martha continued on. "From this realization of 'I Don't Know,' you can move to the top rung which is 'I Know.' From here you can access your natural knowing and hear the voice of the Sage. Dan, on some level, you knew all along that Tim could probably do this call, but your ego wouldn't allow this possibility to enter your conscious awareness. You see, if you think that you know everything, then you'll never get here to the top rung. It's only by climbing the Knowing Ladder that you can become a more effective human being."

Alex studied the graphic. It made intuitive sense, letting go of preconceived notions and ideas to move to a higher level of knowing. He wished she'd cite some statistics to back it up.

Paula's cell phone went off, ringing a jazzy little tune. Taking it out of her pocket, Paula glanced at the caller ID and then switched off the phone.

"Paula, do you realize you have a broken agreement?" Martha began.

"What?"

"Your cell phone went off."

Paula stared straight at Martha. "I turned off my cell phone."

Sarah looked nervously from Paula to Martha and back to Paula.

Martha repeated the question, which prompted a sarcastic reply from Paula. "All right, I have a broken agreement."

"When you gave your word to keep the agreements, did you check to see if your cell phone was off?" Martha asked. "When were you planning to start keeping the agreements? At the break? Later today? Tomorrow morning? What would a person have done who was committed to keeping their word, Paula?"

"I do not like this one bit."

"Yes," Martha acknowledged, "but whether you like it or not is not answering the question. I ask you, however; how is it working for you, feeling the way you feel? Is your reaction giving you the experience that you want? Does breaking agreements work for you? Does defending broken agreements work for you?"

Paula dismissed the questions. If this course didn't get better soon, she told herself, she was so gone.

A memory surfaced from one of the countless times in high school when she had a confrontation with her mother. She was headed out somewhere with friends when her mother started pelting her with questions: "Where are you going? Who are you going with? Who is driving? When will you be home?" Tired of arguing, Paula had learned to silence the questions with a slam of the door. Sometimes it was just better to fold your tent and move on than waste energy arguing with somebody. Life was too short.

Her thoughts were interrupted when Sarah spoke up suddenly. "Excuse me, Martha, but does everything have to involve an argument? I am feeling very uncomfortable with this."

"I'm sure you are, Sarah. So what would you suggest?"

"Why can't you just be nicer to us? We just started the course. And why are you being so hard on Paula?"

"Okay, Sarah, I hear you. Let me ask you, are you arguing for Paula's capability and strengths or are you arguing for her incapability and weaknesses? You see, I believe that Paula is an incredibly powerful woman, and, therefore, I choose to speak to her greatness, not her smallness. Why would you support someone being less than the very best they can be? What would you gain from supporting people to remain incapable individuals? In what other ways, Sarah, do you try to keep people from owning their power?"

Martha paused; Sarah looked away.

"My guess is your whole self-worth is wrapped up in doing for other people and protecting others. This is your way of feeling powerful. Does that sound familiar?"

Hesitantly, Sarah turned her eyes to meet Martha's gaze.

"Just like Paula believes that she's a worthwhile person if she's independent and free, and Dan believes he is worthwhile if he produces results. So, Sarah, what belief would be running you if you thought your personal value were dependent on doing for others?"

"Well…that it's not right to do things for yourself; that you should be doing things for others," she replied.

"And what kind of behavior would be consistent with that thinking?" Martha asked her.

"I help people."

"Yes, and that has become one of your survival strategies. When you look at the results, who ends up being the strong one and who's the weak one? What other results does that behavior produce? And what does a person who thinks this way always have to have around her? Your answers to these questions are pieces to your puzzle, Sarah. It's important for you to find them."

Martha turned to the next chart, a series of concentric circles.

Survive or Thrive?
How Strategies are Formed

Fixed Results

Fixed Behaviors

Fixed Beliefs

YOU

"Let's look at how human beings operate." At the center of the chart was the smallest circle labeled, "You." The next circle was "Beliefs," then "Behaviors," and finally the outer circle labeled "Results."

"When you were born, you came into the world as a relatively clean slate in terms of your beliefs and your decisions about who you are and how life is," Martha explained. "We know that in the uterus, the fetus does form some behavioral patterns, and we know there are genetic tendencies. But a good part of our development starts from birth on.

"As you grew up, you listened, you watched, and you learned what to believe and how to act to survive in this environment. Since survival is the strongest drive we have, these beliefs and behaviors became significant for you. You learned how to get acknowledged and appreciated, and how not to get punished, yelled at, or rejected. You watched your mother and learned what it meant to be a woman. You watched your father and learned what it meant to be a man."

Mom and Dad on the farm, Sarah thought. They both worked so hard and had so little to show for it except what they could put on the table.

"You watched them together and learned about relationships and marriage. You listened to them as they discussed their beliefs about all kinds of things: money, work, values, and, especially, about you. As you heard these beliefs expressed over and over, they became more deeply engrained, and soon they became your own beliefs. These then determined your behaviors, which in turn produced the results you have in your life. Therefore, many of the beliefs you are operating with today were formed when you were three, four, or five years old."

Paula thought of the mixed messages she had received. Her father didn't care what she did as long as she was happy. As for her mother, it didn't matter what Paula did, it would never be good enough.

"In order to access your inner wisdom and get your power back," Martha told them, "you must form an honest relationship with your results. You must identify and sometimes admit 'how it really is,' not how you'd like it to be or how you want others to think it is. Each of us within our own lives has produced workable and unworkable results based on our beliefs and behaviors."

Martha shared about herself. "For example, I grew up in a family where achievement and producing results were valued, as least as far as my mother was concerned. She was the strong one. I learned early that to get my mother's approval, acceptance, and love, I had to achieve—get the gold star, the blue ribbon, and the As on my report card. So the wiring in my head formed a belief that said to be a good person and to get approval, my survival strategy was that I had to achieve. Kind of like you, Dan. You believe that if you bring in that client, if you achieve those results yourself, then that means you're good. If you achieve and bring home the money, then you believe you are a good father and a good husband. Can you relate to what I am saying?"

Dan frowned. "Yeah."

"So when you were growing up, Dan, who did you have to achieve results for to get love, acceptance, and approval?"

"My father," he said.

"Did you ever really get that from him? Did you ever really feel like you accomplished it?"

"No," Dan replied. "No matter what I did, he always wanted more. But don't worry. I'm showing him."

"Okay, Dan. If you want to keep giving your power away to your father, that's your choice."

Dan was taken aback, protesting that he wasn't giving his power away to his father. Martha calmly pointed out that, based on what he'd said himself, Dan ran his life trying to prove something to his father. Dan met her gaze, but said nothing.

"If you honestly face your results—not the results that you'd like to have, but the results you really have—then you will realize that some of your results work for you and some of them don't," Martha continued. "You are a results-achiever, Dan. The workable part of your belief system makes you a reliable producer. If I wanted to get something done, I would go to you, no doubt about it. However, if you take those beliefs to an extreme then you will likely experience unworkable results. For example, how often have you let your drive to achieve keep you from taking the time to build successful work relationships? How often have you found yourself running over others to get your result? Or how has this drive kept you from taking time to be with your kids, walking in the rain or lying on the grass with them on a summer night and looking up at the stars?"

Dan folded his arms tightly across his chest, but didn't look away.

Martha continued: "What beliefs and behaviors would you have to let go if you wanted to produce the results that would have you be financially successful and a strong contributor to your company, and still have time to take care of yourself, your family, and your other relationships? It's not unlike finding a solution to making the phone call and staying in the course for your own growth. Clearly, to find the solution, you will need to be open to thinking differently."

Martha's eyes shifted from Dan to Paula. "So, Paula, who are you giving your power away to? Your mother?"

"No way! She tries to control me, but I won't give in to that!"

"Now really think about this," Martha advised her, and then explained that whenever she reactively and automatically did the opposite of what her mother wanted, Paula was losing her power. "If your mother told you to go left, you'd go right just to spite her, no matter what direction you really wanted to go. You're not necessarily doing what is best for you. You're just a stimulus-response machine still reacting to your mother."

Paula crossed her legs and jiggled her other foot.

"So what about your dad?" Martha asked. "What was he like?"

"He's fun. I love my dad. We're very close."

"So what were you doing and how were you feeling when you felt the closest to your dad?"

"We did a lot of crazy things together," Paula said. "He loved to have a good time. When we were together, I could be myself. There weren't any rules."

When Martha asked what her mother was like, Paula quickly replied that her mother always tried to control everyone. In response, she was rebellious, which angered her mother, prompting Paula to tune her out and rebel even more.

"And how did you feel?" Martha asked.

A smile curled Paula's lips. "I felt pretty satisfied because I knew how to drive her crazy. I was in control."

"Paula, I invite you to take a good look at what voices you are tuned into and how they affect your beliefs and behaviors. It appears to me that what works for you is to be a free, creative, spontaneous, friendly, and social person. However, what doesn't work is to be rebellious, resistant, and overly competitive. Might these be survival tactics that are designed to help you win in a competitive power struggle with your mother? And, I'll bet that you operate the same way with other people in a position of authority—especially someone like me."

Martha paused, noting a flicker of recognition in Paula's eyes.

"Paula, I'm not your mother. You don't have to rebel and fight here to be a valued, powerful woman. When you put me in the same category as your mother, then you keep yourself from being able to have a genuine relationship with who I really am."

Paula raised her eyebrows slightly as she chewed on her bottom lip.

"Sarah," Martha began, turning to her. "My guess is that one of the loud voices in your head is the Helper. It tells you that to be a good person, to be loved and accepted, you have to be giving and supportive, and never draw attention to yourself. The workable result of that belief is that you are probably a loving, supportive person. I'll bet you are a loyal friend who is sensitive to the feelings and wants of others. However, when you take those beliefs to an extreme, what you do for others frequently results in depriving yourself, and that's the unworkable part. Are you as equally kind to yourself as you are to others? Or do you use yourself up and drain yourself dry, all in the name of helping everyone else? Sarah, I'll bet that you feel a lot of resentment inside because of that. Would that be true for you?"

Sarah blinked back a rush of tears. "Yes," she said, her voice barely audible.

"Thank you for your honesty."

Deep down inside, Sarah burned with resentment. She was Bernie's administrative assistant, not his wife's personal gopher. But if Charlotte Colletti snapped her pretty little fingers, Sarah had to jump. Of course, she could never say no to Bernie. He depended on her, and she would never do anything to hurt him.

"Now, let's hear from you, Alex." Martha shifted her focus. "Your wildest dream come true, eh Alex?" she laughed.

Alex sat up straighter in his chair. He knew that he would be next and had rehearsed in his head what he'd say. His responses would be correct, and the conversation about him would be short.

"What do you do at Stellar Point?"

"I'm a manager in Information Technology."

"Okay. If someone asked you to overlook some minor bugs in a program in order to get the job done on time, how would you feel?"

"Uncomfortable."

"Why?"

"Because it's not right," Alex replied. "It should be perfect. It's not acceptable to have mistakes."

Martha shifted the conversation quickly, asking Alex how his parents responded to mistakes when he was a child. Alex replied nervously that his parents didn't tolerate mistakes; they taught him there was a right way to do everything.

"So, Alex, what did one of the voices in your head tell you about being accepted and approved?"

"I should be careful not to make mistakes," he replied matter-of-factly.

"Listen to me closely, Alex. Only the dead don't make mistakes."

Alex looked down at his folded hands resting on the narrow desktop attached to his chair. Was she through asking him questions? he wondered.

"Were emotions, particularly strong emotions, allowed in your home, Alex? Did you see a lot of emotional interaction between your parents? Did they show a lot of emotional feeling toward each other or toward you? I'm not asking if they were good or bad parents, but was there a lot of warmth, cuddling, and passionate expression?"

"They were nice people and good parents," Alex replied, visibly confused.

"I'm sure they were, but that's not what I'm asking. So for example, if you came running into your house and you grabbed your mother and gave her a big hug, or if you exuberantly hugged your dad, what would their responses be? If you came in all excited because you had met a new friend and you started jumping up and down, would they start jumping up and down with you? How would your parents have responded?"

Alex gathered his thoughts. "Why are you asking these questions? It seems unnecessary to me. Are you a psychiatrist or something? What kind of degree or license do you have to be asking these questions?"

"I can tell you all about my degree and my experience, Alex, but I don't know why that would make any difference. What prepares me the most for this work is living life with conscious awareness, by observing myself and others, listening to and learning from great teachers, and developing an honest relationship with reality. It's called tapping into wisdom. All I ask is that you look within yourself and ask whether anything I'm saying is making sense to you or not."

Alex furrowed his brow and said nothing.

"Perhaps it's time for you to connect with the intuition or natural knowing that you have within yourself, Alex. Let's begin by looking at the workable results that your beliefs and behaviors have generated. Believe me, if I was going over a bridge, I would want it to be one that you built, Alex, because I completely trust that it would be totally safe and constructed properly."

Martha winked at Paula. "I would never comfortably go over a bridge that Paula built, although it would be a great-looking bridge. It would probably be painted yellow with pink stripes. Very fun and creative, but maybe not much attention would have been paid to the details. And when she was finished, there would probably be lots of nuts and bolts left over!"

Even Paula had to smile at that comment.

"But not you, Alex. Everything would be done accurately because you would be focused on detail. However, the unworkable part of your beliefs which direct you to give away your power is that you're overly cautious, low-risk, and unwilling to initiate action. Look at the number of times you have let your belief that you shouldn't make a mistake go to an extreme. You go into analysis-paralysis. As for results, I'll bet you have missed a lot of opportunities in life because you didn't take action. Would it be true that you missed out on relationships that could have been, jobs that could have been, or even fun times that could have been because you had to think about it and analyze it for a long time before making a decision? Would it be fair to say that when you finally decide to take an action, that frequently it's too late?"

He needed time to think! What was so wrong with that? Alex argued silently. People made decisions all the time without thinking things through. That's how mistakes were made.

It still angered him to remember when his boss told him about a consultant that had been hired by the company to do team-building exercises. When she asked if Alex wanted to sign up for a day session with his team, he said he'd think about it and he did, weighing the time commitment with the needs of the team. Three weeks later, when he told his boss that, yes, he would like to sign up his team, it was too late. The consultant's time at the company was completely booked. He had taken too long, and the other departments had taken all the available slots.

"All of us," Martha summed up, "have things in our lives that have worked well. You are smart, successful, and high-potential people. That's why you're here. But you also have things that don't work so well because you have given your power away to your survival strategies."

Martha glanced at the clock. "We'll take a twenty-minute break. We'll resume at 11:35. The door will be opened five minutes ahead of time. Dan, I'd like to speak with you for a moment."

"Can we do it in two minutes? I have to make a quick phone call."

"All right," Martha said. "Two minutes—at 11:17."

"Fine," he replied firmly, and dialed his cell phone as he stepped out of the room.

After the others left, Sarah stayed behind. "Do you need anything, Martha?" she asked tentatively. "Can I bring you something to drink? Maybe some coffee or some water?"

"No, thank you, Sarah."

"I see your hands and the way you walk. Do you have rheumatoid arthritis?"

"Yes, I do."

"You know, my sister-in-law has the same thing, and sometimes she's in terrible pain and can hardly do anything for herself. If you'd like me to get anything, I'd be happy to do it."

"Thank you, Sarah," Martha replied. "I appreciate the thought. Today, however, I'd like for you to take care of yourself."

Sarah smiled awkwardly, hesitating before moving toward the door.

A member of the lodge staff was waiting in the doorway. Martha handed something to him and whispered in his ear. Nodding, he left the room quickly.

There was no one to be found in the Great Room when Sarah walked over to the table where two tall coffee carafes stood along with cream and sugar and a tray of biscotti. Sarah poured herself a cup of coffee and then noticed it was getting cold. Grabbing the carafe, she headed to the kitchen to find a way to heat it up. Nobody wanted to drink cold coffee! She'd let the others know as soon as it was hot.

When Sarah left, Dan was waiting to speak with Martha. "Is this going to take long, because I do have several calls to make and we only have twenty minutes for the break," he began.

"You'll have more time to make your phone calls at lunch," Martha replied calmly. "In the meantime, I have a little assignment for you. I ask you to follow the directions exactly."

Martha gave him a short, concisely written note. He was to go out the double-doors of the Great Room to the patio where he would find a path leading from the patio into the meadow. Then he was to take that path to the very end. When he got there, he would find an envelope with his name on it.

"And then what?" Dan asked, wanting to get this over as quickly as possible.

"Look inside the envelope, and then come back. Please do not be late; we will resume promptly at 11:35."

The day was picture perfect with bright sunshine and a virtually cloudless sky. A flagstone path curved from the patio and across the lawn, lined by red and orange begonias. The meadow beyond was uncut grass, rippling in the wind like waves on the ocean. In the distance, a pair of hawks circled and then dove to the ground.

Not seeing any of this, Dan plowed straight ahead, focused only on the path. He cut across the meadow and through a grove of trees beyond. He looked at his watch, timing how long it would take him. Around the next bend, the path ended. It had taken only three minutes.

In front of him, enclosed by a wrought iron fence, was an old cemetery. It was small, only a dozen or so plain stone markers in white or gray stone, the edges worn and crumbled by time. On one marker, the name was no longer legible, erased by the elements over the years. Another, which looked newer than the rest, read simply Jonathon Stewart Pines, 1873-1926, Husband and Father. The tallest monument stood in the center. On the leeside, Dan could read the name "Anderson." At the base, were smaller markers, presumably family members. One read, "Anna." The other was too worn to read, and the third said only "infant son."

At the base of this monument was an envelope with his name on it. Dan picked it up and tore it open. He pulled out a cream colored piece of paper, folded in half. Opening the note, he read the single line: "Cemeteries are filled with indispensable men – Charles de Gaulle."

❖ Chapter Three

Confronting Behaviors

The door opened at 11:30, exactly five minutes before the session would resume. After fussing with the coffee and heating a mug for herself in the microwave, Sarah had tried to offer one to Dan as he walked through the Great Room. He waved her off and headed in the other direction, dialing his cell phone as he walked. Sarah spent the last few moments of the break alone, drinking a cup of coffee that she really didn't want. She made a quick trip to the restroom and was in the classroom at 11:33.

Alex followed and took his seat next to the wall. With his head down, he avoided eye contact with Sarah. Through the open doorway, Dan's voice could be heard as he approached the room, still talking on his phone. He stood outside the door, said a brusque good-bye, and snapped it shut. He sat in his chair, his mind clearly elsewhere, at 11:34.

At 11:35, Martha returned to the classroom and took her place. Her attention settled on Dan for a moment; his eyes locked defiantly on hers. Smiling patiently, she looked away and welcomed the others back to the session. "So, let me ask you, what are you experiencing at this point in the course?" she began.

Alex shrugged. Dan stared at a spot on the wall. Sarah cleared her throat and said, "It's, uh, interesting. Looking forward to hearing more."

At 11:38, Paula breezed in the door. Martha glanced at the clock then looked at Paula. "Do you realize, Paula, that you have a broken agreement?" she asked calmly.

"What? I'm here," Paula said defensively as she looked at the clock.

"Yes, you are here but you are three minutes late."

Paula turned her head away and sat down unwilling to make eye contact with Martha. "I didn't realize you were operating according to a train schedule here." She glanced at the others with a little snicker.

Martha calmly stated the facts: Paula had an agreement to be on time but had come in late and did not do what she said she would. Paula brushed it off with a hasty, "If you say so."

"It's not if I say so, it's the clock that says so. I am only asking you to have a truthful relationship with your results. The reality is that you weren't here when you said you would be here."

Grimacing, Paula muttered a noncommittal response.

"Paula, what was more important than keeping your word?"

"I kept my word. I'm here. I didn't realize we were being timed down to the second," she replied defensively.

Her voice steady, Martha asked Paula if she understood that the agreement was to be in her chair at the end of the break and that she had also made a commitment to keep all the agreements. Reluctantly she said yes to both points.

Paula went on the offensive, snapping back at Martha: "Look, I had phone calls to make. I got something to eat because I got up late and missed breakfast, and then I had to go to the bathroom. I mean, what do you want?" Her voice rose dramatically. "Do you want me to go hungry? Do you want me not to go to the bathroom? I thought I was supposed to keep the agreement to take care of myself. Or am I supposed to break that one?"

"No, I'm not asking you to break any of the agreements. Do you think anybody else here made phone calls or got food and went to the bathroom on the break?" Martha turned her attention to the rest of them. "How many of you did these things? Please raise your hand."

Slouched in his chair, Dan managed to raise a finger a few inches off the desk. Every time they got started, there was some big delay around this annoying woman and her inability to tell time.

Smiling apologetically at Paula, Sarah raised her hand. Martha should have told them that she was going to be so exact. Why was she making it such an issue?

Alex put his hand up for a moment and then put it back down. Paula was so irritating! She didn't care that the whole course was at a standstill again because of her, he thought angrily.

"So, fine! You're all better than I am," Paula snapped.

"No, no one here is better than you are," Martha explained carefully. "They simply kept their word. Every choice they made during the break produced the result of keeping their agreement to be on time. Therefore each kept his or her word. It doesn't make them good and you bad. It doesn't make them right and you wrong. It does mean that they were conscious of their actions during the break and made choices to keep their agreement and you didn't. Let me illustrate what happens with kept and broken agreements."

Turning the page on the flip chart, Martha showed them the Agreements chart.

"When you keep your word, self-confidence, self-worth, self-esteem, and trust go up," Martha explained. "When you break an agreement, all these go down. You don't feel good about yourself.

You feel inadequate. And you violate trust between you and other people who begin to realize that they can't rely on you. Integrity is who you are with people," Martha explained.

Agreements

KEPT

↑

TRUST
Self Confidence
Self Esteem
Self Worth

↓

BROKEN

Dan had seen it countless times at work. After someone failed to meet a deadline or follow through on a project, it was hard to trust that person again. Then from deep in his brain, his wife's angry words echoed accusingly at him. "How can I trust you again?" It had been nearly two years since his affair with Christine, but Donna hadn't been able to forgive him, let alone forget.

"In your life, are you aware of how many agreements you have made and broken? Maybe you had too many things on your plate, and you couldn't handle them all. Maybe you forgot." Martha focused her attention on Paula. "You were three minutes late. Do you know how hard you have to work to be three minutes late on a twenty-minute break? So ask yourself, with your results, what beliefs and survival strategies did you get to be right about?"

"Yeah, but..." Paula started, then didn't finish what she started to say.

"Would they be based in the belief that 'I have to jam in as much as I possibly can?' Or the belief that, 'If I'm a few minutes late, it doesn't matter?' Would it be that 'Nobody can make me? I'll do whatever the heck I want to do anyway.' Does any of this sound familiar? I ask you, Paula, how is it working for you? Is this giving you the experience and the results in life that you are looking for? Or do you quite often feel out of control? What is your inner Sage telling you?"

"Maybe I don't have one of those," Paula smirked.

Martha's eyes rested on her. "Yes, Paula, you do. Everyone does."

Paula kept silent, but mentally ran down the list of "Agreements Broken." She knew all about the negative feelings that were stirred up every time she screwed something up—a project, a friendship, a relationship, a job.

"My guess is that being late and breaking agreements are actually learned behaviors that have become unconscious habits. They are so strongly embedded by continuous reinforcement you don't even think about them anymore. You just automatically make choices that disregard your word."

Paula knew that she was late all the time. Her friends teased her about it. At work they joked about it, although lately she didn't think it was so funny. She still felt the sting of a conversation she overheard between two colleagues about how long something was going to take: "You want that in regular time or Paula time?"

Martha posed a different question: what if being on time meant Paula would receive a million dollars in cash—tax-free—and that she still would have time to do everything she needed to do?

"Well, that's different. It's for money," Paula replied looking around at everyone else with a laugh.

"Okay, so you see, there was a way to do it. Notice what you will do when money is at stake but what you don't do when your self-confidence, self-worth, self-esteem, and trust are at risk." Martha pointed to the drawing on the flip chart. "Every choice you made during the break led to these results. Ask yourself: are these results working or not working for me and the people around me? If the results are not working, you need to make some changes. If you keep doing what you're doing, you'll continue to have what you have. Remember, when you keep your word, you begin to control your life."

Paula sat up in her chair, both feet planted on the floor, her body leaning forward.

"You see, Paula, this is not just about being on time. It's about doing what you said you would do when you said you would do it with no excuses."

"Well, I tried," Paula said with a sigh, slumping back again.

"Exactly. That's what you did. You tried. But you were not committed to being on time."

Martha turned to a fresh sheet of paper on the flip chart and wrote a list of words.

Reading the list of words, Martha asked them to think about how often they heard themselves saying these words. Then she drew a big "X" through the list. "Have you also noticed that these words don't work? They don't give you the results you're looking for."

Walking toward Paula, Martha held a pen in her outstretched hand. "Paula, I want you to try to pick this up." Paula reached out and picked up the pen. "I didn't ask you to pick it up, I asked you to try." This time Paula sat there, looking at the pen, and then she pretended to strain against a great weight as she just touched the pen with her fingertips. "I didn't ask you to not pick it up," Martha said and repeated the instruction to try to pick up the pen. "Don't pick it up and don't not pick it up. Just show me 'try,'" she said. "Show me what 'try' does."

Frustrated, Paula dropped her hands. "I get it. Trying doesn't work. Either I pick it up or I don't."

"That's right. You're always going to be committed to something, Paula, either to picking up the pen or not picking up the pen. Your results will tell you what you're committed to. Trying doesn't work. In fact, the very word 'try' immediately sets up the possibility of what?"

"Failure," Paula replied.

"Exactly," Martha said, nodding. "Powerful, effective people do not set up conditions for failure to occur. They do not use the word 'try' ever!"

Martha set the pen back on the flip chart tray. "There is only one thing that will make something happen in your life and that is your commitment," she told them. "You can always tell what you're committed to by the results. And your results, Paula, indicate that the truth is you were more committed to doing things that would keep you from being on time than you were committed to keeping your word."

Martha turned to the rest of the class. "How many of you feel that I'm being too picky? I'm chastising her. I'm making her wrong. How many of you are judging me for that?"

Dan, Alex, and Sarah raised their hands. Paula shot both hands into the air.

"Yes, and that is certainly one way of looking at it. Another view would be that I am doing what any committed coach would do who believed in the capability of a player and cared about his or her winning," Martha explained. "In a football game if a player drops the ball, a good coach is going to first address that the ball was dropped and, second, that the player realizes what actions he took that resulted in the ball being dropped. The coach will do this so that the player can correct the situation and next time make a touchdown and win the game. If you can understand that scenario, then another way of viewing what's happening here is I am coaching Paula to win. I am supporting her to identify the choices she made that produced unworkable and limiting results—choices that keep her from winning in her life."

On a fresh sheet of paper, Martha drew a circle. "This circle represents Paula's being late."

Martha then divided the circle into two halves, one on the right shaded with the magic marker and the other she left blank. She drew a small circle to the right, shaded it and labeled it "B".

"Paula, this smaller circle, "B," is you. You viewed what I said to you as an attack on you, that I am making you wrong and bad. Is that a fairly accurate description?"

Perception / Reality #1

"Uh-huh!" Paula agreed, crossing her arms.

"When the others raised their hands and said they had the same reaction, how did that feel?"

"It felt like four against one; I was right. You're the one who was wrong."

Martha drew three more small circles next to the first one. "Do you notice that when you have a view about something, you tend to gather an army around you of people who think the same way? Then do you notice that you also tend to gather some facts to prove it, such as why you were three minutes late? It's not that it's right or wrong, good or bad; just notice that's what you do. How many of you realize you do that, too? You take a certain position about something. You gather people around you who more or less agree with you, and then you accumulate facts and data to support your view. If you agree with that self-observation, raise your hand."

Every hand in the room was raised.

"I suggest, however, that your view is just your perception. It is your reality, not the reality, because there are many ways of interpreting a situation. For example, another way of looking at it would be to see that my challenging her lack of impeccability with her agreements is in support of Paula, helping her to take ownership of her life and not let her circumstances run her."

Martha drew a small circle on the left side of the page, next to the half of the larger circle that was blank and labeled it "A"

"This side reflects the perception that what happened was in support of Paula, which is my view. Now I could gather around

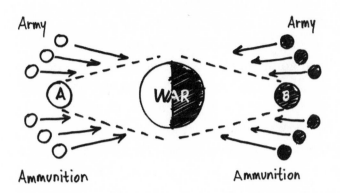

Perception / Reality #2

me a bunch of people who agree with me, and get data and information about it—if I wanted to be right about it," Martha continued. "How many of you frequently find yourself in a situation like this when you have differing opinions with others? You engage your armies against each other and throw ammunition at each other. Eventually, this escalates into war. It happens at your breakfast table with your spouse and children, in the office with your boss and co-workers, and even on the highway. Why? Because you are going to be right no matter what. The survival of your view depends on it. Then egos get involved, and we fight to be right because unconsciously, our wiring thinks our physical survival depends on it. In fact being right is the source of the most insidious and fundamental survival actions of all—hurting, undermining, sabotaging, destroying, and even killing others (as well as ourselves) to be right. We get bigger armies and more ammunition and use all of the resources we can find to overpower the opposition and prove how we are right and others are wrong. How often do we find ourselves willing to do anything to be right? We'll delay projects to be right, quit jobs to be right, and in relationships, sleep on the couch to be right—alone—but right! Being right triggers survival strategies that can be devastating to your organization, others, and most of all yourselves."

Alex frowned. That's what Frank was constantly doing at work. Whenever they started a new project, Frank always thought it should be done his way. It didn't matter if the programming wasn't exactly right, Frank thought his way was the best. Martha noticed the reflective look on his face and invited Alex to share his thoughts.

Alex cleared his throat. "I have a co-worker, Frank is his name, who does that constantly." He spoke in a monotone, measured cadence. "This has been going on for a while, maybe two years. He's always looking for shortcuts. When I point out what's wrong with his ideas, he refuses to see it. The last time, he talked to some of the team behind my back and then went to the boss about it." Alex shook his head. "I told my boss what I told Frank, his approach is flawed. Many of the other people agreed with me. I told him, you can't just take the easy way every time. It's not right."

"Thank you, Alex, that's a good example. And what did you do? What did you do to prove that you were right and he was wrong?" Martha asked him. "Do you notice that you gathered people around you—your own little army who more or less agreed with you? Do you see that you defended your view by gathering a lot of data and information and submitting it to your boss? Do you see, Alex, that you're in the game as much as Frank is? By your own admission, this has been going on for two years. That's a long war, Alex. How's it working for you—your relationship with Frank? Clearly, your survival strategy is to believe that you're right and he is wrong, but are you and Frank—and the project—thriving?"

Alex cast his eyes downward, occupied by his thoughts. There was one fast way to end this long war, as Martha called it. Get rid of Frank! He was the problem, and Alex didn't understand why his boss didn't recognize that.

"So, Sarah," Martha said, turning toward her. "What are some areas of conflict for you?"

"Well, the big issue in our house is the kids don't help. I have three children, and they don't do anything around the house. I ask them to clear the table after dinner, and nine times out of ten, they take off to their rooms without doing it."

"And what do you do?" Martha asked.

"Well, I clear them myself, of course."

Sarah launched into an explanation that soon became a list of complaints: her husband doesn't help around the house either, nor does he make the kids pitch in. With a smile, Martha asked her what would happen if she just left it all undone, including the dishes on the table.

"I can't do that!" Sarah gasped.

"You can't? You mean it's impossible? What book is that written in? Or do you mean to say you won't do it?" Martha questioned.

"Well, when you put it that way, I guess I won't do it."

"Okay. So do you see that in this situation when you say 'can't' you are listening to the Martyr voice in your head. Would it be accurate to say that the Martyr voice echoes all your old beliefs of what you should do and dominates your life, drowning out the wiser, more balanced, truthful voice of your Sage? The Martyr then drags in her buddy, the Victim, and their voices begin to take up room in your head. When you listen to these voices, you're not in charge of your reactions; your limiting beliefs are. When you say 'won't' do you now see how you have some choice in the matter?" Martha paused. "Sarah, when nobody helps you out, what is it that you get to be right about?"

Sarah thought the question over. "That I'm the only one who ever does anything around the house."

"Yes. Can you see that no one helps you because you step in and do it all anyway? In fact, I would guess that you also give a sigh that's loud enough for everyone to hear—especially your husband—and then, with the Martyr and Victim voices egging you on, you complete the task. You make sure that everyone knows, however, that you're doing it. You bang the dishes around, slam a few cabinet doors, and get more resentful by the minute while they're in the other room watching TV, completely ignoring you." Martha smiled.

Sarah gave a thin little laugh.

"My guess is that you do everything yourself because you don't include boundaries with your requests. Then you get to be right about the belief that no one will help you. You get to be right, that 'I'm the only one who does any work around here.' Does any of this sound familiar?"

"Unfortunately, yes."

"Tell me, how do these same beliefs and behaviors show up at work, Sarah?"

She paused, looking around at the group, particularly at Paula, and said in a low voice, "We have confidentiality, right?"

Everyone nodded and Martha reinforced the importance of not sharing anything that anyone said or did in this course.

Hesitantly, but bravely, she began. "I do a lot for Bernie, but that's part of my job. There are times, though, when his wife calls and she has me doing all sorts of things for her. I can't complain about it to Bernie because, after all, it's his wife!"

"I wonder why she repeatedly does this," Martha asked her. "Could it be that you set it up that way just to be right about being a Martyr?"

Sarah's eyes widened, and she opened her mouth to speak but said nothing.

Martha nodded toward Dan and Paula. "I'll bet the two of you have lists a mile long of things you're right about. And I'll also guess that you aren't very quiet about it either. Does that register?"

They both glanced up with a look of recognition in their eyes but offered nothing.

Martha pointed to the two halves of the circle. "Which view of this circle is the right one? Which is the wrong one?"

"There really isn't a right or wrong view," Dan offered. "It's all just your perspective."

"Yes, and it's important to realize that there are three things you need to know about perception and reality. One, that your point of view and your beliefs are your reality, not THE Reality. Two, it's your truth, but not the Capital-T Truth. Three, when you operate as if your views are the Capital-T Truth, things won't work. Mistaking perception for reality gets you off track. This is one place where you can get yourselves into trouble and keep yourselves from seeing and listening to views that are different from yours—the very views that could help you win the game."

Martha turned and looked at each of them, lingering a few seconds on each person. "I am asking you to be willing to open up to a different part of the circle than the part you can see—a different perspective. Going back to our discussion about Paula being late, I'm going to ask you all to consider something: Are you open to the possibility that I'm not making Paula wrong or bad, but, in fact, I'm addressing the very thing she needs to hear to be the powerful, effective woman she can be? Are you open to that possibility?"

The four of them looked back at Martha, but no one spoke at first. "Paula, Sarah, Dan, Alex, are you open to that possibility? I'm not asking that you agree with me. I'm just asking if you are open to the possibility."

"Sure, anything's possible," Dan said.

"Exactly," Martha agreed.

Reaching for a stack of paper and some handouts on a side table, Martha gave a couple of sheets to each person. She instructed them to list the broken agreements in their lives. On the handout was written:

1. Agreements you've broken with other people
2. Agreements you've broken with yourself
3. Agreements that other people have broken with you

"These are your private lists. You don't have to share them with anyone unless you choose to do so. As you write, however, think about the prices you and others have paid internally and externally for those broken agreements. Please begin."

In his fast scrawl, Dan started his lists quickly. He had an agreement with himself to call the client on Friday, and now he had broken that. He reread what he wrote and scratched it out.

No, the truth was the client had to be called. He had just wanted to do it himself because he believed he was the best one at bringing in new business. Now Tim was going to. Tapping the pen against the paper, Dan thought for a moment and then started writing. "Promised to workout when I'm on the road but haven't kept that promise to myself. Agreed to go with Donna to parents' night at Brian's school last week but had to stay late at work." Taking a deep breath, he wrote the biggest agreement he had ever broken. "Had an affair that nearly cost me my marriage. Marriage is still in trouble." Dan wrote several more then glanced around and quickly folded his paper in half.

Paula chewed the end of her pen for a second. My life is one big broken agreement, she laughed to herself, but the realization still stung. "Don't keep deadlines at work. My apartment is a mess even though I tell myself I'll keep it clean. I make and break dates with friends all the time. I overcommit and can't remember half the things I promise to do." She wrote on and on….

Sarah wrote the word "Agreements" across the top of the paper and underlined it. Staring at that word, she could not think of any agreements she failed to keep at work. She was fastidious about deadlines; in fact she was the one who reminded everybody else. At home, well, she kept everything running. Agreements with yourself. Martha's words echoed in her brain. Sarah began to write, "Promised to lose twenty-five pounds, but can't keep on a diet. Promised to exercise regularly but can't find the time." Were those the only agreements she had broken? Sarah thought about Beth who, at twelve, was in full-blown preteen mode. She wanted to pierce her ears, dress like her friends, and buy her own clothes. Sarah wrote down, "Promised to let Beth be more independent but haven't been able to do it."

Alex stared at his blank piece of paper. He prided himself on the quality of his work. There were no broken agreements there. But frequently that meant he had to miss a deadline. He wrote down, "Sometimes miss deadlines at work due to quality-control issues."

The blankness of the paper seemed to mock him. He recalled a scene just a few weeks before when Ann suggested that they get away for a weekend. He had been so surprised by what she said that he said he'd think about it and then hoped Ann would forget. When she brought it up again, he said he was too busy at work to take any time off for a long weekend. It wasn't actually a lie, but the truth was he didn't want to go away. What would they do for a long weekend? He wrote down, "Promised Ann I would think about going away for a weekend but haven't given it much thought."

When they each finished writing, Martha spoke. "Tonight, your assignment is to look at what you've written and really think about the prices that have been paid—by you or someone else—for those broken agreements."

Settling back in her chair, Martha brushed a speck off her slacks. "So speaking of assignments, let's look at the assignment you had last night. Remember, you were asked to DO nothing, to just BE. How did you spend that time?"

Dan recited his automatic routine whenever he traveled. He unpacked systematically, making sure he knew where everything was, and then plugged in his laptop to go through his email. He spent four hours working on a client proposal.

"Okay, Alex, what about you?" Martha inquired. He replied that he had spent the evening doing a little work on his laptop and then read until he fell asleep. Sarah explained she had called her family, put her things away, and then decided to write notes to everyone to welcome them to the course since there wasn't anyone at the lodge when they got there. Paula's evening was spent on the phone with her friends, she said simply. Her things were still in her duffel bag, she added to herself, and would stay there until she could finally leave this place.

Martha continued: "I thought the assignment was to DO nothing and just BE."

Dan shifted in his chair, and Sarah clenched her hands. Paula started chewing on her cuticle. Here comes another lecture, she groaned inwardly. Alex looked at the clock.

"What does it mean to do nothing?" Martha went on. "What does it feel like to do nothing, to just be with your thoughts and feelings?"

"Boring," Paula piped up.

"Uncomfortable," Sarah added.

"A waste of time," Dan muttered.

What would be the purpose? Alex wondered to himself.

"You probably feel that way because doing nothing runs counter to the very survival beliefs that drive you, control you, manipulate you, and essentially run your life. Until you become aware of what it is that drives you, it will control you. You will not be in control of your life; your limiting, survival beliefs will be in control," Martha explained. "So for you, Paula, doing nothing would be boring because you believe life is supposed to be what?"

"Exciting, fun, interesting," Paula responded easily.

"Okay. And for you, Sarah, it would be uncomfortable because your beliefs tell you that the purpose of your life is about ignoring yourself and spending all your time doing something for someone else. For you, Dan, it would be a waste of time because you believe the purpose of your life is all about being efficient and producing results."

Turning to Alex, she said, "And you, Alex, you didn't even answer the question. Is it because you're afraid to say the wrong thing? Looks like you don't want to make a mistake. Could it be that you believe that the purpose of your life is to make sure that mistakes don't happen?"

Martha paused, allowing them to absorb what she had just said. "There were many ways to do nothing last night. You could have sat by the fire in the Great Room or gone outside and sat by the pond and breathed in the fresh air. Or you could have stayed quietly in your room. You could have meditated."

"Wouldn't that be doing something?" Alex spoke up.

Martha blinked in mock surprise. "Alex! You're volunteering!" She smiled at him. "Yes, you would be doing something in terms of sitting and looking at the fire or the pond or meditating. But in terms of a state of being, you could be emptying your mind, keeping it as clear of old limiting beliefs and as open as possible to the voice of your inner wisdom. I want you to begin to notice what goes on in your mind, the 'I think I know' part of your brain, and all the different and often distracting voices that chatter inside your head. That's the noise generated by beliefs which turn into behaviors and survival strategies thereby producing results. And it's your mind that you need to empty out."

Martha continued enthusiastically. "Let me tell you a story. It's about a famous American philosopher who was highly renowned and respected by all who knew him as a foremost authority on life philosophy. Wanting to learn more, he contacted a famous Master philosopher in Japan. The Master invited him to come and meet with him and welcomed him into his home. Once they were seated together on the tatami mat at a low table, the Master asked him, 'Why are you here?'

"The American philosopher explained that he had come to learn. 'I see,' the Master replied, as he placed an empty teacup in front of him. 'So, tell me everything you already know.' At that, the American philosopher began reciting everything he already knew or had studied. As he spoke, the Master began filling the cup with tea. The more the American talked, the longer the Master poured the tea, overflowing the cup and spilling it onto the table, and causing it to drip onto the tatami mat.

"The American philosopher finally stopped his discourse. 'Excuse me, Master,' he blurted out. 'But there is no more room in the cup.' Putting down the teapot, the Japanese Master replied, 'That is true. Just like your mind.'"

Martha smiled as she watched the impact of the story reflect on their faces. "Last night when you were busy 'doing' things, you were filling up your mind with 'stuff' you were already familiar with. When you do this, there's no room to learn. You could have spent the time preparing a clear space open to all possibilities. Now it is time to empty your cup and quietly allow your Sage to speak to you."

The room was so still they could hear the clock click to the next minute.

"One more short story," Martha went on. "Albert Einstein was one of the greatest minds the world has known, and yet it took him twenty years to discover the Theory of Relativity. Why? Because he was encumbered for years by pre-existing theories. One day he decided to throw them out. He allowed himself the luxury of not knowing anything, because he knew that from nothing anything was possible. This allowed his natural knowing to surface. Shortly thereafter he discovered the Theory of Relativity. In fact he once told a friend that some of his best ideas came in the morning when he was just shaving. The mind must relax some of its inner controls and conditioning for new possibilities to emerge. By being and not doing, what discoveries await you?"

Looking at the clock, Martha saw it was 1:20 P.M. She explained that lunch was being served in a small dining room off the kitchen and that they would eat together; she would not join them. After lunch they were free to go anywhere in the building or on the grounds. The course would reconvene in exactly one hour.

The afternoon sun angled through the wide windows of the dining room which looked out onto a grassy slope and the hill behind it. Dan could see what looked like a jogging path across the field and up the hill. He'd love to get a run in later, if there were time, or perhaps he'd go first thing in the morning.

Sarah surveyed the table in the center of which was a large ceramic salad bowl filled with mixed greens, sun-dried tomatoes, cucumber rounds, artichoke hearts, and baby corn, tossed in what smelled like an herb vinaigrette dressing. Beside it was a platter of assorted meats, cheeses, and roasted vegetables with rolls and croissants placed on the side. At each place was a bowl of chicken and lemongrass soup. The aroma was heavenly.

Alex looked at the empty chairs and took one. He started eating his soup before the others sat down.

Paula stood at the window and closed her eyes, soaking in the sun. "God, I feel like I've been locked in that room for a month!" she exclaimed.

Dan took a seat at the other end of the table, snickering to himself as he watched Alex eat his soup in a constant motion: head down and spoon in. Still, he'd rather sit with this antisocial geek than those two annoying women.

Sarah sat down with a sigh and a smile. "So, Dan, may I make you a sandwich?" she asked, holding the platter in one hand and a pair of tongs in another.

"I'll get it later. Thanks."

"I'm holding the platter right now, so I don't mind," Sarah said brightly.

Dan looked directly at her, his jaw tense. "No. Thanks. I'll help myself in a minute."

Sarah swung around in her chair in the other direction. "Alex," she offered, her voice shaky. "Sandwich?"

He looked up at her, frowning slightly. Why did this woman insist on intruding into everyone's thoughts! Without saying a word, he picked up some turkey and cheese and an onion roll and put it on his plate.

Paula wrinkled up her nose at the soup but loaded her plate with salad. "Paula?" Sarah offered.

"No thanks, not now," Paula said, crunching a piece of cucumber.

Sarah started eating her soup and wondered what her kids were going to eat that night. It was Thursday, which meant the beef stew, although they hadn't eaten the goulash on Wednesday. Maybe she'd call Stephen at work and make sure.

"So what do you think of our instructor? Isn't she a piece of work?" Paula remarked. "She's wound up so tight, and they let her teach a course like this. I mean, how the heck are you supposed to learn how to lead your life from someone like that!"

Sarah nodded eagerly, happy that there was some conversation at the table. "Yes, she could be nicer to people, you know. She is awfully direct. And being three minutes late, well, I don't know anyone who would consider that so important. Meetings at work are always at least five or ten minutes late."

Dan took a spoonful of soup and thought for a moment. "Directness doesn't bother me. I actually prefer it when people are direct."

Of course you would, Sarah thought to herself; you're a big bully.

"My problem is I just don't see what the big deal is about this course. I mean I haven't learned anything here that I didn't know. Hell, I could probably teach this course," Dan boasted. Then his attention shifted to the quote in his pocket about "indispensable men." He felt a little tightness in his chest.

"Hey, Alex, you alive down there?" Dan called out. This guy was beyond being a geek; he was some kind of half-man, half-computer like one of those stupid cartoons his son watched.

Alex looked up and cleared his throat. "It's okay," he said, haltingly. "I'd just like to know the basis of her comments. She could have made it all up for all we know."

"Well, I don't care where it comes from, I just don't like this woman's gig at all," Paula said. "She is so picky. She makes my mother look like a wimp."

Her mother, Paula thought angrily. Actually, she'd get along perfectly with Martha. Paula knew that she was a big disappointment in her mother's eyes. Nothing she had ever done had been good enough because she rarely stuck with anything long enough, Paula admitted silently. She never lived up to her potential as far as her mother was concerned. Her potential. A sick feeling crept over Paula. That's exactly what Sylvia had said. Paula pushed away her brooding thoughts. "I wonder what she'd do if we were all five minutes late? She'd probably explode."

"Oh, Lord, Paula, don't even think of it!" Sarah gasped. "We've got to be on time!"

Every time an agreement was broken, it completely derailed the course, Alex grumbled silently. He was going to be there as soon as the door opened so there would be no mistake about the time.

"Just don't fool around, okay? If there is anything to get out of this course, it has to be more than whether or not you can tell time." Dan directed his comment to Paula. With that, he got up and left the table.

"Okay, boss!" Paula crisply saluted as he walked away. "Geez, he's another one."

Not wanting to be left with the two of them, Alex made a second sandwich and wrapped it in his napkin. He left the table abruptly.

Sarah nodded, and then felt guilty for agreeing with everything Paula had said about Martha. "Her arthritis looks so bad," she said quietly. "My sister-in-law has rheumatoid arthritis too. Some days, she can hardly get out of bed. I wonder how Martha manages. She doesn't seem to have anyone here to help her."

Paula shrugged. "It's not my problem." She took her cell phone out of her pocket. "See you later." The voicemail chime on her cell phone started ringing.

"Don't forget, Paula, 2:20! At 2:15 I'll meet you in the Great Room," Sarah called out to her. "Okay? Now don't forget—2:15 in the Great Room!"

"Okay, fine," Paula said, dialing a number as she walked away.

Alone at the table, Sarah helped herself to some more cheese and a roll, which she ate quickly. Hearing a sound in the kitchen, she opened the door and saw a woman in a white chef's coat was working at the counter. Sarah asked if she would like help clearing the table. The woman shook her head and urged Sarah to enjoy the rest of her break.

Sarah walked away, a rush of sadness nearly overcoming her

and feeling a little frightened by the thought that she had nothing to do. When she eventually wandered back to her room, she tried to call Stephen at work to ask about dinner, but she got his voice-mail. She left him a hurried message and instructions for dinner for that night and the next night. Looking at her watch, she saw it was 2:12 and dashed to the Great Room to meet Paula. At 2:15 when the classroom door opened, Alex went in, but Paula was not there. At 2:17, Sarah left the Great Room to look for Paula, running down the hall to her room, looking on the patio outside, and then made a final dash back to Paula's room. It was 2:20 and Paula was nowhere to be found. At 2:22, breathless and flustered, Sarah bustled into the classroom. Paula was sitting there with Dan and Alex, talking with Martha about their lunch together.

"Sarah, are you aware you have a broken agreement?" Martha asked calmly.

"Where were you, Paula?" Sarah snapped, ignoring Martha for the moment. "When you weren't in the Great Room at 2:15, I went looking for you everywhere."

"Sarah, I didn't ask you where Paula was or wasn't, I asked you if you were aware that you had a broken agreement?"

Sarah looked wide-eyed at Martha. "I was in the Great Room at 2:15 ready to come in the classroom. I wouldn't have been late if I hadn't had to look for Paula."

Martha calmly repeated the question, and Sarah's shoulders hunched as if under huge burden. Yes, she admitted, she knew she had a broken agreement.

❖ Chapter Four

The Capital-T Truth

Sarah stood in front of the classroom, not believing what she was hearing and yet knowing full well it was true. She had a broken agreement only because she had run around looking for Paula, not wanting her to be late. If Paula had been where she said she was going to be, none of this would be happening right now, Sarah fumed silently. It was all Paula's fault, and she should be the one being chewed out by Martha—not her!

Resentment bubbling inside her, Sarah watched Paula who was sitting casually in her chair. Well, at least, Paula got there on time, Sarah consoled herself. Feeling exposed and embarrassed, she took her seat.

"So, Sarah, what thinking caused you to have a broken agreement? Was it your belief that you have to help people, even when it's at your own expense?" Martha asked.

Sarah nodded. "Yes. That's just what happened."

"Sarah, when you give and keep your word—including to yourself—that's when phenomenal growth occurs," Martha told her. "When you are committed to keeping your agreements and doing what you said you would do, you will be confronted with the things that you need to learn in order to be a powerful person. People who thrive make big agreements and then they keep them. The space between giving and keeping your word is where you will be challenged to shift, change, and grow. Can you see that one of your lessons is to let go of the unworkable belief that led you to believe it was more important to take care of Paula than to keep your word? For other people, the lesson is to be more flexible or to be attentive to details. Some will need to learn to ask for help. Others will need to learn to delegate, to be creative, to prioritize, to say 'no'... The lessons are endless."

In the momentary pause that followed, Sarah felt the tiniest shift inside, her quick, shallow breaths beginning to relax and deepen. "Yes, it makes sense," she admitted.

It wouldn't be easy, Sarah pondered silently. Doing for others had been the way she was raised. The oldest of six children, she was responsible for the younger ones. She remembered one Christmas when she was a child and money was tight. She had received nothing except a handkerchief on which her mother had embroidered her name. Money was used for the little ones to have a toy or two to play with. Going without, doing for others, missing her turn, giving someone her share...the Martyr. It was deeply engrained in her.

The memories of all the times she had to push her own needs aside for the sake of someone else burned inside her like acid. She pretended to believe that taking care of everyone else made her feel good about herself, but the truth was it made her mad as hell at times, especially lately. Now when Stephen and the kids needed something and she had to drop whatever she was doing, she could practically taste the bile in her throat. And every time Charlotte Colletti called, she wanted to strangle her!

Martha watched the change in Sarah's expression as she sat there, absorbed in thought, and asked if she would like to share any of it. Sarah couldn't possibly admit to the negative thoughts she had been harboring. She gave a tentative reply: "Well, I was thinking that if you are raised to believe that doing for others is good..."

"You are raised? Martha interrupted, pointing to herself. "Are you talking about me, Sarah?"

"No, I'm talking about myself."

Okay, then please use the word, 'I'," Martha told her. "I'd like you speak in the first person."

Sarah drew her breath in slowly. She had half-forgotten what she wanted to say. Speaking slowly and deliberately, trying to use the word, "I", in spite of several stumbles, Sarah felt frustrated with the robotic way she spoke. "I was always taught that drawing attention to, uh, myself or talking about myself was something you—no, I mean I should never do. I always thought it was...I guess...selfish. Gosh, it's hard to use the word 'I'."

"You're doing fine," Martha encouraged. "Just stay conscious of the words you are choosing and keep reminding yourself. Using the word 'I' indicates ownership."

Turning to the rest of the class, she invited sharing from the others, asking them what was going on for each of them. What were they experiencing, and what had they discovered thus far?

"Well, do you want me to be really honest?" Paula asked with a little laugh, relieved that she was not in the hot seat for somehow causing Sarah to break her agreement. She vaguely remembered Sarah saying she'd meet her somewhere, but that woman talked so much it was hard to pay attention to her.

"It has been my experience, Paula, that either you're honest or not. There's no 'really' honest," Martha replied. "Since honesty is the only thing that works, then yes, I want you to be honest."

"Okay, here goes. This whole thing is a mixed bag for me. I mean, there is some good stuff here, but it feels like everything I do is wrong. I feel like you're constantly judging me, just like you're constantly judging everybody else."

"I hear your view of what you think is happening, Paula," Martha replied, her voice even and without emotion. "Let me ask you, what is your experience when you think that?"

"It feels uncomfortable. I feel angry and upset." Paula fixed her eyes on Martha. "I'm ticked off that I'm here and I wish I weren't. I feel sort of…"

"Negative?" Martha suggested.

"You bet!" Paula exclaimed.

"So how's that working for you?" Martha asked.

"It isn't," Paula replied smugly.

"Then I wonder why you choose that experience."

Paula opened her mouth to reply but shook her head instead. She wasn't choosing to have this experience, she thought angrily. It was the way Martha was running this stupid course.

"So, Sarah, what are you experiencing?" Martha asked.

"Well, I have to admit that sometimes it's hard for me to pay attention," she said deliberately. Sighing, her voice became more relaxed and natural. "My mind is preoccupied a lot. I'm really worried about my children and how they're doing at home. Plus, I wonder how things are going at my job. I did everything for my boss before I left, but I still worry that something might have come up…" Her voice trailed off.

"When you are thinking and worrying about everyone else, Sarah, whom are you ignoring?" Martha asked her.

"Myself," Sarah replied.

"And what do you get to avoid looking at when you do that?"

Sarah paused, thought for a moment, and then looked at Martha, "My life."

"Sarah, isn't it time for you to realize what a valuable human being you are? Isn't it time for you to be important, too?" Martha continued. "And notice, what is your experience when you feel the need to always think about everybody else?"

"I'm nervous, worried, afraid… unsure."

"Is that the experience you are looking for in life, Sarah?"

"No," she said meekly.

"Then I wonder why you choose that."

Feeling defensive and still stung from having a broken agreement, Sarah argued that she hadn't chosen that experience. Slowly and softly, Martha repeated what she had said, wondering why Sarah would choose that experience. Sarah sat with her head bowed. Inside, a profound weariness started to envelop her.

Martha shifted her focus this time to Alex, asking him what he was experiencing.

He kept his reply brief, saying that it was "interesting," and then asked Martha where her material came from.

"Like I said before, it comes from life lessons, being aware and conscious, and developing an honest relationship with reality," Martha replied. "I know that's not the answer you want. You're looking for numerous citations of research. But for now, let's just say 'life' and teachers far wiser than I, and leave it at that. So, what are you experiencing in this course? What are you feeling?"

"I think the course should be more structured without all these tangents."

"Thank you for your opinion, but I didn't ask what you think, Alex. I asked what you are feeling."

Flummoxed, Alex searched for the right reply and shared that he noticed each of the participants think differently, probably because they have different backgrounds. "I didn't ask for your point of view on the people here," Martha interrupted. "I asked how you felt. Do you notice how difficult it is for you to talk about how you feel?" She took a step forward toward him, holding his gaze. "Alex," she said softly, "perhaps the lesson for you is to move from your head to your heart."

Alex sat quietly, outwardly impassive but inwardly his mind was going a mile a minute. Martha's question stirred a memory of a discussion he had with Ann just a few weeks before. She had asked him, out of the blue, how he felt about her. He felt just fine, Alex had told her, but he could see on Ann's face that wasn't the right answer either.

Releasing her focus on Alex, Martha turned toward Dan. "Now, let's hear from you, Dan," she invited.

Dan shifted forward in his seat as if ready to spring to his feet. "Well," he began, "I've heard all this stuff before. I don't think there's anything new here."

"Okay, thank you, Dan. Thank you for sharing your view of what you think is happening here," Martha said, nodding at him.

Martha glanced at the clock. "We'll take a twenty-minute break," she told them and reminded them to keep their agreements.

What the hell was this? Why is she ignoring me? Dan thought angrily. He had to sit through Sarah's whining, Paula's inability to take responsibility, and Alex's half-baked comments, and now he wasn't allowed to speak! Maybe, he smiled smugly to himself, he had gotten under Martha's skin by telling her that he already knew this stuff. Guess he won that round.

Martha continued with the same calm tone and easy smile. "All I want you to see at this point is that each of you can interpret this course or anything in your life any way you choose and that it's your interpretation that determines your experience." Turning to Sarah she asked, "Could you stay for just a minute?"

Dan was out of his chair as soon as Martha finished speaking, and Alex left a moment later. Getting up, Paula stretched lazily. Facing the back of the room, she saw a framed photograph on the back wall. It was a stark winter scene of a tree on a barren field of snow with one lone leaf clinging to a branch as if fighting the inevitable. Who would put something like that on the wall? Paula thought. How depressing!

"I'm sorry I was late," Sarah began, hoping to head off a lecture from Martha.

"Thank you, Sarah. I appreciate your apology. Now, I have an assignment for you," Martha said. "In the garden to the right of the patio, you will find a small reflecting pool. It's a beautiful day and the sun is shining. I want you to look carefully into the water for about ten or fifteen minutes and then write down a list of everything you see. When you come back after the break, please share your observations with us."

"Sure," Sarah said, surprised.

With a small notebook and pen in hand, Sarah walked across the patio and into the garden. She mentally took note of everything she saw: miniature boxwoods trimmed into rounded shapes, azaleas with rich waxy green leaves that made her imagine how beautiful they would be in spring when they bloomed, big yellow daisies that her mother had grown in her garden. A spiky blue-green plant gave off a familiar scent as Sarah brushed past it. Lavender, she smiled to herself, and closed her eyes.

In the center of the garden was a small reflecting pool no more than four feet across. She wrote the dimensions in her notebook. It was circular with a white cement bottom. The water was still and glassy like a mirror. There was some kind of aquatic plant in the water, feathery like a fern. Round stones lay in the center. Someone had tossed a penny in the pond. Making a wish? Sarah smiled. She wrote a long list of everything she saw. The warmth of the sun and the peaceful beauty of the garden made it hard to leave, but her ten minutes were up. She walked back into the lodge.

Sarah was the first one in the room and scanned her list of observations with a smile. A minute later, Alex arrived, followed by Dan. With less than thirty seconds to go, Paula sauntered into the room. "Think I'd be late?" she grinned.

"Better not be," Dan grumbled. "Too many distractions in this course as it is."

Martha came in five seconds after Paula was seated in her chair.

"We're all here," Paula said smiling. "Are you surprised?"

"No, Paula, I'm not surprised when people keep their word and honor their agreements. I expect it."

For a moment, a look of disappointment clouded Paula's face.

Martha explained to the others that, during the break, Sarah had an assignment to spend some time at the reflecting pool in the garden. Her task was to look into the water and share with them everything she saw.

Excitedly, Sarah began reciting a long list, from a tiny bug that had landed momentarily on the surface of the water to the reflection of the sky and clouds on the surface of the water. She sat back, pleased that she had managed to find twenty-three things.

"Sarah, I think you missed something," Martha said. "Did you notice anything else?"

Sarah scanned her list. "I don't think there was anything else to see!" she laughed. "I was hoping another bug would fly by to make an even two dozen things."

"Sarah, are you sure you didn't see anything else?"

Sarah shook her head. She had followed Martha's instructions exactly, she assured herself, so she couldn't possibly have done it wrong.

"Sarah, did you see your own reflection in the pool?" Martha asked her.

"I don't know. I was leaning over the water to make sure I could see everything," she explained.

"And did you see yourself?"

"I don't know. I suppose so," she said quietly.

"So it would be probable, or at least highly likely, that you saw your own reflection. And yet, if that is the case, you didn't notice. You took careful note about a tiny bug but didn't pay any attention to yourself." Martha's voice softened; she spoke almost tenderly. "Your name is not on your list, is it Sarah?"

Tears brimmed in Sarah's eyes.

"If you could hear the voice of your Sage right now, what would it be telling you? I am worth noticing…I am important. I count… My only measure is not what I can do for other people. Is that what your Sage might be saying?"

Sarah nodded her head, afraid that if she opened her mouth she would start to cry.

"Perhaps the lesson for you, Sarah, is to learn to appreciate yourself and not to find your value only by doing for others. Constantly giving to others empties you out. Then that void begins to fill with resentment. Could it be that this strategy, which you learned early in life to survive in your childhood, no longer works for you? In fact my guess is it hasn't been working for a long time."

She nodded, closing her eyes.

Martha turned the page on the flip chart. "So let's move on," she continued. The graphic on the next page was labeled Life View Filter.

LIFE VIEW FILTER

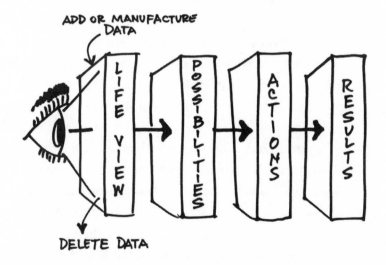

ADD OR MANUFACTURE DATA

LIFE VIEW → POSSIBILITIES → ACTIONS → RESULTS

DELETE DATA

Alex perked up as Martha began explaining how a human being is constantly being bombarded by huge amounts of sensory input. Based on scientific research, she shared, each person hears, sees, feels, touches, tastes, and perceives up to about 10 million stimuli messages every ten seconds. "That's a huge amount of information, and if we let it all in, we'd be blithering idiots. Therefore, we have a filtering system that allows some information in but filters out the rest."

Martha continued: "We all have our life-view filters through which we look at everything. This filter determines who we think we are and what we think is true about life and the world around us. Your filters developed primarily during the formative years of childhood. Please tell me who or what influenced your filter and view of life?"

"Parents," Dan responded. His father had hammered his life view into everyone around him.

"Yes, in fact human beings are one of the few species on the planet whose physical survival is dependent upon their parents for a very long time. Since their approval of us is subconsciously linked to life or death, the beliefs and behaviors of our parents became strong influences on us. Our instincts told us we needed to fit in with them to just survive."

Martha asked for some more influencers, and one by one they offered replies: Teachers. Siblings. Religion. Media. Societal values. Socioeconomic conditions. Gender. Race.

"And many more. They all have helped to shape us in one way or another, particularly in our early years, ultimately forming our filters," Martha summarized, pointing to each box on the chart as she spoke. "Once this filter is formed, it determines what each person sees as possible. Based on our filters, we take actions, and those actions produce results. So for instance, if the influences in my childhood led me to believe that I could do anything, then I would perceive the world as a place of countless possibilities. My confidence would be constantly reinforced as my successes are acknowledged. Mistakes would be viewed as learning opportunities. Then, when I met a challenge, I would look for ways to resolve it. This would be an example of a thriving strategy."

Nobody was brought up in a dream world like that, Dan grumbled to himself. His old man saw the world one way: life was all about what you could get faster and do better than the next guy. And what about Brian and Brigitte? Dan's thoughts turned abruptly. What kind of filter had he and Donna given them? He never stopped to think about that before.

"On the other hand, if I were brought up in a home where I had been taught and came to believe that I was incompetent, incapable, and should be seen and not heard, then I would have a different filter. If I were punished, demeaned, or hurt each time I expressed a view, then I would quickly learn to believe that I had limited capabilities. I would view the world very differently," Martha went on. "Later in life, because of the preconditioned wiring, I would see fewer possibilities for resolution when meeting a challenge. This would limit the actions I would take and would ultimately produce limited results. My limited results would in turn reinforce my limited filter—the belief that I was incapable and unimportant—and I'd get to be right. And because this strategy always keeps me flying under the radar, it keeps me safe and helps me survive. But there is no experience of joy, fulfillment, or freedom. I am not thriving."

Or you grow up with double vision, Paula thought to herself. There was her mother's world with rules for everything and standards that no one could meet. And then there was her dad's world where everything was about having a good time. Neither view served her very well, she admitted. Rebelling against her mother, she had blown off as many rules as she could. Taking her dad's view was a lot more fun, but what did she have to show for her life? Paula squirmed in her seat. What brought up all that?

"Whatever results I produce will always be consistent with my filter. It's a closed system." Martha turned to another graphic on the flip chart.

Making a circular motion with her hand, Martha traced the loop

BELIEF / ACTION CYCLE

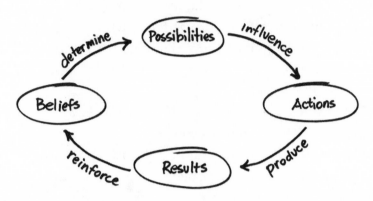

of the graphic. "What this shows is that I will always be right about my filter. I will gather armies and evidence, whatever I need to prove that I'm right, even if I produce limited results. I will then manufacture and add the data I need to back up my view. If it doesn't fit my view, I'll just make it up!"

No one can just manufacture data! Alex disagreed silently. *Sure, the politicians sometimes use facts and figures to their advantage, but data are facts, and facts are indisputable. This just proved that nothing Martha said was scientifically based.*

"Let me give you an example. Let's say I believe that I'm ugly. Then one day this great-looking man comes toward me, and I want him to notice me. So, I give him my best smile. But he walks right past me and goes down the corridor to speak to someone else who I think is ten times better looking than I am. Now what will I make up about his behavior? What story will I tell myself? That the reason he passed me by without even acknowledging me was because I'm ugly. But was that the Capital-T Truth, or was that just my truth? Maybe he was engrossed in a work project that he had to get done by five o'clock and he needed to speak to that woman before she left for the afternoon. Maybe he was so preoccupied with his thoughts that he really didn't see me or think about me one way or the other. However, my filter won't allow me to think about these possibilities. We will make up our own stories, interpreting events in a way that is consistent with our beliefs."

Kelly does that all the time when we're out together, Paula thought. She's so self-conscious about the way she looks. If she tries to make eye contact with a guy and he doesn't see her or pay attention to her, Kelly jumps to the conclusion that it's because she should lose five pounds, or do something else with her hair, or wear different clothes.

"Not only do we manufacture and add data, but we'll also delete data that doesn't fit our filter," Martha explained. "Let's say the exact scenario occurred. I believe that I'm ugly, but when I smile at the attractive man, this time he gives me a big smile back. Then he says, 'Hey, you look great today!' What would my filter require me to think? I couldn't accept the compliment, could I? Instead, I'd be thinking, 'What does he want?' Or 'He's just trying to make me feel good because he feels sorry for me.' Anything that did not fit my filter would have to be deleted so that I could be right about my beliefs."

Her gaze swept across the four desks. "I wonder what's in front of you right now that you're not seeing or hearing because your filter won't let it in. I wonder what you're making up that isn't even there."

Martha turned back a few pages on the flip chart to the Perception/Reality chart showing the divided circle, half shaded and half clear. "Is there a right and wrong on this chart?" She watched them shake their heads. "Exactly. It all depends upon your perception. And remember, it is just perception, although we don't operate our lives in that way. Yes, there is a Reality with a capital 'R', but what I view through my filter is my perception. That is not the Reality. In terms of perception, I don't own the Capital-T Truth. I only have my truth, with a small 't'. I do not see the Reality; I only see my reality, which is my interpretation."

Martha flipped the chart to a fresh page and wrote the third principle.

Principle #3
How's the view from your view?

"This principle reminds us that our perceptions are based on a particular viewpoint. It's just our perception, not the 'Capital-T Truth.' What we see and experience around us gives us a particular 'view.' Although our view may be different from someone else's, it's not better or worse. Adopting this principle, we actively seek input from others, to share their perceptions from their viewpoint." She paused, letting them absorb her words.

"This principle also calls us to move beyond our limited thinking—such as 'I can't,' 'It's not possible,' 'There's only one way to look at something—my way,' and 'I'm right and you're wrong.' By inviting other people to share their viewpoints, we stay open-minded and continually seek new possibilities for solutions. We acknowledge that the experiences we have are the direct result of our perceptions."

Martha asked them to consider the experiences and results they were producing in their lives. If the results and experiences were what they wanted, she told them, then they should keep doing what they've been doing. If not, then they should look at how they are interpreting and viewing things. "It may be that your filter needs some cleaning out and that you need to view things differently."

"Okay, so what do I need to do to change the filter?" Dan interjected.

"Dan, notice that you immediately want to jump into action. Do you see how impatient you are to DO something? And you're not alone. Most of Western society wants to know what to DO. We are a very 'doing' culture, and that can be a problem because the need to take action frequently keeps us from thinking things through."

"You were the one who said the filter needed some cleaning out," Dan challenged her. "I was just asking how that could be done."

"It's a good question, Dan; however, we need to get a few more things in place before answering it. Going to action too quickly is one of the biggest mistakes that people make. Taking actions without thinking will produce results that will reinforce the filter. Instead, we need to go to the filter itself and change the filter, if we want lasting, effective results. Ask yourself, 'What am I thinking and how am I thinking? How am I being and what does this drive me to do? What is my strategy?' When you open yourself to your natural knowing, you can change those limiting beliefs to empowering beliefs, then effective actions and results will naturally follow."

It sounded so simple, Sarah thought, and then remembered how difficult it had been to say the word "I" instead of using "you." She looked down at her lap and felt the bulk of her body around the middle and through the thighs. Changing how she looked at things would be like going on a diet: small changes every day to make steady progress. Sarah smiled to herself; perhaps she could just think herself thin! But the answer was in her next thought: She could maybe loose weight if she kept her agreements with herself. Why haven't I done that? Sarah thought sadly. If I could, then that would really be a gift in my life.

It's just your perception... That sounded like some kind of New Age bumper sticker, Dan thought cynically, but the words captured his attention. He knew that in negotiations the manner in which things were said and perceived could certainly influence the outcome. He fully appreciated the power of words in that regard.

Paula read the words of the principle. But I like my view! I like the way I am. I don't want to change how I look at things, she argued with herself. She was happy and fun-loving, not negative and sad all the time. Except, she admitted, when she looked at how much better off everyone else seemed to be. Being twenty-eight years old, living in a one-bedroom apartment she could hardly afford, and working at a job that she liked well enough but would probably get tired of pretty soon, did not really make her happy. It was the story of her life.

Way too simplistic, Alex decided as he studied the words. And yet what about the Einstein story? If one of the most brilliant human beings ever to walk the planet had to change his thinking to reach the next level of discovery, then perhaps there was something to it. As for himself, he was certainly a logical thinker who was strong in deductive reasoning. He enjoyed puzzling out a problem and finding out the right solution. But that made him see the world as definitive, linear, with no margin for error. The world—even nature—was erratic, unpredictable, chaotic, and yet in the wild there could also be perfect balance. He replayed what Martha said in his mind: The experiences we have are the direct result of our perceptions. It did sound pretty subjective, he thought, but then again there was Einstein… His mouth curled into the slightest smile.

"As we wrap up for the day, I'm going to give you an assignment," Martha began.

Dan glanced at the clock. It was only 4:15 p.m. He could get a ton of work done and brief Tim for tomorrow morning's call. Maybe he'd have time to take a run before dinner.

"Remember, we all have beliefs that have helped us to survive. You recall that many of these beliefs came from our parents on whom we were once totally dependent for our survival. These beliefs are deeply engrained. They are second nature to you. The voices in your head echo them. Now it's time to examine them. Based on your beliefs, what do you think you have needed to do to fit in, be accepted, be loved, and be a 'good person?' What beliefs are controlling your life right now? Be prepared to share your discoveries."

Paula drew her feet together, ready to spring out of her seat. She remembered what it felt like in high school when she had study hall last period and could cut out early.

"Dinner will be served at seven this evening, and you will be dining together. From now until dinner, I encourage you to go outside and enjoy nature. It's a beautiful day. I will see you tomorrow morning at eight o'clock sharp. Before you go, I do have two special assignments to hand out."

Martha stepped forward toward Alex. "I'd like you to go out into nature, Alex, and find something that invokes feeling for you. Anything at all. Then I'd like you to write a poem about it and share it with the group tomorrow. It needs to be a poem that comes from your heart."

"I'm no poet," he said sheepishly.

"Maybe you're a great poet, Alex. Maybe you've got poems inside you that are dying to be written. Will you be open to the possibility that your Sage knows what to say?"

Shaking his head slightly, Alex got out of his seat and left the room. If he was going outside, he'd better change into his sneakers.

"Is that it?" Paula asked eagerly. Her body felt tightly coiled. She had energy to burn, and, before she did anything, she was going for a run.

"That's it for you. You, too, Sarah, and remember your assignment is to think about your beliefs as well as your agreements made and broken. And, Sarah, would you please go back out to the reflecting pool? You'll find a note there with your name on it."

Martha turned her attention to Dan. "Why don't you and I take a little walk? I'll meet you by the fireplace in the Great Room in five minutes."

Dan glanced at the clock, hoping this wasn't going to take the rest of the afternoon. He had a dozen things to do, starting with a run. "Sure. I'll be there in five minutes." Dan walked quickly back to his room, checking his voicemails on his phone. Four minutes later, he was on his way to the Great Room.

Curious about the note, Sarah walked purposefully across the grass to the perennial garden. Was it another assignment? That was her best guess although she wondered why Martha wouldn't have given her instructions like she did the last time. She'd soon find out, Sarah thought, as she spied a small cream-colored envelope at the edge of the reflecting pool. Nervously eager, she tore open the envelope and pulled out a folded note. On it was a single handwritten line: "Self-esteem isn't everything; it's just that there's nothing without it. – Gloria Steinem"

Sarah sat on a rock beside the pool, reading and rereading the line, feeling the warmth of the sun on the back of her neck and smelling the fragrance of lavender in the air. Then, gazing into the pool, she caught sight of her own reflection, her own eyes looking back at her. Taking note of every feature, Sarah studied her face as if seeing it for the first time.

❖ Chapter Five

Filters Begin to Clear

Paula raced back to her room and kicked the door shut behind her as she pulled her shirt over her head. In five minutes flat she changed into her running clothes. She stretched one leg and then the other but decided to skip her usual warm-up. She couldn't wait to get moving.

The day was warm, definitely above sixty degrees, and although the sun angled toward the hill, there would be plenty of daylight left. The ground felt springy under her feet as she set out on a trail behind the lodge, through a field and toward a hill. Her pulse beat a steady rhythm inside her body: freedom, freedom, freedom. She pushed steadily on, feeling her muscles become more fluid, her arms and legs pumping.

The trail turned straight up the hill, and Paula was forced to slow down. Leaning forward against the steep grade, she worked to keep a steady pace. Just when she thought she'd have to walk the rest of the way, she mounted the crest of the hill. The view was beautiful: rolling hills giving way to gentle valleys where fall colors were just beginning to appear among the green. She stopped at the top, first to catch her breath and then paced back and forth as her pulse slowed. She decided to sit for a moment to savor the view.

From deep in her memory an image emerged of another day in fall. Paula had been young, maybe in kindergarten, and she and her younger brother had gone to a farm somewhere to get pumpkins. Paula sat on the ground, remembering running through cornstalk mazes and climbing on bales of hay. They had picked out pumpkins, big and round and much too heavy for a child to carry. She had struggled to the point of tears to pick one up until her mother handed her a beautiful round little pumpkin, just the right size. Still Paula had looked back at her prize. "Oh, don't worry, we'll get the big one, too," her mother had laughed. "I'll carry that one if you carry this one."

Where had her father been? Paula wondered, trying to place him in the memory, but it was clear: her mother had been the one to take them. Why weren't there more memories like this, of her mother smiling and having fun? The answer crept up on her like a sudden chill. Her mother had to go back to work because her father had another bad year in his sales job. Outgoing and friendly, he easily connected with people, but when it came to closing the deal, he rarely came through. That was about the same time he started drinking.

She and her brother were still in school, and her mother had to work through lunch so she could leave early to be there when they got off the bus and then start dinner and the laundry. That's when her mother changed. She was tired and struggled with all of the responsibilities in her life, and there was no more time for pumpkin patches. Paula hugged her knees to her chest and looked out toward the horizon, not at the scenery, but at the memories that flooded her mind.

Standing near the fireplace Dan had been watching someone—Paula perhaps—running along the trail. He'd be there himself if it weren't for Martha's need for this little chat. Lost in his brooding thoughts, he didn't hear Martha approach. "Ready?" she asked brightly.

Walking with Martha was an exercise in agony for Dan. The woman moved so slowly that several times he found he was two or three steps ahead of her. Then he'd have to stop and wait for her to catch up.

"What a beautiful day," Martha said, ignoring his impatience as easily as she seemed to overlook her arthritis, and appreciatively breathed in the warm, fragrant air. "I always love teaching at this place, especially when I have a chance to go outside. There is so much to learn from nature. Do you remember learning in school about the balance of nature, Dan?"

Two steps ahead of her, Dan had only heard about half of what she said but figured he got the drift of it. He stopped and waited for her, trying again to move at her pace. This better be a short walk, he complained silently, because otherwise it would take forever. Around the next bend, Dan could see a pond ringed with a walking path and a few benches. Their logical destination, he said to himself.

Martha passed by the first bench and moved on to the second one. "I like the view from here." Same view as the other bench, Dan thought to himself as he looked across the meadow to a grove of trees.

She sat down and took in a deep breath, silently absorbing the beauty around her. Eager to talk and get this thing over with, Dan blurted out, "So, what's up?" She turned slowly toward him and took a moment to study his face. Dan shifted on the bench and looked away. "How's it going, Dan?" she asked.

"Fine. No problems here."

"So, Dan, what have you been unwilling to look at that has been causing conflict in your life?"

He was a little taken aback by her abrupt question although by this time he should have been used to her directness. "Well, I have a very busy job with heavy responsibilities. It requires long hours and a lot of travel. I suppose that does cause some stress although that's to be expected."

"What about at home?"

The question hung in the air. Dan drew his breath in slowly feeling his resistance cracking. "Well, let's just say that things between my wife and me haven't been very good these days."

"I'm sure."

Giving her an uneasy sideways glance, he continued, "We've been married for eleven years. We nearly split up a couple years ago, but we stayed together. She wanted us to go to a counselor, but I'm not going to any shrink."

"The problem hasn't gone away, has it?"

"No." Dan batted his hand in the air, as if dismissing the subject. Then, for some unknown reason, he opened up: "I had an affair two years ago which lasted about six months. When Donna found out, she threatened to divorce me, but that wasn't what I wanted. As for the affair," he explained, "I had just needed a break from all the pressure—the job, the house, her spending. God, if I told you how much we spend every month, you'd die. So I slipped up and I'm sorry. I shouldn't have done it, but I can't undo it either. And Donna never misses a chance to throw it in my face."

"Did the affair give you the connection you were hoping for?" Martha asked, her tone of voice easy and without judgment.

"I doubt it," Dan replied icily.

"The answer is 'no,' Dan. You never solve problems within your relationship by getting involved with someone outside of it." Martha paused and watched as a songbird lit on the branch of a nearby shrub, cocked its head toward them, and then took off. "Why are you so afraid of real intimacy with your wife, Dan? Why don't you show your love? Why are you so afraid to show you care for people?"

"I love my kids. They know that."

"Are you there for them when you say you will be? Or do you put your job first and break commitments to them?"

"Like I said, my job puts so much pressure on me sometimes I don't have any choice."

"You say that like it's the Capital-T Truth! Is it? Is it true that you don't have any choice, Dan?" She let him sit with this thought for a moment then continued. "So when you think you don't have a choice and when you're stressed and start to feel like you're out of control, how do you react?"

"Naturally I try to get back in control. I tell people how I want things done. I give out orders."

"I see, so in actuality, you are pretty much out of control all of the time."

Dan abruptly looked at her and, without giving any thought to what she said, defended himself. As far as he was concerned, he was very much in control.

Martha's explanation was gentle but direct: Dan was controlled by his need to be in control. That, in fact, made him the one who was the most out of control.

The momentary silence between them was interrupted only by the sound of a splash as something broke the surface of the water.

"Dan, how have you twisted the rules at work for your own benefit and at the cost of others?"

Dan gave her a quick, furtive look. "What are we talking about?"

"I think you know, Dan."

He shook his head. There was a long silence, and Martha waited patiently for a response. "I mean, I have to entertain clients, okay?" Dan's voice bristled with defensiveness. "I don't do anything a lot of other people don't do."

When Martha asked him to be more specific, Dan gave the expense report as an example. "You can't put down what you really spend the money on," he said.

"You can't? Why not?"

Dan shrugged his shoulders and looked into the distance.

"Dan, how much integrity and self-respect have you lost by twisting the rules? How much connection, intimacy, and love have you lost as a result of needing control? What are the prices that you, your team, and others have paid for your survival strategies to be in control and do everything your own way?"

When Martha paused, Dan did not answer, explain, or defend himself.

She continued, "Do the people around you feel strong? Or do you always have to be the strong one? Does everything have to go your way? Do you make all the decisions? Do you truly empower people, or are they just puppets to you? Do you give them the space to be smarter than you, or do you always have to come out on top, to win?"

Each question pierced the armor Dan wore into battle each day. He knew he treated people like subordinates who had better do it his way. As much as he hated to admit it, he was just like his father. Except, he realized suddenly, there was one essential difference: He was sitting on a bench listening to someone tell him about his life, exactly as it was—ironically a woman who could barely get around. His father never would have tolerated that.

"What would you have to let go of to allow the loving, caring, and supportive human being that's within you to be heard?" Martha asked.

The answer came swiftly, uninvited: control. From deep within, a path seemed to be clearing. For once he would have to admit that he was vulnerable. He would have to face his biggest fear, that he could lose Donna and the kids. Oh, God, they meant more to him than he could ever tell them. That stupid affair was nothing more than an escape. But instead of letting Donna see how much it pained him, he had given her the cold treatment, hoping that time would give them enough momentum to move past the rough times in their marriage. It wasn't working. And things weren't going the way he planned at work, either. They weren't about to promote him anytime soon. Sure, he could bring in the client money, but nobody really wanted to report to him. He wasn't what the company would consider senior leadership material.

Dan's line of thinking raced forward to its logical, dreaded conclusion: He was a failure.

Martha's voice broke his desolation. "Goals are pretty important to you, aren't they, Dan?"

"Yeah," Dan said hoarsely.

"Remember what they say, Dan: 'Life is about the journey, not just the destination.' You'll get to the destination soon enough. It's a six-foot hole in the ground. They'll drop you in there and then go back to your house for creamed chicken casserole and finger sandwiches. Your destination will have been reached. Until then there is a game that's being played; the game called life."

"So is that why you sent me to the cemetery?" Dan looked straight ahead. "To remind me of my mortality?"

"Is that what you took away from that experience?"

"To be honest, when I first read that note I thought it was a slam, letting me know I wasn't such a big, important deal after all."

"Dan, have I done or said anything to you or anyone else in this course that you would honestly consider to be a 'slam'?" she asked quietly.

Dan exhaled and leaned forward, his arms on his thighs. "No."

"So where would that interpretation come from?"

"From a voice in my own head. I guess you'd call it the Self-Critic. It doesn't hesitate to tell me when I'm not measuring up. I guess I learned that by listening to my father's criticism all my life."

"And if you silenced that critical voice inside you, what else could that note mean? How does the Sage interpret it?"

Dan recalled the line: 'Cemeteries are full of indispensable men.' "The obvious meaning is that no one is really indispensable. Everybody can be replaced."

"It sounds like your Judgment voice only sees this as punitive," Martha said.

"Well, it feels like that to me," Dan admitted. "But I suppose it could mean not being indispensable. That I can stop carrying the whole burden alone."

When Martha asked him what that experience would be like, Dan released a little laugh. His first thought was it would be a relief. He had to admit he was tired of doing the same thing over and over.

Measuring the expressions on his face, she asked, "Do you like football, Dan?"

"Used to play it in high school and as a freshman in college."

"Let's look at what they do in football," Martha began, using the metaphor of what happens on the field as the players tackle, pass, run, catch, and intercept. When their team makes a touchdown, the fans cheer, and then they go get hotdogs and drinks. As for the players, they go back to the kick-off and start all over again.

"We want to make goals, Dan," she continued. "That's part of the game. But the heart of the game is what happens on the field between touchdowns. How you play the game determines not only the results but also the journey. How are you playing your game, Dan? You get results, but how many people have you stepped on and run through to accomplish them? How often do you ignore your wife and children? How often do you ignore your own health and well being? Sure, you bring in the client money, but look at how you've been playing the game on the field to get that money."

A warm breeze rippled the surface of the pond, and the cattails at the edges nodded their heads.

"You know, Dan, there are different ways to deal with power. You can have power that is overpowering, the kind that dominates, directs, separates, and hurts. Or you can have the kind of power that empowers, unites, connects, strengthens, and supports. What kind of power do you think would build a great team?"

Dan only knew one kind of power, the kind that took charge and got things done.

"My guess is you have a lot to think about," Martha said quietly, rising to her feet. "What if you did have a choice, Dan? What if you could choose a life that really works for you? You know the answers; they're all inside you."

Dan watched her walk slowly and steadily toward the little cottage on the edge of the pond where she was staying. Leaning back, he opened his arms and rested them on the back of the bench. Christine wasn't the problem; she was a symptom he realized suddenly. He was the problem, and he had to change. Leaning forward, he covered his face with his hands. He was just like his father, and he was going end up a bitter old man, alone and disliked by everybody—even his own children.

It wasn't just in his personal life, Dan told himself. He knew he also had to change his ways at work. Many bright people reported to him, and it was time to let go and see what happens. His heart racing, he got up from the bench. He had to move.

Looking out across the field, he saw someone approaching, walking slowly. It was Paula. He started to raise his arm to acknowledge her wave but turned away quickly and went in the opposite direction.

Sarah sat under the tree, eyes closed and her body completely relaxed. Unsure of what to do, she had stayed in her room for a half hour and then went in search of a snack that she really didn't want. Finally she had gone for a walk. Following the twisting driveway she headed away from the lodge, not intending to go more than a short distance. It was so quiet, nothing around her but birds in the trees and somewhere overhead a plane droning in the distance. The sun shone through the leaves, leaving mottled shadows on the roadway. No one was calling her name, asking her to do something, make something, or fix something… She was completely by herself and it was delicious.

Then she had set off across the field and headed toward a big old oak tree. Seated under it for the past hour, she had let her mind drift. She might have even nodded off for a moment or two. Opening her eyes now, Sarah drank in the simple beauty of field and forest around her. She needed this time away from everyone, including her children who meant more to her than anything in her life. It was time for her to look inside at what she imagined to be a big empty space she tried to stuff with food.

Where had that empty place come from? Sarah wondered. Her childhood for sure, but she had to admit that while money was tight, they certainly weren't impoverished. While her parents didn't believe in spending money needlessly, they didn't really go without necessities like shoes and winter coats—even if they were hand-me-downs.

Sarah recalled again one of her saddest memories. When she was eight, her parents had decided she was old enough to know the truth about Santa Claus and the harsh reality that Christmas presents were budgeted and paid for out of the household money. It had been a bad year on the farm. Her father had to buy feed for the cattle, which meant there was no spare cash for anything. She remembered her mother crying as she counted out a few meager dollars to buy cheap toys for the younger ones. That had been the year she received nothing but a handkerchief on which her mother embroidered her name in blue and pink thread.

Each time she remembered that story, she felt that old sadness, but this time there was a new revelation. The handkerchief had her name on it! She could picture her mother stitching carefully, making the swirling "S" for Sarah and the little daisies made of thread after the "h." Her mother had given her the best gift that she could and one that bore her own name. Her name. This was a gift her mother had taken a great deal of time and attention to make with her own hands. Maybe what her mother was telling her was that she really did matter.

Inside the lodge, Paula stopped in the kitchen for a glass of water. It was nearly six o'clock, but she was in no hurry to do anything except drink in the surroundings. Through the window she saw Martha sitting on the porch of her little cottage just looking at the pond. Paula stepped out of the lodge and headed toward her. Just then Martha got up and was slowly making her way into the building. Paula called out to her.

"Martha, can I see you for a minute?" Paula asked.

Looking up, Martha gave a big wave. "Of course. Come inside and join me."

Martha invited her into a small sitting room. It was rustic but very comfortable and cozy. One of the lodge staff had made a crackling fire in the fireplace for her. "So, what's on your mind, Paula?" Martha asked, settling into a comfortable wingback chair by the fireplace, angled away from the window so she could give Paula her full attention. She beckoned Paula to sit on the couch.

"I went running after the session today. I couldn't wait to get out of there. But I didn't get very far," Paula began. "I made it up to the top of the hill. I was looking out at a farm, and that triggered this memory of when I was little and my mother took my brother and me to get pumpkins. I realized that my mother tried, she really did. But she was so stressed all the time in her life and in her marriage. Sure, I love my dad, but I imagine it has been hard on her to be married to him. He doesn't take his responsibilities very seriously."

Paula's voice trailed off for a moment. "Anyway, what I wanted to tell you was I understand her so much more now. I was fighting against my mother because I thought she didn't approve of me. What I see now is that she just wanted the best for me. She didn't want me to end up like my dad—or stressed out like her."

Martha listened carefully and waited for a moment after Paula had finished before speaking. "It seems like you've opened up to the wisdom inside you, allowing you to see your mother's thinking and her beliefs about you from another perspective—from the other side of the circle."

Martha shifted her focus slowly, gazing into the fire. "I also find it interesting that after today's session you couldn't wait to go running. It seems to me that you're always running in one way or another." She looked up. "Do you ever have that feeling?"

"Yeah. It's how I live my life. Always on the go. Gotta keep things moving..."

"What do you suppose you're running away from?"

"I don't know ... responsibility... things I don't want to do." She shrugged her shoulders. "Myself."

Martha nodded. "So how's that been working for you?"

"It doesn't. I knew I wasn't measuring up, but instead of doing something about it, I just said to heck with it. I tried to convince myself that it didn't really matter." Paula shook her head. "But I'm twenty-eight now. That's not twenty-one you know?"

Martha looked at her with understanding. "Maybe it's time to stop running away."

Paula looked away for a moment, then back to Martha. "There's something else. I want to apologize to you. From the beginning, I saw you like my mother: negative, judging me, judging everybody, being too hard on us. Now I understand that you are supporting me to wake up to my own life. Truthfully, I have broken agreements all over the place: with my friends, with my boss, with myself. I couldn't see that before, or maybe I didn't want to see it."

"What else have you realized?" Martha asked gently.

"I realize that I have a lot of potential. You see that potential, and that's why you were tough on me. You are being the coach who wants the best for me. Just like Sylvia, my boss. That's why she sent me here to this course. Maybe my mother has seen that potential in me, too."

"The important thing, Paula, is that you see the potential in yourself and that you want to tap into that potential," Martha added.

Paula nodded. "Yes, I do. And I'm not going to push it away or pretend that it doesn't matter."

"Even if it means not measuring up sometimes?" Martha asked.

"Yes. I don't want to keep living the way I have been with surface friendships and relationships that don't go anywhere and jobs that I'm easily bored with and quit." Paula looked directly at Martha and smiled. "I'm committed to changing my interpretation so I can have the experiences and results that I really want."

"Those are powerful words," Martha smiled back.

"I know," Paula said. "I've been saying them all the way back down the hill."

Alex lay on the grass, looking up at the trees. The sun was starting to set, and it was time to go back to the lodge. Sitting up, he held a leaf by its stem, looking at its five outstretched points that identified it unmistakably as a maple leaf. It was the object he had been searching for.

After leaving the lodge, Alex had walked a long way, trying to do his assignment, searching the ground for an object—any object—that invoked feeling. The more he thought, the less sense it had made. He looked at dozens of rocks, countless trees, even the sky itself. But nothing seemed to fit with this assignment. Frustrated, he had flopped back on the grass and stopped thinking.

Lying there, looking at the sky, he had watched the trees bend slightly in the breeze, rustling the leaves that were still mostly green but just starting to turn color. It was the change in temperature that caused the chlorophyll to die, bringing out the colored pigment in the leaves. To him the excitement over fall colors was not a big deal. It was just a simple scientific process.

Then he had noticed one leaf, the leaf he now held in his hand.

Dislodged by the wind, it had floated down toward him, spiraling slowly like a miniature glider. His eyes had traced the leaf's flight to earth, watching it flutter and spin until it landed on his chest. Rising up on one elbow, he picked it up and looked at it closely. It was wide and broad, its green center turning a yellowish orange. There was a ragged split in the leaf, perhaps where it had rubbed against a branch and a brown spot like a callous near the stem.

It was far from perfect, and yet it didn't need to be. Even with rips, tears, and a callous, that leaf had done its job, collecting sunlight and carbon dioxide to produce food for the tree and giving off oxygen that replenished the planet. In spite of all its imperfections, it was a still a perfect leaf. It was doing what leaves do, and like all leaves it had fallen to the ground where it would rot and replenish the soil. Even when disintegrating it was a perfect leaf. It represented life, perfect in its imperfections.

Getting to his feet, Alex walked back toward the lodge, the first lines of his poem composed in his head.

❖ Chapter Six

Victims No More

Alex, Sarah, and Paula stood around the breakfast buffet in the Great Room on Friday morning, talking and sharing their experiences of the previous day. Dan grimaced at their laughter as he leaned against the wall, his arms folded across his chest. All this pleasant chatter was really getting on his nerves. As the door to the meeting room opened, Alex called out to Dan, "You coming?"

"Yeah. In a minute," Dan muttered, waiting to move until he saw Martha headed toward the room.

The class began.

"Good morning," Martha began warmly. "When we started this course, I told you that the value you received—just as in life—would come from your participation. If you put a lot into life, you're going to get a lot out of life. If you don't, you won't. The same holds true at work and in your relationships. Participation means being fully engaged, both in sharing and in feedback, including giving and receiving it. So this morning who is ready to fully participate? Who is ready to jump in and go for it?"

Sarah and Paula raised their hands, but Alex quickly rose to his feet, a piece of paper clutched in his hands. Martha beckoned him to come up front. Dan sat back, his arms folded again, and watched.

Standing in front of the others, Alex took in a deep breath. "My assignment was to go out and write a poem. So I did."

"Yes, and it was to be a very special kind of poem—one that came from your heart," Martha affirmed.

Alex's hands trembled as he held the paper. Standing in front of the others, he felt more vulnerable than ever before in his life. Noticing his nervousness, Martha gently asked him what was going on. Alex felt the tightness in his throat as he admitted how uncomfortable this was for him.

"And yet, here you stand, facing your fears and moving through them," Martha said, nodding. "So tell me, what are you afraid of?"

"That people will think this is stupid."

"Are you afraid that they will then think that you are stupid?" she asked. Alex nodded, and Martha continued. "I can see why that would be scary for anyone and especially for you since until now the key to your survival has been your brain and your intellect. Let me ask you a question, Alex. When you were in school were you known for your athletic abilities?"

"No-o-o-o," he said, shaking his head back and forth for emphasis. "In fact, in gym class, I was always the last one to be picked for a team."

"And I'll bet that you were never particularly comfortable in social situations either. Maybe you ate alone in the lunchroom or at a table with the others who didn't fit in with the popular kids. Would that be true?"

Alex agreed, studying the floor.

"And how did it feel when you waited for your name to be called to be for a team and it never came? How did it feel to sit alone? How did it feel to be the butt of name-calling? Even more, how did it feel to be the target of racial slurs and jokes?"

"I suppose it hurt at the time, but I got used to it."

"Did you? Or did you decide that you'd been hurt enough, and you weren't going to be hurt like that anymore? So your inner Protector helped you build a big wall around your heart, brick by brick. Your Protector listened to your 'I Have to Be Smart to Survive' voice, and you developed your mind because that's where you could really distinguish yourself. The problem is that it looks like you went a little too far, to the point where you were so separated from your feelings that you couldn't connect with others in your relationships and at work."

"That's right," Alex said hoarsely, turning toward Martha.

"People who go beyond survival realize they must risk in order to thrive. Are you willing to take the risk of regaining that emotional connection? I use the word risk because you never know how people will respond," Martha said. "They might laugh at you. And yes, they might think your poem is stupid. That possibility exists. You're going to have to move through that ego-fear if you want to be free. Up until now you've given your fear a lot of power. You've moved over it, under it, and around it. You've let it run you and shut you down. Yet, the only way to manage that fear is to go through it. If you want to thrive, then you're going have to jump out of the box that you've put yourself in and trust that your Sage will guide you to a safe landing."

Looking at the paper Alex held in his sweaty grip, Martha asked him if he was ready to leave the safety of his comfort zone and get his power back. He took in a deep breath and looked at her squarely. "I'm ready," he said firmly.

Glancing up from the paper at the three people seated in the classroom, their attention focused fully on him, Alex began in a quivering voice. "I call the poem 'A Perfect Leaf'." Clearing his throat, he started reading, his voice becoming stronger and more assured as he continued.

A leaf that flies in the wind
Not discarded, but set free
From the only home it has known.
I watched its flight,
Riding the currents of the wind
As it drifted toward the Earth.
It made a perfect landing on my chest,
As if I was its destination.
I looked closely at the leaf as it really was:
Flawed, torn, and calloused.
It carried the scars of its brief life
And yet in spite of those imperfections
In the history of all the world,
There had never been a leaf exactly like it
And there would never be one like it again.
Ever.
It was pure inspiration to me.

The room was silent. Alex looked up at their faces, taking in the smiles and the nods. Sarah mouthed the word, "Beautiful."

"Thank you, Alex, for your honesty. You opened your heart to us and that took courage," Martha said, her eyes glistening. "I don't know if you realize it or not, but underneath your chest, where the leaf landed, is your heart. Maybe there are no accidents after all." Smiling, she asked him what he was experiencing right then.

Alex grinned. "I feel good."

"Empowered? Confident?" Martha offered, and Alex quickly agreed.

Martha mirrored his confident face back to him. "You made it through because of your commitment to truly live life and not just survive as a stimulus-response machine driven by your fears of judgment about imperfection. Also notice your hands have stopped shaking! The people out there in the world are going to think whatever they think. We humans are judgment machines. I don't need to tell you, a man of color, that there are plenty of people who will still call you names and try to hurt you, but their judgments are only judgments; they aren't the Capital-T Truth! They are driven by their own fear of people who are different than they are. Hold onto your confidence, face your fears, tap into your inner wisdom, and don't let the judgments of others harden your heart."

Turning toward the others, Martha asked, "How many of you feel more emotionally connected to Alex than when you first met him?" All three of them raised their hands. As Alex took his seat, Paula got up. Looking over at Alex and composing herself, she said, "When I first saw you, I thought you were such a nerd. You seemed to be such a know-it-all, and you didn't want to connect with any of us. In fact I thought you felt you were superior to the rest of us. I judged you and I just want to say, I'm sorry. That was a beautiful poem." She put her hands over her heart then extended them toward him.

"Thanks, Paula," Alex replied, a little self-consciously. He paused for a moment. "You know, you're right. I am a 'know-it-all,' and I didn't want to connect with any of you. So I judged you, too. But now I'm not thinking of myself as separate." He glanced over at Martha. "I'm not feeling that way either."

Martha stepped forward and asked, "How many of you know you are a nerd?" Alex raised his hand first, and then Paula and Sarah put their hands up.

"You know, there are only two types of people in this world. Those who are nerds…" And turning her attention to Dan said, "and those who are pretending they're not nerds!"

Dan just looked back at her, his expression not changing. She smiled gently at him.

"We're all nerds," Martha continued. "We're all caught up in our own little life dramas. Yet inside, we frequently feel awkward and uncomfortable. We pretend that we're slick and cool, but underneath we sometimes feel insecure and incompetent. We're afraid that people will find out that we're real human beings and that we sometimes do nerdy things. Wise and powerful human beings aren't afraid to admit that."

Dan bent over, his arms resting on his legs, staring at the floor.

"The moment you accept yourself exactly the way you are, own up to your imperfections and differences, and realize that they are part of being human, then no one can hurt you with their judgments of you," Martha went on. "You're not afraid that anyone will find you out. You've already admitted your shortcomings. You've already acknowledged that we don't look and act the same. You don't have to pretend, hide, defend, or avoid. Like the leaf, you are how you are—perfect in your imperfections and differences, with no apologies."

Martha stepped back, giving Paula the chance to speak.

"I know now why I'm here, and why my boss, Sylvia, wanted me to come. I get it now that there is so much more to me than I've been willing to see in myself. I've been afraid to be as good as I can be. I know that it will require some hard work and a commitment to the details." Paula's voice shook. "I've been running from that all my life, and it has cost me in every area of my life—relationships, friendships, job promotions. It has cost me peace of mind and feeling good about myself. Now, I want to stop paying that price. I want to stop running."

Martha listened patiently as Paula spoke, giving her the time and space she needed to express what had been so tightly bottled up inside. Then Martha asked her if she was ready to stop being a reactive child and assume adult behavior. Was she ready to take full ownership of herself and her personal power? Was she committed to becoming the person she was capable of being? With each question Paula nodded more and more firmly. "Yes!" she said, clenching her fist.

"Do you know it's going to take some rewiring? You'll need to pay close attention because until now you've been addicted to a carefree 'fly-by-the-seat-of-your-pants' attitude, and sometimes your unconsciousness has allowed you to operate carelessly." Martha continued. "Like an addiction, that way of thinking and operating has run you. And it has hurt you."

"I know," Paula acknowledged.

Taking this step would require some shifts in behavior, she told Paula, closing off old escape routes, and facing tasks and completing them instead of running away. "What lies ahead is hard work, but I promise you, the payoffs will outweigh the cost."

"I am committed to changing my thinking and to doing the hard work," Paula stated, looking Martha in the eye. "Starting now, this moment."

Martha steadily kept her gaze, a slight smile on her face. Finally she said, "Thank you for sharing your honest self-awareness, Paula."

Sarah glanced over at Dan as he ignored everyone, clenching his right fist in his left hand. "I want to go next," she announced. Standing in front of the room, Sarah radiated with new energy and determination. "All my life, I've let people run right over me. I've taken a backseat, not spoken up, and always come last. I've done everything they've asked and then some. But I'm not going to let that happen any more. I've done things for people that I didn't want to do, at work and at home. I let them take advantage of me because I thought I should. In my role as an administrative assistant—and as a wife and mother, too—I've been ruled by all the 'shoulds' and 'have tos.' And you know what? The truth is they're not part of my job or role descriptions. I made them up!"

Sarah spoke with clarity and honesty, commanding the others' attention. She spoke of her anger: at her boss, her boss's wife, and even at her family. "But I'm the one who let them do it! I see it now. I set it up that way," she admitted, and laughed, her voice full and strong. "I feel so powerful and 'I' matter—and I do mean the word 'I'."

Paula and Alex gave her a little applause. "Great, Sarah," Martha echoed. "It's interesting what happens when you admit those things you have been pretending you didn't know."

"Oh, and there's another thing," Sarah continued, looking at Dan, "I have to say I learned this from you, Dan."

His body frozen, he moved only his eyes to look at her.

"I've been thinking about how you didn't want to let anyone else make that call to your client, how you have to take care of everything yourself. Well, I do the same thing with my children. I don't let them take on any responsibility, even though it would be good for them. I have to thank you, Dan, because I learned that from you!"

Dan looked away.

Martha glanced at Dan, and then turned her full focus to Sarah. She acknowledged Sarah for facing her fear of confrontation, for being honest with herself and standing up for her wants and needs, and for challenging the limiting belief that taking care of herself was bad, and that owning her power was wrong. "Now you are realizing that looking out for your own self-interest as well as that of others is one of the greatest gifts you can give to another person. Why? Because it's honest, and honesty is what builds relationships, rather than the dishonesty of pretending that everything is fine and holding in all that resentment."

Paula blurted out, "I have to say, Sarah, that all the times you were trying to help everybody and take care of us have been uncomfortable. I just felt smothered."

"I know," Sarah admitted. "I understand that now. I thought if I took care of all of you, you'd like me. I do like helping people. That is part of who I am. But I just have to keep it in perspective."

"It all comes down to balance," Martha interjected. "When you take your caring too far, it becomes smothering and it doesn't work."

Sarah smiled confidently, voicing how much better she felt for finally expressing what had been building up inside for years.

Martha turned toward Dan and looked at him for a moment. "Are you ready, Dan, or do you want to fight it some more?"

Dan sat focused on the ceiling. In that silence, the minutes that passed felt like hours to him. Martha waited patiently. No one moved. Finally, he started to talk: "I don't know what to say," he started quietly. "Let's just say I don't like myself too much right now. I, uh…" He cleared his throat. "I have been looking at some things in my life, things I've done that I wish I hadn't…" His words trailed off. "Look, I'm glad that you're all doing great, and now you're all happy." His voice crackled with anger and got louder as he spoke. "But you know, my life just isn't like that. Right now, my life sucks, and I hate it. I don't have anything more to say."

"Okay, Dan. I hear you. Whenever you're ready to let go of control, I am ready to listen." Martha turned toward the others: "Let's take a twenty-minute break. During that time I have a special assignment for Paula."

After the others had filed out of the room, Martha handed Paula a blank piece of paper and a pencil and explained the assignment. "Behind the lodge, there are a series of paths. Down these paths are small sheds. Inside one of them is a lawnmower."

"So am I doing a little yard work?" Paula joked, but clearly eager to launch into whatever she had to do with newfound energy and enthusiasm.

"Listen carefully, Paula, to all the instructions," Martha replied playfully. "Inside one of the three sheds is a lawnmower. First, you need to find where the lawnmower is. Then I want you to write detailed instructions so that any other person could go directly to that shed from the lodge and immediately find the lawnmower."

"Can't I just draw a map?" Paula asked. "I'm very good at drawing,"

"No. You must write detailed instructions, step-by-step, on how to find the lawnmower. You have seventeen minutes left in the break. I expect you to complete the assignment and be back here in that time."

Dan walked away from the others and headed out the front door of the lodge, his cell phone in hand. Calling the office, he left a voicemail for Tim. He stared at the phone for a few seconds and then punched in another number.

Paula took off out the back door to the patio and headed down the center path. It then split off to the left and the right, but Paula continued straight. Around the first bend was a shed. The door was locked. She peered through a window; there was no lawnmower. Sprinting back up the path, Paula decided quickly between the two remaining choices: She took the path to her right. There was another shed about thirty yards down the path, hidden amongst some trees. The door was unlocked and ajar about an inch. Inside was the lawnmower.

"Bingo!" Paula said smiling and ran back to the patio. She had ten minutes left and didn't want to be late. Plus she had to go to the bathroom. Paula sat on the edge of the patio step, tipping up on her toes to use her lap as a desk.

"Step one, go out the back door to the patio."

"Step two, take the path in front of you." Wait a minute! She remembered the path that led straight wasn't where the shed was. She had turned right. She wrote down the directions quickly: "When the path splits, go right. Follow the path to the shed. Shed door is unlocked. Lawnmower is inside." Folding the instructions as she walked, Paula hurried back inside the lodge. She had just enough time to stop in the restroom and grab a bottle of water.

When the break was over, all four of them were in the room and waiting for Martha. When she arrived, Paula proudly handed in her assignment, on time and completed.

Turning her attention to all four of them, Martha began: "What you are each starting to realize is you are accountable and responsible for the results that show up in your lives. Most of us, however, have spent quite a bit of time listening to the voices in our heads that would keep us from being accountable and responsible: the Victim, the Wounded Child, the Martyr, the Judge, the Critic… When we tap into these negative, controlling voices, we see ourselves as the victims of the circumstances, events, and situations of our lives. When we buy into this perception as 'truth,' we allow our circumstances to be bigger than we are. Does this sound familiar?"

Heads nodded, but their faces showed they were still wrestling with the concept.

"To explain, start by recalling a time in your own life, in the fairly recent past, when you really felt like a victim, or when you felt hurt or taken advantage of by someone. Or perhaps something happened that you believed was unfair or you didn't see coming," Martha explained. "Then I want you to tell your 'victim story' with all the drama you can muster. When the others are convinced that you are a world-class victim, they'll raise their hands."

Sarah offered to begin. "Okay, I'm the assistant to our CFO, Bernie Coletti, and he relies on me to do a lot of things for him—even personal stuff like remembering his kids' birthdays and doctors appointments. I don't mind doing that, really, because it's my job. But his wife—and I know we have confidentiality in this room—really imposes on me. Just because I'm Bernie's assistant, she thinks she can ask me to do things for her." Paula raised her hand. "I'm not just talking about once in a while, either. I bet she calls me at least twice a week to do something for her—dinner reservations, booking flights, nail appointments. She even had me look into spas for her and her sister!" Dan and Alex raised their hands. "And the same thing happens at home. I'm the one who is stuck doing everything because the kids won't pick up after themselves and my husband never steps in to help me. And then there are my husband's parents…"

"Okay, Sarah," Martha interrupted. "That's a great victim story. You can stop now. They're convinced! Who's next?"

Alex volunteered. "Frank is always undermining me and my projects. Every week, he gets more aggressive about it. He doesn't even try to hide it any more. He talks to the other team members about me, and he goes to the boss about me. He points out anything and everything he thinks I'm doing wrong. I'd be pretty happy if it wasn't for him. It's getting so I can't even do my job with him around." Sarah, Dan, and Paula all raised their hands.

"All right, Alex. You've convinced them. Paula?"

"Okay, people are always complaining about me and yelling at me," she began. "They complain that I'm always late—which I am— and that I lose things and that things don't get done on time." She looked around hopefully, but no hands were raised. "Okay, here's one. My landlord has now demanded that I pay my rent in advance with a certified bank check just because one time my check accidentally bounced because I forgot to deposit my paycheck. One time! And I've lived there three years, and I gave him a security deposit when I first moved in. It's not fair what he's doing to me." Alex, Sarah, and Dan raised their hands.

"Okay, Paula, you got it. Dan, you're up," Martha told him.

Starting in a monotone, Dan began. "Okay, so I think my team is not doing what it could. They don't take responsibility. They expect me to do everything. Except Tim. I guess he's okay..." He paused. This was just more crap, and he knew it.

Martha waited several moments, then gently coached him: "Maybe now is the time, Dan. If it isn't working for you any more, maybe it's time to stop making the same choices—shutting down, shutting out, pretending that you don't have a heart, that all you have to offer anyone are your results...."

He drew in his breath, and then blurted out from his gut: "I am always the guy who has to do everything. They screw up and drop the ball, and who gets the blame? Me! That's why I stay late—because they don't, and I can't make them. I'm the one who is putting in the long hours so I can make a good living for my family. I'm killing myself at work so my family can have the beautiful house and the pool in the backyard to keep up with the Joneses." He spoke bitterly, his voice just below a shout. "But while they're relaxing in the $300 lawn chairs,

I'm at work. And do they ever say thank you?" He slapped the desk with his hand. "No! All they do is complain that I'm not home!"

At this point, all hands were raised but Dan went on.

"Victim? Damn right, I'm a victim. First my old man. Then every coach and every boss and every customer and client..." He ticked off each name on his fingers. "And now myself. I'm the one who screwed up my life." The words hung in the air.

The others sat quietly, listening carefully to what he had said.

Martha thanked him, turned to a fresh sheet on the flip chart, and drew a line down the center. On the right side she wrote the word, "Victim." "Tell me, what does it feel like to be a victim? What are the thoughts, emotions, and feelings that you have? What are the reactions in your physical body?" she asked them.

As they called out the words, Martha wrote the list on the paper.

	Victim
	Powerless
	Angry
	Hurt
	Upset
	Frustrated
	Abused
	Betrayed
	Set up
	Irritated
	Stressed

Reading the list aloud, she said, "That's exactly the experience you will always have when you are a victim. However, there is an alternative to feeling like a victim: that is, being accountable." Turning to a fresh page on the chart, she wrote:

ACCOUNTABILITY = The awareness that I contribute to or cause (directly or indirectly) the events around me as a result of my actions or inactions Without Judgment

"Accountability is not to be confused with responsibility," she added. "Responsibility is task-oriented; it is the degree to which you are responsible for accomplishing something or completing a task.

"When I am accountable, I can account for my connection to events as they occur, and I recognize that I have an ability to choose my response," Martha explained. "Further, I emphasize WITHOUT JUDGMENT because this is not about blaming yourself." In other words," she continued,

Accountability ≠ Blame

"When you are accountable, you simply acknowledge the choices you made that produced the results. Not good. Not bad. Not right. Not wrong. It's just that you acknowledge the choices were yours. Accountability is a reflection of a Universal Truth. Whether we recognize it and accept it or not, we are all accountable."

Turning to the next page, Martha drew another illustration: a horizontal line with an X at each end. Along the line she drew hash

CHOICES and RESULTS

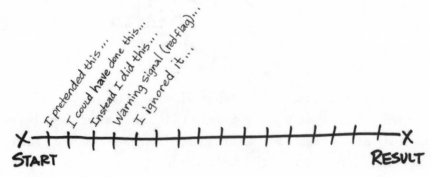

marks, an inch or two apart.

"The X on the left is where I start. The X on the right is my result. Each of the slashes along this line is a choice I made along the way. I pretended this... I could have done this, but I didn't... Instead I did this.... And every one of those choices I made along the way led to the results I have today. When I am accountable, I fully recognize how my choices connected me to events as they happened, and I recognize that I have chosen my responses to those events," Martha continued. "Nobody forced me to make the choices I made. There are no accidents. Every choice you made in your life, and every choice I made in my life, led us to be here in this room at this time."

Alex nodded as he listened. Logically, this made sense to him. It was as if long lost puzzle pieces were finally coming together.

"You already know there are many ways to interpret an event. So who would like to tell their story differently and step to the other side, from victim to accountable?" Martha invited. "When you tell your story from this viewpoint, you will likely see that there are some details that you conveniently 'forgot' to tell in the victim story. You'll see that there were some red and yellow flags along the way, and you chose to ignore them. After you identify these choices, you begin to take ownership of your results because these were the choices that produced them."

She cautioned them to watch out for the Judge and Self-Critic who would want to make them feel guilty or feel bad for the choices they made. All they had to do was honestly recite all the facts and choices they made without judging them as right or wrong or good or bad. "If you feel that you've done something wrong, then you will feel guilty and blame yourself. That's not accountability. That's being a victim of yourself," Martha coached them.

Alex volunteered to go first and, studying the words on the flip chart, he began: "Without judgment, I see how I have everything to do with the outcome. I am accountable for the situation with Frank." He stopped himself. Did he really believe that he was personally accountable for what Frank did at work?

"Are you having difficulty listening to a different voice in your head, other than the judgmental Critic that would make you right and Frank wrong?" Martha coaxed.

"Uh-huh. I'm stuck. I mean, I get it intellectually, but I don't know if I believe it."

"That's okay. Let's see if we can walk through this together. For example, have you looked at things from Frank's point of view, or do you shoot down everything he says before you even consider it?"

"I refute what he says. I've never really sat down and listened to why he thinks the way he does." He shook his head. "Okay, I'm starting to understand it."

"Remember, there's no judgment involved here," Martha reminded him gently.

Alex looked at the chart as he spoke. "I see how I've built my army against him, while he's built his army against me." He shook his head a little sheepishly. "I do see how I have everything to do with the results because I've made him the enemy. In fact, there were a couple of times he tried to talk with me, but I was so ticked off at him, I ignored him."

Acknowledging the step he had taken, Martha referred back to the Life View Filter chart. Now that he had cleared his filter and had a different framework of thinking, he was open to the natural knowing inside him which would allow him to see new possibilities, and then take different actions.

"I need to meet with Frank. I need to apologize for my role in perpetuating this problem between us," Alex continued. "I need to listen to his point of view and see if he's willing to listen to mine. I have to end this war and see if there is some way to work it out so we can coexist in the same department without fighting."

"Yes. You need to initiate this communication, and that's not what you have been inclined to do in the past," Martha interjected.

"I know. That's what I have to do," Alex said firmly.

Paula was next. "Oh, I get this. I see that I am accountable for the outcome because I've screwed around so much. I always have too much going on, and that's why I'm late or I act crazy. And nobody is making me do it. I really get this! I'm responsible for my own results. Also," she added with a grin, "I didn't tell you that more than one check bounced on my apartment. I only bounced one rental payment, but my security deposit check also bounced."

"I see. How convenient to forget that detail," Martha teased. "What do you realize now that you can do differently?"

"At work and with my friends I have to say 'no' sometimes. I don't want to because I like saying yes to everything. But I want honesty and integrity. I want people to respect me. And I want that more than just doing stuff. With my apartment, I have to make sure I operate with integrity, write only good checks, and be on time with them. I have to keep my agreements, and I've gotta clean up all the broken ones."

Martha agreed, explaining that apologizing and asking for forgiveness for something that they had done or not done which has hurt a relationship would be very healing for themselves and others. But this should not be communicated from a place in which they were feeling wrong or bad. They simply did something that didn't work.

Sarah stirred in her seat, drawing in a deep sigh before she began. "I see that it's all my fault."

"Whoa! Wait a minute, Sarah," Martha interrupted. "Do you hear those words coming from your mouth? It's my fault?"

"Oh, I forgot," she continued, a little flustered. "Okay, I see how I have everything to do with the outcome."

"Remember," Martha interjected, "no judgment. You haven't done anything wrong or bad. It's not your fault. Fault implies blame. You just made choices that didn't work out. If you feel guilty or bad, you are now a victim of yourself."

"Okay," Sarah began again, "I see I have everything to do with the outcome—without judgment—because I always tell Bernie's wife that 'it's no problem,' and 'I'm happy to do this.' Or 'Ask me any time.' It was my choice to say all those things. Then I feel all this resentment toward her because…" Sarah bit her lip. "I feel resentment toward her because Charlotte Coletti knows how to take care of herself and I don't. That's really why I hate making the reservations for the spa and booking flights for their family getaways. These are things I should be doing for myself and my family."

Sarah went on, admitting that if she were truthful, she would explain to Charlotte that she didn't have time to do all these things for her because Bernie kept her so busy. She never says "no" to anybody, however, because she is afraid of hurting someone else's feelings. While she constantly complains that no one helps her, Sarah could see how she does not keep boundaries with herself, others, and even her children and husband. "In fact, what I think I'm really afraid of is that they're going to hurt *my* feelings," she realized. "That's why I feel like a victim all the time, every minute of the day. I see that because of the choices I'm making, I have set that up to happen."

"Now that you're open to new possibilities and you're changing your filter, what do you need to do?" Martha asked.

Sarah saw the choices and possibilities clearly. She needed to be honest with others, to set boundaries, and then to respect them herself, and to acknowledge that she and her feelings were important. Plus, she admitted sheepishly, she needed to respect other peoples' boundaries and not be a helper to the point of smothering.

"And who is the person you most need to apologize to?" Martha asked.

"Myself," she acknowledged.

"Yes. If you don't hold yourself as important and respect yourself, how do you expect other people to?"

"I'm not going to keep doing things to please people at my own expense," Sarah continued firmly. "But I still like to help people."

"Of course, it's part of who you are: being helpful and kind. But when you do things at your own expense, you're hurting yourself, and that's when you've gone too far. You're out of balance, and resentment begins."

Everyone waited. Dan was next, but no one looked at him except Martha. Without being asked this time, Dan rose to his feet. Every head turned toward him. He spoke slowly and deliberately: "I see that I have everything to do with the results and with my experience of the results. When it comes to my team, I've overpowered them. Because of that, they've been afraid to take risks. Now I need to empower them. I need to listen to them and delegate." He took in a deep breath as he composed himself.

"And at home, I need to change things." Dan stood with his hands on his hips, nodding to them all as if they were making a group decision. "I made a call at the break. I told Donna that I want us to work things out. I don't know how she feels right now, but," he said with a hopeful smile, "this is what I'm choosing to commit myself to. I need to include her and treat her like a true partner."

Dan paced back and forth. "And I need to spend more time with my kids. Play ball with them. As a kid I loved playing ball, but my father was always too busy to play with me." No one interrupted as he related his memories of how, when his father showed up for his games, all he ever heard was the constant criticism. With his own kids Dan was committed to go out and play every weekend. "And I mean play. If they drop the ball or swing and miss, who cares? This is something I need to do for them—and myself."

"Thank you for your honesty, Dan. I acknowledge you for listening to your Wise Man within," Martha said sincerely. "It all comes down to balance, doesn't it? Do you see that when you are in the extremes, you don't achieve the results and the experiences that you're looking for?"

She moved to the chart that had the Victim list on it. At the top of the left-hand column she wrote "Accountability." Then she asked them, "What do you experience when you tell your story from this point of view?"

She wrote the words on the chart as quickly as they blurted them out:

Accountability	Victim
Honest	Powerless
Strong	Angry
Free	Hurt
Clear	Upset
Energized	Frustrated
Peaceful	Abused
Empowered	Betrayed
Loving	Set up
Powerful	Irritated
Relaxed	Stressed

After reading both lists aloud, she asked: "Now for the million dollar question, which list is right, and which one is wrong?"

"There is no right or wrong view. It's all just personal perception," Alex offered. "We all get to choose which way we want to tell our stories."

"Exactly, Alex. We can gather evidence and data and people to support either view. The question is this: What is the experience you are looking for? If you want to feel powerless, angry, hurt, upset, frustrated, abused, betrayed, set up, irritated, and stressed, then tell your victim story. Have at it! Roll in it! But just don't complain that you feel this way because you are choosing it!"

Then pointing to the left side of the chart she said, "If, on the other hand, you would like to have the experience of being honest, strong, free, clean, energized, peaceful, empowered, loving, powerful, and relaxed, then tell the story from the accountable view. It doesn't matter to me which one you choose. It is your life. All I want you to see at this point is this : First, you have a choice between two views, accountable and victim. Second, the choice is yours to make. Third, the view you choose will determine your experience. Fourth, your experience determines the quality of your life. The ability to choose your life experience is the root of your personal power."

For emphasis, she wrote on the flip chart:

Personal POWER = The ability to choose my life experience

After a moment, she turned to a clean sheet and wrote down the fourth principle.

Principle #4
Got results?

"'Got results?' is a reminder that you must take full accountability, without blame, for your results and that the actions, reactions, and choices you made that produced them are yours and yours alone. Results don't lie. They are the clearest indication in your life of the choices you have made. No one forced you to make the choices you did, and every choice has led directly to the results you have. Look around you. What results do you have? What feedback do others give you? What feedback is the world around you delivering? As empowered human beings, we choose to take full accountability for everything."

Dan broke in. "Okay, wait a minute here. What do you mean for everything? I'm getting how I have everything to do with the outcome in my own life, but you can't possibly expect me to be accountable for something like the war in the Middle East!"

"Dan, I consciously wrote the word 'everything.' Remember, I don't mean blame."

Dan just shook his head in disagreement.

"It's an interesting question, Dan, and I'd like you think about it."

Martha then suggested they take a fifteen-minute break and asked Paula and Alex to stay behind for a moment. As they came to the front, Martha explained to Alex that she had given Paula an assignment. Paula started to interrupt, but Martha firmly instructed her not to say anything. Now it was Alex's turn for an assignment: He was to take Paula's instructions and find the specific location of a lawnmower behind the lodge. If Paula had done the assignment correctly, he should be able to follow her directions and find it easily.

Martha handed him the instructions. "You have 13 minutes to complete the assignment," she told Alex. "I expect you to be back in the room on time, regardless of whether you successfully complete the assignment or not."

Paula lingered in the room after Alex left.

"Is there a problem?" Martha asked her.

"I don't know," she admitted. "My directions and Alex's might be, well, a little different."

"Different?" Martha asked.

"You know, accuracy-wise."

"We'll see, "Martha said. "I suggest that you take your break and let Alex do his part of the assignment."

❖ Chapter Seven

Synergy and Alignment

Standing outside on the patio, Alex unfolded Paula's directions. "Take the path in front of you." This was a little disconcerting as it didn't state the starting point, but he pushed his irritation aside since there was only one main path leading off the patio. When he came to the fork in the path, Alex felt his irritation rising. Following directions from Paula didn't give him much confidence, especially since her instructions were simple, way too simple. "When the path splits, go right."

"We'll see," he muttered aloud. Wrapped up in his annoyance and judgmental thoughts about Paula's competence, he didn't see the sharp, pointed object protruding from the soft ground underfoot. An Indian arrowhead jutted out of the earth, pointing to the left. Never seeing it Alex stepped on it, pushing it back into the ground, and took the fork to the right.

When he saw a shed along the path, he was amazed that he had found it so easily. Anticipating a quick completion to the exercise, he pulled on the door. It was locked. He read the instructions again,

"Shed door is unlocked. Lawnmower is inside."

Frustrated, he pulled again rattling the handle back and forth. It wouldn't budge. He walked around the back looking for another way in and then peered through the window, which was sealed shut. The shed was completely empty. Clenching his jaw, he could feel his blood pressure rising as he read the directions for a third time. How could anyone screw up something so simple, he thought angrily.

Knowing he followed the instructions exactly, Alex decided to look farther down the path in case there was a second shed. He walked through the trees and into the meadow beyond, but there were no more buildings. Hurriedly he returned to the first shed and then retraced his steps back to the split in the path. There were only five minutes left in the break.

Martha had said to follow the directions exactly as written, Alex fumed silently, but with Paula anything could happen. Maybe she didn't know left from right! Alex headed off in the other direction. He set off at a jogging pace down the path. Was the shed on the left or the right? The directions didn't say. He looked carefully on both sides and, sure enough, he saw another shed barely visible behind some trees. Of course, just as he had thought! This one was unlocked, and this one had the lawnmower in it. If Paula had told him to go left—and not right—he'd have found that lawnmower ten minutes ago, and he would have had time to enjoy a little of the break. Now, running back down the path, he made it back into the lodge with only a minute to spare.

"So how'd you do?" Paula asked him, grinning nervously as he came into the room.

"Left and right are pretty easy concepts, Paula," he replied icily.

Martha entered a moment later. Seeing Paula's grimace and Alex looking visibly tense, she invited them both to come to the front of the room. She explained the two assignments to the others.

Paula made a funny face and giggled. Alex set his mouth in a hard line.

"So, Alex, did you find the lawnmower?" Martha asked.

"Yes, but not by following her directions!" he snapped.

"Alex, the assignment was to follow Paula's directions exactly as they were written. Did you do that?" Martha asked calmly.

"Yes. I followed them to the letter," Alex retorted. "Just like the directions said, I took the path directly in front of the patio. When the path split off, I took the right path."

"Left!" Paula blurted out. "Oh, God, I can't believe I did that! When you leave the lodge, it's a left. I was coming the other way because I went down the center path to the first shed. That's when I turned right."

"Uh-huh. I figured that out," Alex said sarcastically. "When I took the path that went right, I found a locked shed and no lawnmower. When I came back to the split and went the other way—which would have been a left coming from the lodge—I found the unlocked shed and the lawnmower. Unfortunately, it took me a while, and I missed the whole break!"

"Geez, I'm sorry, Alex. I can't believe I did that." Paula shot him a sheepish grin.

"But you did do that, Paula." Martha looked at her directly. "The result of your actions is that Alex took the wrong path. A simple exercise that should have taken five minutes took him the entire break. Alex didn't get a break like you did because of your error."

"Okay. I said I was sorry," Paula replied defensively.

"This isn't about being wrong or bad," Martha reminded her. "It's just looking at the result of your actions." Martha turned to Alex. "So how are you feeling right now?"

"Annoyed and frustrated," he replied. When Martha asked him what else he was feeling, he admitted that he also felt vindicated. "As soon as you gave me Paula's directions, I knew there was going to be a problem. She never stops to think things through, so I wasn't that surprised."

"So there are some people you automatically expect to make mistakes, and then when they do, how do you feel?" Martha observed.

Alex relaxed his rigid posture. "Superior, I suppose. It makes me right and the other person wrong." He looked over at Paula. "I know you didn't make that mistake on purpose. When I made it back to the where the paths split off, I figured out exactly what you had done."

"Paula, do you see that if you had taken the time to really think it out—if you had reviewed what you had written, if you had followed your own directions—it wouldn't have happened," Martha commented. "When you do this kind of thing, it makes other people think you're incompetent or, worse yet, that you're stupid. And, you're not. You're a very intelligent and capable woman, Paula. The results, however, also show that your lack of attention to detail can sometimes be viewed as irresponsible. I don't think you realize the impact of your carelessness on other people. When you don't pay attention to details, when you miss a deadline, when you fail to hold up your end of the bargain, when you bounce a check, other people pay the price—and in the long term so do you. As you become accountable for your choices and actions, you will see how you impact others. Remember, this isn't about being wrong or bad. It's just looking at the choices you made to produce the result."

Turning to the whole group, Martha continued: "In life, there are specific and implied agreements. When you accept an assignment, there is an implied agreement that you will do your best to be accurate and do it well. When you are careless or when you fail to complete it, when you rush through, it is a broken implied agreement."

Paula admitted that now she understood the impact of her actions on others and apologized sincerely to Alex. He accepted her apology with a faint smile.

"Alex, can you also see that when other people make mistakes or are careless, your behavior is to immediately jump to judgment, making them wrong and you right?" Martha continued. "This way, you get to think of yourself as better while seeing them as less.

When you do this, do you realize how that affects your emotional reactions? You allow yourself to remain a stimulus-response machine. Do you also see the barriers you build between yourself and others? As a leader in your company, if you were to have some empathy and sensitivity toward your colleagues, how would you utilize this experience and turn it into a positive?"

Alex thought for a moment. "I suppose I could use it as an opportunity to control my reactions and to mentor someone."

"Yes, and you can be successful if you are willing to stop making others wrong so you can be right and if you are willing to risk and allow yourself to care about people." Martha looked at him directly.

"From now on I'll try harder to pay attention to the details," Paula said with conviction, and then slapped her hand over her mouth. "Ooops! No trying, right? I *will* pay attention to the details."

Martha winked. "Nice catch."

As they both headed toward their chairs, Paula's eyes rested on something she had not seen before: a picture on the side wall, this one of the same tree in spring as it was just starting to bud. "Has that picture always been there?" she asked.

Martha nodded, explaining that nothing had been added or removed from the room.

Paula stared for a moment at the picture. "The first day I saw the one in the back of the room of the tree in winter. Are you sure someone didn't put up that springtime picture today?"

"It's always been there, Paula," Martha explained patiently. "But it appears that your filter deleted it. Perhaps you could see the winter scene of the last leaf hanging on to the tree because that was consistent with your filter and the belief of clinging to the past. Now that you're clearing out your filter, you will begin to see things that have always been right there in front of you—literally and figuratively. I find it interesting that you are just now noticing the picture of the tree in springtime, a time that represents a new beginning. It seems so appropriate. And yet, I wonder what else has been right in front of you that you haven't seen before, or what has been said that your filter wouldn't allow you to hear. Cues and clues are around us all the time if we will only take the time to observe with open minds and without judgment."

Paula looked a little pensive as she sat down.

Martha explained that people who thrive have relatively clean filters and, therefore, can take in more information. Conscious and self-aware, they are willing to let go of "thinking they know," and they are willing to listen to their inner wisdom. Therefore, they can more readily see the solutions that are right in front of them and have more resources available to make the most effective decisions. They thrive. Whereas people who disconnect from their Sage can't see solutions because their filters that are influenced by fearful and limiting voices keep them from letting wisdom in, she added. They can't see the possibilities that are available to them. They can only survive.

Martha felt the mood in the room rise as they absorbed the lesson that had just been presented. "One thing I noticed as I came into the room is that you were all here on time," she acknowledged. "Now, I ask you: How does it feel when everyone does what they said they would when they said they would do it?

"It feels great," Paula said quickly. The realization made her smile. After all her years of purposeful rebellion—against her mother, teachers, bosses, and anyone who wanted to impose rules on her—she realized how self-limiting that had all been. Keeping her word, in this case, being on time, was far more empowering than she could ever have imagined.

"I feel like we're really beginning to work together," Sarah commented.

"We're a team," Alex added. He liked this feeling of connectedness and thought about how he could change the way he interacted with his team members when he returned to work on Monday.

"What you're experiencing is everyone moving in the same direction," Martha explained. "When people are in alignment and keeping their word, it builds a synergy that is more powerful than individual energy. Let me show you a visual of what I'm saying."

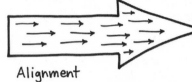

ALIGNMENT

Misalignment

Alignment

"Imagine the larger arrow is your organization, and the smaller arrows are the departments, divisions, and individuals," Martha explained. She pointed to the top illustration that showed a large wobbly arrow containing a myriad of small arrows angling off in various directions.

"When people within the organization are misaligned, going off in different directions without a thorough understanding and agreement of what is expected of them, it creates an unstable environment. The same, of course, would apply with your home and family," she went on. "The top arrow shows a disorganized company that is not charting a clear strategic direction for others to follow. There are no agreements spelled out about what game they're playing or how they should play it. The culture is chaotic at worst and confusing at best. To say the least, this results in an unstable organization that is producing at unacceptable levels or a dysfunctional family that produces unhappiness."

Pointing to the second illustration, a large straight arrow in which all the smaller arrows pointed in the same direction as the larger one, Martha continued: "Here the organization is clear about its course of direction, and the vision is well communicated. Everyone is onboard, aligned, and in agreement. This shows a stable, solid, and healthy company. The people within it are likely satisfied, productive employees who know what is expected of them. This company is growing steadily and creating a culture that fosters peak performance.

Aligned energy creates synergy. When people work together, they have a greater total effect than the sum of their individual efforts. The same, of course, applies to your home and family."

She turned to the four of them and asked how they felt now that they were experiencing what it was like to be part of an aligned team. Alex was the first to respond, with a little grin to Paula: When everyone is aligned, everything runs more smoothly, he observed. Sarah chimed in that they were all moving in the same direction.

"And what made the difference, Sarah?" Martha asked.

"All of us keeping our agreement to participate and tell the truth openly and honestly," she replied, then smiled gently at Dan.

"Being able to keep our agreement to be on time." Paula looked over at Dan and added, "Plus being able to keep all our agreements like sharing and being open and honest."

"Everyone is able. That's not the issue. Rather it's all about your willingness. This feeling of alignment that you're experiencing re-flects your willingness and commitment to do what it takes to keep your word," Martha explained. "So how does it feel for this level of trust to be built in this room among four strangers?"

"Really good," Alex responded.

"Do you see that to maintain your commitment to keep your word that you had to pay attention to detail?" Martha asked. "To keep from getting distracted, you had to remember your priorities, and you had to put the agreement to keep your word at the top of the list. To participate fully you also had to risk. In short, keeping your agreements meant that you had to face your fears and practice self-discipline in order to make choices that would be consistent with your word."

Sarah spoke up again. To keep her agreements she had to stop worrying about everyone else and start taking care of herself.

"The essential thing," Martha said, "was to pay attention and stay conscious. If they broke their word—even though it was only one agreement, such as being on time—it puts all the agreements into question. Can you understand how someone might think, 'if this person didn't pay attention to being on time, then how can I trust that he or she will honor the other agreements, like confidentiality?' Breaking one agreement affects all the agreements, and trust diminishes."

It is important to take stock, periodically, of the agreements made in one's life and how well they are being kept, Martha went on. Just like the leaf in Alex's poem, humans are "perfectly imperfect," and from time to time anyone can become careless and allow themselves to go "unconscious." The result may be broken agreements. But by building a track record of consistently keeping their word and demonstrating themselves to be trustworthy, then even during those momentary lapses of consciousness, when they disconnect from their natural knowing, they will not lose significant credibility.

"It will be a yellow flag, not a red one," she explained. "When this occurs, always apologize immediately. Never make excuses. If you do, you give the excuses power. In fact, the excuse can become so powerful it can keep you from keeping your commitment and your word. When that happens, you allow circumstances to be bigger than you are, and they begin to run your life."

Martha wrote the word CIRCUMSTANCES in huge capital letters on the flip chart and beside it the word "me" in tiny letters.

"Can you recall times in your lives when you have let circum-

CIRCUMSTANCES/me

stances be bigger than you? Perhaps it seemed easier at the time to rely on excuses than to be accountable or to tell the truth."

They all nodded as she spoke.

"When you own your power, however, then you are bigger than your circumstances," she went on. "You don't let them stop you or direct your behavior or interfere with your agreements."

She wrote the word ME in huge capitals, and circumstances in tiny letters

$$ME/circumstances$$

and asked them how it would feel to live this way—not allowing circumstances to overpower them. Paula, Alex and Sarah responded with: in control, great, responsible, and honoring of myself.

"So that brings us to Dan's question," Martha said. "Before the break, Dan, you said you didn't understand how you could be accountable for everything that happens. And I asked you to think about it."

"I can understand each of the principles we've learned so far as they apply to my life, my actions, and the way I choose to view things," Dan replied. "I can see how I am responsible for myself. But I still don't get how I'm accountable for everything that happens on the planet! I think that's going too far."

Martha turned back to the flip chart where she had written about

$$Accountability \neq \begin{cases} Blame \\ Obligation \\ or\ Burden \end{cases}$$

accountability not equaling blame and added a few words:

"Let me show you a couple of diagrams, Dan, and that may help you understand just how connected you are to everything that happens."

Drawing a series of concentric circles, Martha labeled the first one in the center You. The next was Family, followed by Community, City, State, Country, Continent, and World.

Then she drew an arrow from World to You. "We already discussed earlier about how we, as children, were born into an existing world that influenced our thinking and behaviors and told us

CIRCLES of INFLUENCE #1

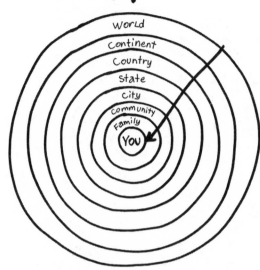

who we are and how life is. Through our commitment to survive in that environment, we conformed. We learned what were acceptable and unacceptable beliefs and behaviors, and we adapted to those interpretations. Most of the time it was unconscious.

"We are always conforming, and conforming implies that we're not choosing. We are acting out what we were programmed to do. We have certain genetic tendencies, but the person you have become is mostly a function of the interpretation you were born into. Had you been brought up in Rwanda, Japan, Afghanistan, the desert or the tundra, you would think and act differently, and you would BE different. The idea that we are separate from what we believe is a myth. We are a series of interpretations, from world to continent to country and all the way down."

Silently, their eyes traced the path from the outside world to their own inner circles.

"I suggest that there is no objectively existing world. It is an occurring world that is subject to our interpretation. Therefore, the idea that we are fixed characters doomed to a certain way of being is a myth. Minus genetics, we are pure possibility. We get to make it up! This is why being conscious and aware is so important. Who we have decided to be and how we have decided to act—through our own choices—also has a great deal of influence in the other direction."

She drew a second set of circles like the last.

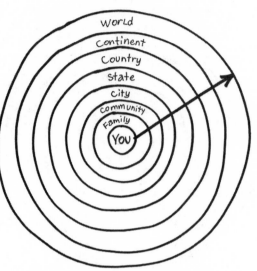

CIRCLES of INFLUENCE #2

World
Continent
Country
State
City
Community
Family
YOU

"Let's start here with 'You.' Do you see how the choices you make and the manner in which you operate within your own home affects your family both positively and negatively?" Martha asked.

"Sure," Dan agreed quickly.

Martha went to the next circle, asking Dan if he could see how the way his family operates affects the community. For example, she noted, there are families that participate in neighborhood projects, pick up trash when they see it, are kind to their neighbors, and are a positive force in the community while others neglect their yards and maintain no control over their un-disciplined, problem children. Dan nodded, although he had never thought about it in those terms before.

"Now do you see how the behaviors within your community influence your city? For example, if a city has many high-crime neighborhoods, then the reputation of the city goes down, people don't want to live there, and property values go down. Everyone is affected. The opposite is also true, of course."

Martha moved to the next circle, asking him if he could see how his city affects his state. Two cities in any state may be very different: one very cosmopolitan and the other provincial. Both have an impact on the state by their character, their needs, the sizes of their populations, their demographics, and so forth. Together, the cities contribute to a "framework of thinking" in the state.

"As you know, thinking may vary greatly from state to state," Martha continued. "The people who live in Maine have a culturally different framework of thinking from those who live in Mississippi or California. It's not good or bad, better or worse; it's just different. The cities and the people who live in them affect the framework of thinking on the state level."

The next circle was marked Country, which reflects the combined framework of thinking of all the states. The U.S., with a particular history, culture, and framework of thinking is quite different from Mexico and Canada, and yet the three countries combined makeup the continent of North America, which has its own framework of thinking.

Moving to the next circle labeled Continent, she commented that North America is quite different from South America, Europe, Africa, Asia, and Australia, each of which reflects the framework of thinking and acceptable behaviors of the countries that make up those continents.

"As we open our minds and allow different views from other continents to influence us and vice versa, we gradually change our own habits and our views. They in turn change theirs. We influence one another." Martha pointed to the outermost circle labeled World. "Together they create a world context. The world context and framework of thinking is no more or less than what a critical mass of individuals determine it to be."

Looking at the concentric circles, Alex thought of the ripples that formed when a stone was dropped into the water. From the place of impact, the center, the waves rippled out, affecting a wide area.

"Now can you see that no matter how miniscule, your actions have some connection with world behavior? The greater the number of people who act with honesty and integrity and who make a commitment to confront dishonesty when they see it, the greater our chances of having a healthy world," Martha stated. "Likewise, the more people who think and act in ways that are consistent with accountability, the fewer victims we have."

They listened intently as Martha painted a vision for the world that seemed so logical, so realistic: When people stop blaming others, believing that everything is someone else's fault; when more people take accountability for their behaviors and take a stand for integrity, the world will be a different place, she observed. War, corruption, and crime exist because a critical mass of people either: 1) support it or 2) allow it and aren't willing to do what it takes to stop it. Martha paused, allowing them time to process these concepts through their new filters of understanding. "So how am I accountable for the war in the Middle East? First, I must account for my connection to it. If I have war in my own heart, then that mindset is part of my reality. Combined with others who also have war in their hearts, it creates the reality of war on the planet."

"So what you're saying is, 'Change your thinking and you change your life,'" Dan acknowledged.

"Yes, I am," Martha replied. "Taking that to the next level, you could say that when you change your thinking you help change the world. That doesn't mean you lie awake at night worrying about everything happening on the planet. That would be a waste of your time. Remember, accountability does not equal blame, obligation, or burden. But you can respond to the reality of war, starvation, and crime, for example. You can begin, here, at the center." She pointed to the "You" in the middle of the concentric circles.

Martha offered realistic ways that this could be done by cleaning up their own lives. As much as possible, remove any conflict. She advised them to live with abundance instead of hoarding. Act with honesty and integrity. Take a stand for mutual respect in their families, justice in their communities, accountability in the workplace, honesty from politicians, and whatever else is meaningful to each of them. Talk to other people. Interrupt negativity. Don't engage in gossip. Become involved. Write letters. Make their views known.

"Remember, in any game participation is the key and how you

participate makes all the difference in how the game ends. It may feel like a minute contribution—" Martha went on.

"But every little bit helps!" Sarah interjected enthusiastically, making everyone else smile. "Just like they say, if everyone did even one small thing, when combined, it adds up to something much bigger."

Martha sat back in her chair. "Think of the world as big bucket of white paint and you are one small dollop of blue. If you jump into that white paint, it may not look different, but on some miniscule level, it has been changed. If enough dollops of blue jump into that white paint, it begins to take on a different tone and hue. Your voice matters. Your vote counts. Your framework of thinking makes a difference, because it's all part of the world mindset. The world only operates as it does because, through their choices, enough people make it so."

Alex studied the chart, his hand on his chin. Where the stone is dropped into the water the first ripples are the biggest, the most pronounced. "Not only do we have a cumulative impact by our thoughts and actions, but what we say and do is also strongly felt in the inner circles that are closest to us."

"Yes, Alex. On a very practical level, can you see how the way you think and operate in your company—regardless of whether you're the CEO or a mailroom clerk—makes a difference?" Martha asked. "We all know the ripple effect of someone's negative actions. Now imagine the same ripple effect of being positive and respectful toward others."

"It sure would increase productivity," Dan reflected.

To illustrate this principle in action, Martha used a true story of a consultant working with NASA in the 1960s when the U.S. was committed to landing a man on the Moon. Recognizing the importance and influence that an organization's culture has on the results produced, the consultant first assessed the attitudes and behaviors of employees throughout NASA. He interviewed a random selection of people and asked them a series of questions. He started with the janitor. When he asked the man what his job was, he replied, "My job is to help put a man on the Moon."

The consultant was surprised. He had never before heard of a janitor who so directly and proudly linked his job with the vision of the organization. By keeping the workplace clean and organized and by eliminating clutter and emptying the trash, he provided an environment in which others could do their work without distractions. As he went about his daily job with a purpose that was aligned with the corporate vision, he allowed others to do the same. The consultant found this attitude throughout the organization. Putting a man on the Moon wasn't just the job of a select group of individuals. Everyone held that vision as a part of their personal job description, and people fully understood how their jobs linked to it. Martha smiled: "Now that's synergy."

"That was JFK's vision," Alex spoke up. "I've always been struck by his words: 'I believe this nation should commit itself to achieving the goal before this decade is out of landing a man on the Moon and returning him safely to Earth.' That was in 1961, before the technology even existed."

Martha nodded. "When people are aligned behind a common goal, practically anything is possible."

What would it take to have that kind of thinking at the Stellar Point? Dan asked himself. What impact could his team have on achieving the company's goals if everyone took full ownership of the vision?

Noticing that Dan appeared to be mentally working through something, Martha invited him to share. "I was just thinking what it would take to inspire that kind of attitude in my company," he replied.

"It starts with you and how you interact with your boss, co-workers, and direct reports. Are you controlling, self-righteous, and judgmental? Or are you cooperative, responsible, and personally accountable? Regardless of your position, whether you're the team leader or a team member, that's where it begins. Like they say, 'If it's to be, it's up to me.' Act in a way that is consistent with account-ability and support others to do the same," she explained.

Martha scanned their faces, taking in their thoughtful expressions. "At this point, we've gone through four of the eight principles. How eager are you to learn the rest?"

"Let's go," said Alex enthusiastically.

Martha smiled warmly at him. "We're ready to find out right now. But first, we're going to play a game."

❖ Chapter Eight

How to Win

A little surprised yet enthused with the change in direction, the four of them listened intently to Martha's instructions: "Get into pairs, Dan and Alex, Paula with Sarah, and arrange your chairs to face each other." They started moving around and sat down. "Now put your right elbows on your desks and clasp your hands together."

"Arm wrestling!" Paula announced as she flexed her bicep. Sarah laughed again and shook her head.

Dan flexed his hand and stretched his arms. "I haven't been working out much lately."

Alex grinned at him. "Computer programmers are tougher than you think."

Martha gave each person an empty paper cup. The two teams were then given a third cup holding ten M&M candies. "Now listen carefully," she told them. "The object of this game is to win. Winning is determined by getting the maximum number of M&M's into your individual cups by the end of the game. Each time the back of your partner's hand touches the desk, you get to put an M&M into your own cup. I'll time you, and when I say 'stop,' we'll count up the M&M's in your cups and see who wins. Any questions?"

It seemed so straightforward and self-explanatory that the teams were ready to go. Clasping hands, Sarah and Paula struggled briefly. Paula gritted her teeth and pushed harder against Sarah, who resisted for only a few seconds before relaxing her hand and letting it fall to the desk. Gleefully, Paula took an M&M. In the next round, the same thing happened, and Paula took another M&M. Shaking her head, Sarah dumped all the M&Ms into Paula's cup. "Here," she said. "You win!" They laughed together.

Dan and Alex were locked in an all-out battle. Sarah and Paula turned in their chairs and watched the two men struggle, their faces showing their physical strain. Dan pushed Alex's hand a few inches away from the desk, only to have Alex power back and then push Dan's hand close to the desk. After two minutes, Martha called time.

"You put up quite a fight," Dan laughed, playfully punching Alex in the upper arm and feeling a little embarrassed that he couldn't overpower a computer guy.

"I wasn't going to give in if that's what you mean," Alex retorted, stretching out his arm.

Paula jiggled the ten M&M's in her cup. "Too bad they're not gold coins." Sarah chuckled at the sight of Paula's happy face.

Martha observed them closely. "Now let's take a look at your results. Paula, you have ten M&M's and Sarah you have none. Based on that, it appears that Paula won and Sarah lost. Would that be correct?"

"Yes," the two women said in unison, giggling.

"Now, Dan and Alex, neither of you have any M&M's in your cups. So in other words, based on the rules of the game, that means you both lost. Would that be correct?" Martha said.

Dan protested, "It's a tie!"

"Yes, it is, and neither of you have any M&M's. Therefore, you both lost."

Both men slowly nodded, the smiles fading from their faces.

"Remember life is a game. Relationships are a game. Work is a game. And you just played another game. Just as in life, work, and relationships, there are different ways to play the game," Martha explained. "Everyone has a life strategy. Let's take a look at the results that you achieved because as we know, your results are an indication of how you think. This in turn reveals your life strategy."

On a blank sheet of the flip chart, Martha wrote the words:

I Win / You Lose

In this framework of thinking, she explained, for someone to win, someone else has to lose. "That's what winning means in the I Win/You Lose context. That strategy says, 'I get my way, and you don't get yours.' A person with this thinking will use manipulation, credentials, brute strength, force, intimidation, or whatever it takes to win. They will use their power to overpower others."

Looking over at Dan and Alex, she commented that it appeared the two of them had played with an I Win/You Lose strategy; for one of them to win, the other had to lose. Both men agreed.

"Your results, however, show a different kind of game was actually played out, and that is I Lose/You Lose," Martha explained. She added the phrase to the list.

I Win / You Lose
I Lose / You Lose

"I Lose/You Lose happens when two stubborn, ego-invested people interact. They battle hard but eventually both lose," she continued. "They both will become vindictive and want to get back at the other in some way. They perpetuate the war. When you play with someone who operates with this strategy, you had best watch your back."

Martha turned her attention to Paula. "It appears that your results may also have been based on an I Win/You Lose framework of thinking: I win at someone else's expense. You may have also been playing the game another way, which is just plain I Win. You don't necessarily want someone else to lose, but you don't do much about it. You just want to make sure that you win, and let everyone else figure it out for themselves. Would that be accurate?"

Grinning, Paula nodded.

Martha added I Win to the list.

I Win / You Lose

I Lose / You Lose

I Win

"You found the perfect partner in Sarah because during this game she forgot that she was going to take a stand for herself. She went back to her old filter and let herself lose again. Right, Sarah?" Martha added another phrase to the list:

I Win / You Lose

I Lose / You Lose

I Win

I Lose / You Win

Based upon her results, it appeared Sarah followed the I Lose/You Win strategy when she played. These players don't maintain a solid set of personal standards, Martha continued. They don't establish boundaries, and they operate with low expectations for themselves to win. People who play this way are quick to please or appease and often put themselves last. "Does that sound familiar, Sarah?"

"Yes," she said laughing at herself. "I did it again!"

Martha explained the mindset for I Lose/You Win: "Go ahead, have it your way. Step on me again; everyone else does. I'm a peace-maker, and I'll do anything to keep the peace." I Lose/You Win players have little courage to express their feelings and are eas-ily intimidated, but they build up resentment inside because once again, they go last after everyone else. "I Win/You Lose people and I Lose/You Win people love to play together because they keep each other's game going," Martha glanced at Sarah. "It's codependent behavior and it's destructive."

Facing the realization of how quickly they had fallen back to their old patterns, the four of them sat silently. The high, optimistic en-ergy of the early morning had slightly lessened, replaced by the reality of how much work it would take to stay disciplined in the eight principles to thrive instead of slipping into their old survival behaviors.

Martha smiled encouragingly as she explained that there is an entirely different way of playing the game. It requires a higher level of social consciousness and constantly seeks mutual benefit in all human interaction. Behavior is collaborative, based on a thriving framework of thinking that there is plenty for everyone and that one person's success does not need to be at the expense or exclusion of the other. "It's called I Win/You Win. I'm sure you've heard of it, but too few people play the game according to this strategy." She wrote the phrase in capital letters at the top of the list.

I WIN / YOU WIN

I Win/You Win requires committed, proactive thinking and behavior as well as persistent and compassionate action, she continued. It means "I am going to win; after all I respect myself. But not at the expense of another." I Win/You Win players, in fact, believe that no one wins until everyone wins. They make sure they win, and they also make sure the other person wins. People who operate with the I Win/You Win framework of thinking make sure that their actions are consistent with their words. It makes for a different kind of world.

"Only by examining your framework of thinking can you get to this higher level of consciousness," Martha told them. "So let's examine your results again."

Neither Alex nor Dan had any M&M's in their cups because each was unwilling to let the other win. They were afraid of losing, but both ended up losing anyway. I Win/You Lose was the framework of thinking that drove their actions, but the result of those actions was I Lose/You Lose, Martha explained. Based on Paula's results, it appeared it was more important to her that she won than it was to make sure Sarah also won. Sarah, once again, gave up winning to someone else without regard to her own desire or need.

"Remember, this is not about berating yourself," Martha reminded them. "You're not wrong or bad for having played the way that you did. But as any good coach who is supporting you to win, I am bringing this to your attention so that you can begin to recognize how deeply this framework of thinking is embedded in the unconscious."

"So how would I Win/You Win work in a situation like this?" Dan asked. "The object of the game was to arm wrestle."

Martha shook her head. "I never said the words 'arm wrestling.' Your survival instincts and competitive filter brought that interpretation to the exercise. I only said that the object of the game was to win and that winning was determined by getting the maximum number of M&M's into your individual cups. The first step is to look at what winning means. Does it mean that you have to hurt someone else? Or does it mean finding a solution that allows you both to win? Now, step into a framework of thinking of I Win/You Win. This kind of player always enters the game asking, 'How can both people win?' How would you answer that question if you could listen to your Sage instead of the Driver who wants to win, no matter what?"

The answer was so obvious it caused them all to smile. Clasping hands again, Alex and Dan spontaneously demonstrated. Dan let go of his resistance, and, without effort, Alex pushed his hand to the desk. An M&M went into Alex's cup. Then it was Alex's turn to cooperate. Dan easily pushed Alex's hand to the desk. Plunk went the M&M in Dan's cup. Like a seesaw, the action was fluid, effortless, as they went back and forth without resistance, allowing each other to win.

"Exactly," Martha smiled. "You both won. You both earned five M&M's. You each got the maximum number of M&M's into your cups. You are not exhausted or hurting. It was easy and fast, and everyone is satisfied. And, Paula, do you agree that five M&M's would be enough to win? Do you have to get ten when someone else gets none?"

Dan had a perplexed look. "Where does competition fit into all of this? Are you suggesting that a business shouldn't compete?"

"Certainly not," Martha responded. "We live and participate in a global economy. It is important to note, however, that there are healthy and unhealthy ways to compete. With the unhealthy way, a person is constantly trying to undermine, sabotage, and manipulate others. They will do anything they can to win at any cost. They're not so interested in being their best; they just want to beat the other guy even if it means being unethical, immoral, and dishonest. People who compete in this manner view every situation as a potential for one-upmanship and every person becomes a potential opponent. Paradoxically, people who compete this way lack self-confidence, which is why they feel the need to continually prove themselves as better."

"I always thought that the best leaders were those who were the best competitors," Dan added.

One's ability to compete successfully certainly is critical for business success, Martha agreed. However, cheating, stealing, or breaking the law to do so will destroy a person's reputation—and a company as well; witness the demise of Enron and Worldcom. Highly competitive leaders also often create a culture of competition within their ranks that fosters an atmosphere of distrust as work associates are treated like opponents instead of allies. This thinking is counterproductive since the company's ranks are the one place where collaboration, not competition, is needed. Moreover, competitive leaders rarely listen to others and frequently try to push their own ideas, often at the expense of organizational success.

"Interesting," Dan said.

"Healthy competition, on the other hand, is fun and personally challenging," Martha went on. "With healthy competition, a person should be aware of the positioning of the other person or company. However, they use that information to better channel their efforts to perform at their personal best."

She used the analogy of playing golf, in which the real competition for the individual player is with the course itself, not the other players. She talked about Roger Federer, the great Swiss tennis champion who had won the Wimbleton Cup three times and had been a three-time U.S. Open champion, as well as the champion of at least nine major events. When asked why he was such a good competitor, he answered that he measures the quality of his game against himself, not against his opponent.

In business, if one company is enjoying far more success than another, all that says is one firm has found a winning strategy, and the other hasn't. Healthy, thriving competitors see this as an intellectual challenge, not against the competitor necessarily, but within themselves: to think ahead, think smart, fully understand their business as well as the market, understand the customer's wants, anticipate their future needs, and figure out how to serve them the best way possible.

"People who compete in this manner are creative and proactive in their thinking. They are responsive but not reactive to the other guy. I even know of some companies that seek ways to collaborate with other firms to provide excellence to the customer," Martha told them. "True leaders build corporate cultures that value collaboration. Trust is developed. People aren't afraid to share information or express their ideas. It makes for a completely different climate for success."

"Okay, since you brought it up, let's talk about sports." Dan challenged. "I mean competition is what it's all about."

"I couldn't agree more. I also think it's healthy. That's part of the fun. In fact if you play cards with me, get ready. I have every intention of winning but not by cheating or showing a mean spirit that leaves everyone with a bad feeling. The exciting challenge is to anticipate everyone else's strategy, to sharpen my own, and to stay alert and adept enough to shift strategies if necessary. Most important, I enjoy the process."

In sports, business, or a game like cards, always remember that you chose to play a game that involves competition, she continued; no one made you. It's a healthy, stimulating game if everyone plays for all it's worth without sacrificing honor, integrity, and respect for themselves and others. With I Win/You Win, each player makes sure everyone leaves the evening having had a good time, wanting to play again.

At this point, Martha wrote the next principle on the flip chart.

Principle #5
Everybody gets a prize

"Can you see how this phrase embodies the win/win attitude? This is not winner take all. Everybody ends up with more than they started with. 'Everybody Gets a Prize', including you." Martha looked directly at Sarah. "Can you see how the fifth principle builds relationships, not only with others but also with yourself? Why would you ever participate in a game in which you are going to ultimately lose? Why does anyone have to lose?"

Martha sat back in her chair. "I want to tell you a true story about Everybody Gets a Prize," she began, and started to tell them of the time she moved to St. Louis. From the time she decided to move, Martha had a clear and specific vision in her mind of where she was going to live, to the point that she called her realtor Sue and described it to her in detail. It was a large loft apartment with big exposed beams, old brick, high ceilings, and a great view of the city. Two weeks later Sue called and excitedly reported that she had indeed found it. Martha flew to St. Louis to have a look and discovered that it was exactly what she wanted, from the ten foot front doors that had been on an old church building to a view of the entire city skyline. It was a spectacular place in every way. The owner accepted her purchase offer, and Martha few back to California very satisfied.

That night, however, Sue called with some disappointing news. She had just discovered that the owner of the whole building, who owned every apartment in that building except this one, had the right of first refusal to buy the loft. And he wanted to buy it. Martha went to bed discouraged but woke up the next morning with the realization that the game was being played out in a way that the building owner would win and she would lose. "That wasn't okay with me," Martha explained. "I wanted to find a solution that would allow us both to get a prize."

Dan smiled. Man, she just doesn't give up, he thought.

Returning to St. Louis on business, Martha met with the owner of the building—a very high-profile attorney—in his offices on the top floor of one of the tallest buildings in the city. The conference room windows looked out onto dramatic sweeping views of the famous Arch, which only seemed a few yards away.

"Once we were all seated at one end of the huge table in this 'meant-to-impress' wood-paneled room, I looked at him and said, 'You and I are both powerful, capable people. We've produced impressive results in our lives. Right now we both want the same thing. You have all four aces in your hand because you have a legal agreement that gives you the right to purchase the property. Nonetheless, I would like to approach this from the view that allows both of us to walk away from the table winning more than either one of us has right now'," Martha explained. "The concept was obviously appealing to him, and why wouldn't it be? He couldn't lose. Of course he was interested in discovering how he could win even more than what he had."

Sarah was listening to every word. She couldn't imagine herself negotiating real estate deals, not at this point in her life anyway. But could she empower herself enough to play I Win/You Win in her own life, at work and at home?

As they explored possibilities, it became clear that the building owner really didn't want to put up the money at that time to buy the apartment. Ideally he wanted to buy it in three years. The timing was perfect for Martha since she was only going to be living there for about three years. The I Win/You Win framework of thinking unearthed this information. If she had given into I Win/You Lose, she never would have discovered his underlying desire to delay the purchase. The solution was a deal known in financial terms as a "put option." In three years time, if he wanted to buy it, Martha would have to sell, and if he wanted to sell, she would have to buy.

"I got to live in that extraordinary loft apartment for three years, and he didn't have to part with his money right away," Martha smiled. "At the end of three years, I sold it to him, exactly as we had agreed. It was an I Win/You Win solution that allowed us both to walk away with more than what we had when we started."

Alex's thoughts returned to his nagging problem with Frank. In trying to shut out Frank at every turn, they had both ended up losing. So much time was wasted that could have been spent on managing projects. No doubt Frank was frustrated too, and as much as they disagreed, Alex had to admit the man was an intelligent and gifted programmer. Playing I Win/You Win, they could both get what they wanted with less effort and better results.

"Does this strategy always give you the win you're looking for? Not always. Some people are so rigid, fearful, selfish, and self-righteous they are completely unwilling to discuss possibilities. Move away from these people as they are negative energy. On the other hand, sometimes a person is willing to look, but a win/win solution cannot be found because one or both parties are unwilling to agree to the proposed solution for a variety of reasons. These are the times you must let go and trust that there's a reason that is bigger than what you can comprehend in the moment. But you will succeed more often than you may think," Martha continued.

Looking at the problem or situation from a different angle can lead to the negotiation of a different result, one that reflects a commitment to each person winning. When she negotiated with the building owner, Martha told them, she had to be genuinely committed to him winning, which meant that he would end up with more than he had originally, while at the same time she was going to win, too. "There must be an equal commitment to each person winning," she emphasized.

Dan posed a question: "Sometimes in negotiations you don't want to leave any money on the table. How does that work with this principle?"

"You must be willing to let go of whatever you leave on the table," Martha explained. "It's about you winning and the other person winning, not about squeezing out every possible dime in a deal. If you're satisfied with only a short-term relationship with a client and if you're not worried about the kind of reputation you generate, then sure, you can focus on not leaving any money on the table so that every deal is of maximum benefit just to you. But if you are interested in building long-term relationships with clients and establishing a reputation as a fair player operating with a high level of integrity, then you play in a way that everybody wins. Everybody gets a prize."

Martha invited them to consider how they had been playing all of their games—be it I Win/You Lose, I Lose/You Win, or I Lose/ You Lose—at work, in their families, and even in their communities. Turning back to the Circles of Influence chart, which illustrated the impact of an individual's actions from home to community and eventually to the world, she asked them to consider how their framework of thinking affects not only them but also their families, communities, cities, states, and so forth. Their framework of thinking, she explained, was revealed in their attitudes: for example, the thinking that says, "All I care about is my kids going to good schools and to heck with the kids in the poor neighborhoods." The ideal is to be accountable and seek solutions for all children in every community to win. Otherwise, eventually everyone is going to lose.

She gave another example: people who choose to be unaccountable for what happens to the environment as long as they can have all the material goods they desire. They use all the energy they want while supporting industries that pollute the air and water, so they can produce products cheaply. Doing so rapes the environment, however, and eventually this will turn into an I Lose/You Lose result. "Future generations will lose, the environment will lose, and as it becomes depleted, the world will lose as the balance of nature is destroyed...the ultimate I Lose/You Lose!" she observed.

In that moment each of them felt their direct connection to the world around them. Martha saw it in their expressions: they were thinking beyond the small spheres of consciousness in which they had previously operated and were beginning to consider the broader implications of their attitudes, behaviors, and actions.

"It's sometimes difficult to relate to the reality that 'my choices affect the world.' Let's connect in more immediate terms," Martha suggested. "Think about how your framework of thinking affects your workplace. Do you seek ways in which you make sure everyone wins, or do you just look out for yourself? Do you participate in office gossip in order to fit in with the crowd, or do you refuse to participate because it is hurting someone else?"

For example, she offered, if you don't agree with a decision upper management has made, do you bad-mouth management behind their backs and subtly sabotage them, or do you get on board and make their ideas successful? Do you choose to proactively share information, or do you make people come to you so that you can be in control and look and feel important? What about the corporate culture? Is it driven by a context that pits employees against one another, or does the context foster an environment in which everyone wins?

Alex leaned forward in his chair. "Everything we've learned thus far is all related. One principle is connected to the next. Being truthful with myself and others supports me to keep my word. That in turn supports me to play the game in a way that honors and respects others and myself and everyone to get a prize. When I acknowledge that my experience is determined by how I chose to interpret events and that my results are determined by my choices, then I can be personally accountable for all of it. All the parts fit together."

"Yes. Thank you, Alex. Life, work, and relationships will continuously challenge you to step up to a bigger way of playing the game. When you understand that, you can connect with your higher, natural, authentic self; truly become empowered; and seek successful, positive outcomes for all."

Martha glanced at the clock and suggested a one-hour break for lunch, which was being served outdoors on the patio. "And Dan," she smiled at him, "do you have a phone call to make?"

Raising his eyebrows, Dan's expression was half grimace, half smile. "Yeah, let's see if this principle really works."

As they were leaving, Martha called Paula and Alex over and handed them each a sealed envelope. She told them to open them at any time they were alone.

Paula found a quiet corner in the Great Room to open hers. Tearing it eagerly, she found a sheet of paper, folded in two, on which was a riddle:

What Am I?
You cannot see me by running past
So slow yourself down, don't go so fast.
There's no place to run, there's no place to hide.
Let go of your carelessness and regain your pride.

Inside me is a woman both wise and smart.
Will you be still long enough to hear my heart?
Examine me closely and you will see
The person you've always wanted to be.

The real you awaits within my space.
It's time to surrender; some things you must face.
I invite you in, but only you have the key.
Will you let me out? Will you set yourself free?
(Clue: I am an object somewhere in the lodge.)
(Clue: You will know it when you find me.
There will be no doubt.)

She read it again and eagerly began looking around the Great Room, at the pictures on the wall, the books on the shelves, even inside a decorative box on a side table. "You will know it when you find me." Well, she hadn't found it yet.

Alex walked out the front door and sat on the steps. Carefully, he slid his finger under the sealed flap of his envelope. Inside, was a sheet of paper, folded in two, on which was written a single sentence: "People with high levels of personal mastery cannot afford to choose between reason and intuition, or head and heart, any more than they would choose to walk on one leg or see with one eye. —Peter Senge"

Leaning back against the steps, looking out over the landscape that had become so familiar to him over the past two days, Alex smiled, then laughed aloud.

Sarah and Dan were already seated on the patio, eating sandwiches and drinking iced tea, when Alex joined them. Paula arrived a few minutes later and flopped in a chair with the note still in her hand. "What a treat to be outside." Paula tipped her head back to feel the sun on her face.

"It's really beautiful here," Alex commented, surveying the rolling hills. "Growing up in Chicago, I never stopped to think about the landscape being anything but flat."

"That's because where we are right now, a few million years ago the glaciers dumped some of what they dug out of the Great Lakes," Sarah explained.

"Amateur geologist, Sarah?" Dan inquired.

"Nope. Fourth-grade science. I help my son with his homework." Sarah turned to Alex. "Whereabouts in Chicago did you grow up?"

"South Side." Alex felt a familiar tightness in his chest as he talked about where he had grown up, ever conscious of how he was different from the others. His parents were hardworking, honest, decent folks who lived in a small but immaculate apartment in a three-flat. Yet Alex knew that being a black man in Chicago was something the others couldn't understand.

"I grew up in Iowa on a farm." Sarah gazed off in the distance. "Nothing but fields stretching out as far as you could see. What about you, Paula?"

"I was born in New Jersey, went to grammar school in Pennsylvania and Ohio, high school in Indiana, but graduated in Illinois." She ticked the states off on her fingers.

"Wow. That's a lot of traveling," Dan said. "Your parents in the military?"

Paula shook her head. "Let's just say my father had a less than illustrious career, and a new opportunity was always some place else." She watched the beads of condensation trickle down the side of her glass. "But Chicago is my home now. I feel so alive there. And I love running along the lake. I can turn my back on the city and just look out over the water."

"Ever think of doing a marathon?" Dan asked. "That's one of my goals, to run the Chicago Marathon."

"Every year I think I should run, but haven't done it—yet." Paula gave Dan a sly grin. "So you want to do it? We could train together, or at least keep tabs on each other."

Dan smiled and nodded. "It's an idea."

"I can't do a marathon, but maybe I could take up jogging," Sarah said. "What about you, Alex?"

"Not me," he said, shaking his head. "I'm not what you'd call the athletic type." He paused, remembering the one thing that had always brought him joy. Why had he ever given it up?

"Well, maybe you could consider it." Sarah smiled warmly at him.

"Maybe," Alex said, and drank deeply from his glass of iced tea.

"So how about it, Dan?" Paula persisted. "You and I training for the marathon."

"I don't know," Dan replied carefully. "Training is going to take a lot of my time. But I tell you what. I'll give it some careful thought. How's that?"

Glancing at her watch, Paula told everyone that she had a riddle to figure out and excused herself.

Then Dan got up from the table. "And if you'll excuse me, I have a phone call to make."

"Good luck," Sarah said.

"Yeah, let us know what happens," Alex added.

"Oh, don't worry," Dan smiled. "You'll hear all about it."

❖ Chapter Nine

Shifting Resistance

For the rest of the lunch break, Paula searched the lodge. At first, she thought the object might be a magazine in which she would find a picture of a "put-together" business woman, someone trapped within the pages who needed to be set free. But there was not one photo that she "knew" was the right one. She turned and walked down the hall. On the wall was a copy of an old Vermeer painting of a woman with a pitcher. She stood in front of it and looked for some connection, something that spoke of the woman she wanted to be. One of the clues had told her that she would have no doubt when she found it. She felt nothing looking at the art piece. A little frustrated, she read the whole riddle again.

And what about this key? The only key she had was to her room. Could it be something in her room? She ran up the stairs. Looking around her room, she saw her bed, dresser, and desk. Nothing there. The closet didn't contain anything either. As she was about to leave, she caught a glimpse of herself in the mirror. Reading the riddle again, she stopped herself before quickly leaving. "Inside me is a woman both wise and smart. Will you be still long enough to hear my heart? Examine me closely and you will see the person you've always wanted to be..."

She could feel her heart beating as she took the time to study her reflection in the mirror over the tiny dresser in her room. She didn't look different, and yet, she did. Taking a step nearer, Paula looked into her own eyes and in them saw something that made her smile: the wisdom of a woman who is beginning to understand herself. "You have the key. Will you let me out? Will you set yourself free?" Paula knew she had solved the riddle.

A note was taped to the open door of the meeting room, telling them that the afternoon session would be held by the pond. Paula was the first to arrive, finding beach blankets and cushions spread out on the grass. She chose a purple pillow with tassels on the corners and sat down to watch two pairs of ducks in the reeds across the pond.

Sarah and Alex walked up the path together. Alex listened patiently as Sarah talked. Paula put her finger to her lips and pointed to the ducks. "I think there are four of them," she whispered.

The ducks emerged tentatively from the reeds, revealing not four but six. Sarah and Alex quietly sat down on their cushions. Hearing a voice, they looked up and saw Dan on the path. They motioned to him to be quiet. He stopped where he was and ended his call, flipped the phone shut and stuffed it back into his pocket.

Paula pointed to the pond as he approached quietly.

"What kind are they?" he whispered, looking at Sarah.

"Hooded Merganser," Sarah replied proudly. "See how the male has a large black head with a white stripe and the black-and-white striped breast? The females are mostly brown and gray."

"I'm impressed." Dan winked at her.

"Hey, I'm a farm girl. I know my ducks and geese," Sarah grinned.

They sat silently, watching the ducks skim effortlessly in unison across the pond. Then, stirred by some unseen force, they took off together in a flutter of wings.

"Nature has her own mode of doing each thing." At the sound of Martha's voice they turned their heads. "And she has somewhere told it plainly, if we will keep our eyes and ears open." She paused on the path, pleased that she remembered the quote and added with a playful flair, "Ralph Waldo Emerson."

Accepting help from Alex, Martha took a seat on a cushion and turned to look out over the pond. They sat quietly for several minutes, watching the sun reflect on the water and catching a glimpse of a dragonfly's iridescent wings as it hovered a moment in their midst.

"Nature is the greatest teacher," Martha began, "if we'll only listen. All living things have within them an inherent sense of balance: the trees, the birds, the plants. Even the tiniest insects are all part of a cycle as old as life itself. Humankind is the only creature that can willfully upset that balance environmentally as well as within itself. To regain that balance all we have to do is return to nature and observe, listen, and learn."

Martha turned toward her flip chart, which was propped up against a small boulder near the blanket. "Nature's tripod," she laughed. "So what have you experienced sitting here?"

"Just being." Paula breathed in deeply. "Not doing or thinking or wishing I was someplace else. Just being here." A large flock of geese in V-formation flew overhead, low enough for them to see the feathers on their outstretched wings.

"There's a signal from nature that fall is near." Martha shielded her eyes with her hand as she watched the geese disappear over the tops of the trees.

Alex put on his sunglasses and looked up. "The V-formation is aerodynamic, cutting through the air currents without resistance so the flock can go faster and farther with less effort. In fact, did you know that by flying in a V the whole flock adds seventy-one percent greater flying range than if each bird flew alone? In addition, when the leader tires, it drops back into the flock and another bird takes over."

"Interesting," Martha said. "By sharing the leadership they are all stronger. Nature's lessons are right in front of us, waiting for us to learn them."

Martha's eyes met Dan's. "Do you have something to share, Dan?"

"Yes," he began, slowly. "You might say that I learned it was time to drop back into the flock and let someone else take the lead. I spoke with Tim after lunch. He did great. You should have heard him! He was so excited."

"So he landed the account?" Alex inquired.

"Yes, and more. The client is actually going to increase the amount of money they're investing. That's great for the company, but it's also good for the client, because now they'll pay lower management fees. So everybody wins: the company, the client, Tim…"

"You," Sarah added, nudging him with her elbow.

"Exactly. By allowing Tim to make that call, I got to be here," Dan said. "Watching a bunch of ducks, which is far more productive than I ever would have guessed." They all laughed.

"May I suggest that you didn't allow Tim to make that call," Martha interjected. "It was bigger than that. You empowered him to make the call. That's what a true leader does. They empower others, which in turn, increases the effort tenfold. One person can't do it all any more than one goose can lead the flock from the North to the South. So how does it feel to realize that one of your team is capable of leadership and, in fact, may have even been more successful than you might have been?"

Dan plucked a tall stalk of grass and began folding it accordion-style, over and back on itself. "Honestly, it's humbling. But in a way it feels pretty good. I'm actually beginning to see how I can give more responsibility to Tim and to the others, which will really lighten my load. Still, I have to admit that my ego is hurting a little because I always saw myself as the big deal maker. But I have to say, I'm very happy the way this turned out."

Paula extended her hand palm upward toward Dan, and they exchanged a high-five. "You better lighten your load if you're going to train for the marathon with me," she smiled.

"And play ball with my kids. And spend more time with my wife." Dan rolled his eyes and groaned. "What am I getting myself into?"

"You'll do great," Sarah assured him. "I mean that."

Dan studied Sarah's face. "Thanks. "

Martha observed the exchange, nodding. "Now think back to yesterday morning when we were having a very different discussion. You were on your feet and headed toward the door. You were pretty resistant when I told you that to remain in the course, you needed to 'do what you said you would do' and keep your agreement to be present. That meant finding another way to handle the call. And Paula, do you remember how resistant you were to me the first day?"

Paula laughed. "Oh yeah, I remember."

Martha wrote on the flip chart:

RESIST = What I do when I want someone or something to be different than how it is

"Think of some circumstance that you don't like, something or someone you would like to be some other way than the way they are. Tell me what comes to mind."

Alex quickly offered the situation with Frank at work. Paula blurted out, "My mother." Dan explained that he had been locking horns with some managers over the long-term strategic direction of the company. Sarah said she didn't like the whole dynamic in her department where no one shared information, keeping as much as possible to themselves. Martha wrote each response on the flip chart.

"Tell me more," Martha urged. "Put yourself back into your day-to-day life. Think of the people, situations, events, and circumstances that really get under your skin, that you wish were different somehow."

Self-centered in-laws, time-consuming performance reviews, automated answering services, annoying neighbors, paying bills, taxes, and mortgage payments...the resistance list grew quickly.

"So how do you feel when you deal with all of these?" Martha asked. As they responded, she wrote on the flip chart:

Frustrated
Controlled
Negative
Unimportant
Used
Forced

"Hmmm," she said with pursed lips. "Sounds an awful lot like a victim to me."

"Uh-oh." Paula held her head and fell back on the pillows. "Here we go again."

"That's right. It looks like you've been giving away your personal power to these people, situations, and events. If you want to get it back, then you must listen very carefully as I share the next chart. It is critically important for having the experience you want in your life and work. It's a little complicated, but if you take it one step at a time, you'll understand. Without that understanding, we cannot move to the sixth principle."

She turned the page of the flip chart to a diagram, a four-step cycle labeled Resistance Cycle.

RESISTANCE CYCLE

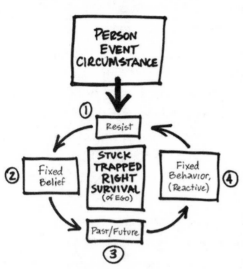

"What you've just described are people or situations that you resist. Before going further, I want to tell you about something that I once resisted." Martha's voice softened as she began the story. "At age nineteen, I was a vibrant and vital young woman. I was a confident athlete. I loved the strength and coordination I could feel in the movement of my body. Then overnight, rheumatoid arthritis hit, severely debilitating me to the point that very often I could not walk. When having a flare-up, I would be hospitalized for days at a time in pain so severe that I could not even bear the weight of the sheets on my body. I couldn't turn myself over in bed. For years I fought this disease. I hated it and was determined to fight it to the finish. Despite all my fighting and resistance, it never left. In fact, the more I fought it, the worse it got. I was caught in the Resistance Cycle."

Martha turned to the resistance illustration on the flip chart. Starting at Number One, Resist, she traced the cycle counterclockwise as she explained. "I was determined to resist having arthritis."

She moved to Number Two, which was Fixed Belief. "My resistance was based on the fixed belief that having arthritis was bad. I believed it was my enemy and I had to get rid of it to be happy." Continuing the cycle to Number Three, Past/Future, she continued: "This belief was based on what I had learned in the past, that having this disease or any disease was bad. And it fed into my fear of the future that if I didn't fight it, the disease would get worse, and I would be doomed to a dismal life ahead."

Moving to Number Four, Fixed Behavior/Reactive, she continued: "As you can imagine, my reaction was anger. I hated this disease and I fought it. However, this brought me right back to resistance because I didn't like feeling the anger, and this kept me revolving around the Resistance Cycle." She pointed to each phase, one through four, as she circled around the chart. "I resisted living my life with anger, bitterness, and fighting because I believed that none of that was good for me. This was something I had learned from the past and was afraid to carry into the future because I knew if I kept feeling and acting that way, it could get worse. So I reacted with another response, which was to feel sorry for myself. After a good session of that, I cycled back." She pointed to phase one again. "And, of course, I then resisted feeling sorry for myself. My fixed belief told me that self-pity was also destructive; it was something I had learned from the past to resist because I was afraid it could lead to constant misery. So I moved to another behavior, which was to be a martyr. Then not liking being a martyr, I resisted that, too, and so on and so on..."

Martha wrote three words in the center of the Resistance Cycle: Stuck. Trapped. Right.

"Because of my resistance and as a result of my fixed beliefs and behaviors, I felt stuck and trapped. But look at this!" She pointed to the word "Right." "I also got to be right about all of my beliefs: Arthritis was a terrible disease to have. It was my enemy. My life was doomed. It was unfair. I was too young... I was a true victim of the disease. It was slowly destroying my life, and I was powerless against it."

She paused. A warm breeze stirred the trees and ruffled the tall grass in the meadow beyond the pond.

"That's what happens when you resist people and situations in your life," Martha explained. "You feel stuck and trapped, but, you know what? You also get to be right. If you ask me, that's a pretty heavy price to pay to be right. Now let's take some of your examples and see how you've been locked in this cycle."

Alex went first, explaining how he resisted Frank because he was uncooperative and not a team player. Tracing the Resistance Cycle, Martha led Alex through the four phases. The first phase was Alex's resistance of Frank for being uncooperative. Second, this was based on a fixed belief that Frank should be cooperative. Third, that belief was rooted in what Alex had learned in the past about how co-workers and teams should work together. Alex nodded in agreement as he studied the chart carefully.

"So what are you afraid might happen in the future if you don't resist Frank's uncooperativeness?"

"That it'll get worse," he said.

"That brings you to Number Four, Fixed Behavior. How do you react to Frank when he's uncooperative?"

"I argue with him and try to prove that he's wrong."

Continuing to track his responses around the Resistance Cycle, she returned to Resist. Alex resisted arguing with Frank because he hated arguing; it was exhausting and nothing good ever came of it. Moving to the Fixed Beliefs phase, Alex saw how this was rooted in the belief that arguing all the time was pointless and accomplished nothing.

"Yes, and that's a belief you have learned from the past," Martha continued. "But if you don't argue with him, what are you afraid will happen in the future?"

"Well, then I'm afraid he'll get his way," Alex said. This cycle explained so much of the anger and frustration he felt at work. It was easy to blame Frank, but now he could see how he was responsible for his own cycle of resistance.

"So then I try a new behavior. I avoid him." His eyes followed the path of the Resistance Cycle as he spoke. "Then I resist avoiding him because I have a fixed belief that I shouldn't avoid a coworker, and so on."

"Do you feel stuck and trapped?" Martha asked.

"Very much so," Alex agreed.

"But you also get to be right about your belief that Frank shouldn't be uncooperative, that he should collaborate. Congratulations, Alex. You get to be right, but you also get to be stuck and trapped. How's it working for you?"

"Oh, just great!" he laughed

Turning to Dan, who was obviously deep in thought, Martha used his example of resisting the company's strategic direction. Dan quickly explained that he didn't feel the strategic plan went far enough and that Stellar Point should be expanding the kind of investment products it will offer in the future. "But nobody else sees it. And this one guy from the New York office is such a brownnose; he'll agree with whatever everybody else says, no matter what. So I end up locking horns with him."

Again Martha moved around the Resistance Cycle: Dan's fixed belief was that the company's strategic focus was not aggressive enough. That's based on something he learned in the past about what he thought successful companies do.

"That's right. If you want to get out in front of the competition, you have to take off the blinders and really go for it." Dan folded his arms across his chest.

"Would you agree that your resistance is also based on your fear of the future?" Martha suggested, pointing to the third phase.

"Exactly. My fear is that if we don't diversify faster, the company won't be as successful as it could be, which means I won't reach my goals if I stay there." A scowl knotted Dan's brow.

"And that leads to the fixed behavior of fighting with other managers over the issue," Martha added, leading him around the cycle again.

"Sometimes I get so frustrated with them that I don't say anything. I mean, let them fall flat on their faces, and then maybe they'll see what I've been talking about!" Dan snapped.

"After doing that for awhile, do you notice yourself resisting that behavior too?" Martha began to retrace the Resistance Cycle with her hand.

Dan admitted he resisted that behavior because he didn't want the company to fall short of its potential, and he certainly didn't want that for himself either. In the end he felt frustrated and angry.

"Would you also describe it as stuck and trapped?" Martha offered.

Dan sighed, his shoulders relaxing slightly. "Yeah, you could say that."

"But then again, you also get to be right in your belief about the company's strategic focus. When they won't listen to you, you'll fight them or else you'll sit back and do nothing. Either way it's resistance. So, Dan, are you being effective with your resistance? Is anyone listening to your views? Is it working for you?" Martha inquired.

"It's not," he admitted.

"But congratulations. You win your game: You get to be right about your views on how the company should operate. Is it worth it? Are you really winning anything?"

There was no sound except the wind and a crow cawing in the distance. A fish broke the surface of the water, creating ripples that spread out until the surface was smooth again.

"There are three things about resistance that you should know." She wrote:

- Your resistance perpetuates the existence of the very thing or situation that you resist

- Your resistance is the source of all of your Life's upsets

- What you resist, persists

"These statements reflect the nature of resistance, one is connected to the other. They are all summed up by the last one," Martha explained. "The more you resist a person, event, situation, or circumstance, the more you hand over your power to that problem, conflict, or dynamic. No matter how much you resist, it persists."

"Look around you," Martha invited them. "Do you see resistance anywhere here? Do the birds fight against their natural migration patterns? Do the animals complain when it's time to hibernate? Do the squirrels grumble and groan as the seasons change and winter approaches. No! They just go out and get some nuts! They are all an integral part of the natural cycle of change around them. They may lack the intellect of humans, but in many ways they are far wiser than we are. Maybe it's because they don't have egos and they don't have to be right."

Overhead a hawk soared, dipping and gliding on the air currents as it rode higher, becoming little more than a speck against a bright blue sky.

Martha used the example of river rafting. One of the first things a guide tells the passengers if they should fall out of the raft is, don't fight the river. Anyone who fights the river will likely lose. Instead, go with the river—on your back, feet first, and head raised. This way there is a much better chance of influencing the outcome, in this case getting to shore safely.

"How many of you," Martha continued, "frequently feel like you're going against the current, fighting the river of life? You feel and look like you're doing a lot of work. In fact you are doing a lot of work, but you notice you're not getting anywhere. You're probably exhausted, but you fight on. Then you start taking in water, and that means that pretty soon you'll start to sink. You'll go down fighting, but you'll still go down. What you need to do is let go. Stop resisting and go with the flow. It is what it is. You wanting it to be some other way is meaningless. The river isn't going to change direction just because you want it to. When you go with the flow, your chances of being able to influence the situation increase significantly.

"Who knows what possibilities exist for you down the river that you would have missed if you had kept fighting? Like a sandbar or a branch you can grab to pull yourself ashore. In your river of life, what opportunities do you have to influence change?"

The next page on the flip chart was another illustration, this one titled Acceptance Cycle. The four points, clockwise from the bottom, were labeled: Accept, Desired Experience, Present, and Interpret Differently/Be Creative.

"The first step requires you to accept. What is, is. You like it; you

ACCEPTANCE CYCLE

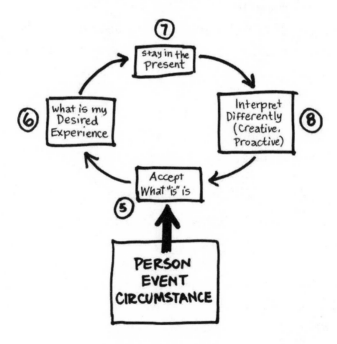

don't like it. It doesn't matter. It is how it is," Martha explained. "You not liking it and you fighting it doesn't make any difference. Your resistance doesn't matter. If your resistance isn't working for you, then it's time to drop it. Surrender to and accept what is. Please note, and this is very important, when I say surrender and accept, I do not mean give up, give in, or condone. What I mean is 'go with.' To do so, we must let go of our egos and our need to be right. Then perhaps we, too, can align ourselves with the changes as they occur. It is only by doing this that we can be in harmony with reality."

An image came to Alex's mind of a tree, its branches bending in the wind. It didn't need to fight the wind to be rooted where it was. Even when the winds were strong enough to snap a limb or a violent storm toppled the tree, it was just nature allowing one thing to give way to another: the tree going back to the earth.

"Now, let me tell you the rest of my story," Martha continued. "For years, I fought having rheumatoid arthritis. It wasn't until a wise person shared this work with me that I began to see my arthritis differently. To be free, I had to accept it totally. I had to come face-to-face with the reality of the disease, not how I wished it would be or how I wanted it to be, but how it really was. I had to admit and accept that this was how it was in my life. Then I asked myself, what was my desired experience? What was I looking for in the present moment? I wanted to feel vibrant, alive, and at peace. To achieve this, I had to let go of the past and my fear of the future and be totally in the present moment. This brought me to the third phase of the Acceptance Cycle, being Present. I had to let go of how things had been in the past and how they might be in the future. I had to be present and focused *in the moment* for each moment as it occurred. From here I could move to the fourth phase: a new beginning where I could choose to interpret my disease differently. Instead of seeing it as an enemy, I decided to see it as a gift."

Martha peered into each set of eyes. "Yes," she said softly, responding to their unspoken incredulity. "It was quite possible. When I saw my arthritis as something that, however unexpectedly, was empowering me, I began to realize all that I could learn from it."

Martha held up her hands, the fingers gnarled and twisted by arthritis. "You may see these hands as deformed and ugly. I look at these hands and say 'thank you.'" She touched her hands lovingly.

"These hands teach me compassion, understanding, tenacity, and courage. Constantly, they teach me patience and acceptance. And I say thank you for the opportunity to have such a teacher with me every minute of the day."

There was perfect silence, as if nature had stopped to listen, too.

"When I let go of fighting and resisting, I could surrender to acceptance, and that helped me to embrace my arthritis. Then I could totally accept the very thing I had feared the most. I had been terrified that if I didn't fight it, it would consume me. But you see, it was consuming me anyway. To be free, I had to let go of being right about arthritis being bad. I had to interpret the arthritis not as a problem but as an opportunity to learn. I needed to see it not as a curse, but as a gift."

From a place of complete acceptance, Martha told them, she had the most amazing experience: she felt as if some voice was saying: "Finally, after all these years, I have your attention. I had to give you a loud message for you to learn these lessons because you didn't hear what was offered quietly. Now you have heard it, and the arthritis can relax."

"And it did," she continued. "The war within me, the fighting and resisting, quieted, and amazingly, so did a lot of the pain. That was many years ago. To be sure, it's a progressive disease. I still have it and I am accountable to seek the finest medical advice. However, I know that doctors and medicine can only do so much. My role is to be a responsible patient and build a healthy relationship with my disease. Therefore, I have accepted it to the point that I've even said 'I love you' to my arthritis many times because of how it has helped me grow as a human being."

Martha turned to a blank page and drew three ovals. "This could only happen, however, by being in the present moment."

She labeled the oval in the center Present. The one on the left was Past, and the one on the right Future. Each oval represented the three basic time frames in which people operate: past, present, and future.

Dividing each oval in half, she wrote, "what is" in the top half of the Present. "That's what's happening right now."

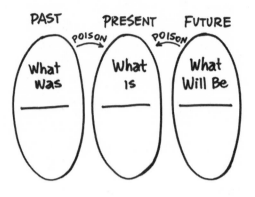

Moving to the Past, she wrote, "what was" in the top half. In the top half of the Future, she wrote, "what will be."

"We have a tendency to poison the present moment by dragging in old fears and baggage from the past as well as unconscious habits and behaviors. Then we bring into the present moment whatever frightens us about the future and poison it again," Martha continued. "The present moment is a space of pure possibility that we continuously limit. This is linear thinking: what is, what was, what will be. It's the way most people view time. But there is another way of thinking," she explained.

In the bottom half of the Present, Martha wrote, "what is," explaining that everything in this moment is what it is. In the bottom half of the Past, she wrote, "what isn't." In bottom half of the Future, which isn't here yet, she also wrote "what isn't."

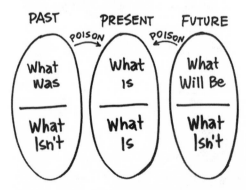

"Neither the future nor the past exists. All we ever have is *right now*. Now that moment is gone. Was it everything that you wanted it to be? I hope so, because you'll never get it back. But you do have a new present moment *right now*. How you spend every moment determines your life. Your life is simply a series of present moments."

Wasn't that the truth! Sarah thought. She spent so much time wishing things had been different in the past or worrying about the future, particularly where her kids were concerned, that she didn't enjoy the moment. No wonder she felt so out of control.

"When you are in the present moment, you can consciously choose to be whoever you want to be and to act however you want to act. Instead of embracing this, however, we become encumbered by what we drag in from the past and what we are afraid might happen in the future. To be in full control of your life right now, you must let go of the past and the future and just be here now. Peak performers are those who can best do this no matter what is going on around them. I am reminded of the story about the reporter who asked Ted Williams what his secret was for being one of the greatest baseball hitters of all time. He answered, 'When the ball comes over the plate, I can see the stitches!'"

Paula wondered if she could ever be that aware. Clearly, it wasn't going to be as easy as flipping the switch. Yet, if she committed to change, then she knew she was going to need to rigorously practice the art of being here now.

Turning back to the illustration, Martha explained that once you are in the present moment and accept that "it is what it is," you can then move to the next phase of the Acceptance Cycle—"Interpret Differently/Be Creative." At this point people begin to look at things from another perspective. They get creative and proactive. "Remember Principle #3: 'How's the View from Your View?' and the need to remain open to other ways of seeing things. You can't always change the circumstances, but you can choose how you interpret those circumstances and thereby determine your own experience and results."

In this phase it is time again to act, but with a different perspective and a willingness to see things from another point of view, which unlocks a wealth of creativity, she continued. That, in turn, completes the cycle back to acceptance, which gives the experience

THRIVE or SURVIVE?

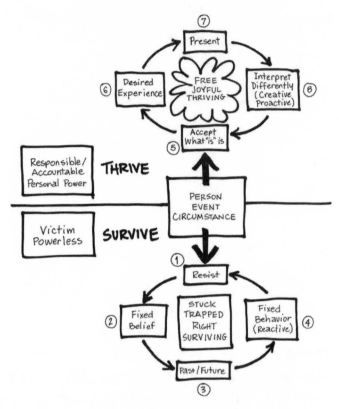

of being free, joyful, and effective. For emphasis, Martha wrote the three words—free, joyful, and effective—in the center of the Acceptance Cycle.

Using the same examples, Martha led them through the Acceptance Cycle, beginning with Alex, who now could see how his resistance to Frank had perpetuated his problem. The first step, Martha coached, was to accept that Frank is the way he is. This kind of acceptance did not mean condone, give up, or give in, she repeated, but rather "go with."

"Are you willing to stop resisting and go with the reality that he is uncooperative?" Martha asked him.

"Yes," Alex replied firmly. "Frank is how he is. Two years of fighting him pretty much means that my resistance has been futile."

From here the second phase was to identify the desired experience. Alex explained that what he wanted was for all of his team—and especially Frank and him—to get along and work together.

"For that to happen, you need to get into the present moment, which is the third phase. Let go of what happened between you in the past and what might happen in the future. Be here now. Moving to the fourth phase, how could you interpret things differently?"

"Well, maybe Frank is feeling frustrated because he doesn't feel heard. Maybe he has some ideas, but nobody is listening to them, including me," Alex said.

Martha then invited him to get creative, to really look at things from a new perspective and to react to Frank differently.

Alex narrowed his eyes as he studied the Acceptance Cycle. "I could approach him and ask him to share his views with me. I guess I could really listen to him for a change and see if he's willing to find a solution that has no losers."

"I would guess that as you take creative action with him, you will get very different results. Your shift to acceptance may very well prompt Frank to shift too, and as I suggested," she smiled, "joy, freedom, and effectiveness will immediately follow."

She turned her attention to Dan. "Can you see that fighting with the other managers hasn't moved you forward? You're still stuck and trapped. And when you decide to withhold your ideas, hoping that they'll fall flat on their faces, you're also stuck and trapped. Either way, you are fighting against the river."

After Dan agreed, Martha suggested that if he were willing to go with the flow, he would have more influence on the outcome. That meant listening to others' ideas, asking questions, and drawing them out. "You will be relaxed, participating and a part of the flow, rather than flailing away, fighting this force you have set up to block the way of creativity. As you move with the current, you will likely be able to exert more influence over the situation. Because everyone is working more freely, you will be able to see more of their talent and nurture it, which will make people more open to listening to your ideas and suggestions. You know, Dan, it's hard for people to listen to someone who is always making them wrong. A different result can only happen if you 'presence yourself,' forget the past and the future and start to interpret things differently."

Smiling, Martha told them another story, this time about her mother who was an ex-schoolteacher from Boston. She had all the characteristics of her New England heritage, from her sensible shoes, tweed skirt, and wingback chair to the clipped speech pattern that sounded a little like Katharine Hepburn. Many years ago, Martha told them, she published a newsletter every month. Wanting her mother to be proud of her, Martha sent her a copy. Each time she called her mother, however, she heard the same thing: "It was lovely, deah, very nice," Martha mimicked. "But did you see the spelling error in the third column?"

Month after month, following her usual comment of "It was lovely, deah," there was another criticism: maybe an article was too long, or perhaps the colors were too bright. Martha admitted that she got so frustrated with these calls that one time, after she had hung up, she started yelling at the phone, an inanimate object!

"That's when I saw the proverbial light," she continued. "I knew that, at seventy-five, my mother wasn't going to change. I had to accept the way she was."

Martha turned to the Acceptance chart and outlined each phase: "When I accepted that my mother wasn't going to change, I moved to my desired experience. I knew what I wanted was to feel connected with my mother. I wanted us to share something. I knew I had to let go of the past and how she had acted and get into the present moment. From here I could go to the next phase in the cycle and interpret her actions differently. Perhaps her criticism was her desire for me to be seen in the best light possible. Maybe, my mother's criticisms were her way of saying 'I love you. I care. I want you to succeed.' Before, I thought her behavior was negative and judgmental. I felt she was making me wrong. But when I was willing to interpret it differently I then saw it as her way of supporting me."

With this new perspective, the next time she called her mother and received the inevitable feedback, Martha focused on her desired experience of feeling more connected with her mother. "So I told her, 'Thanks, Mom. I appreciate your view. Thank you for sharing it. Most important, I appreciate the love that is behind that comment.' A little taken back, she said, 'Of course! You know I love you.' After hanging up the phone this time, instead of being irritated, I felt grateful. Instead of my mother determining how I felt, I was the one who was in charge of my reaction. I was beginning to master my own experience."

"Did she still criticize every newsletter you ever sent her?" Dan asked, wondering if he could ever see his father's bullying in a different light.

"Yes, she did. It was as predictable as water running downhill. Believe me, Dan, like your dad, my mother was a formidable river! Because of this I needed to go with the flow, and this prompted me to get even more creative," Martha explained.

Her solution, she said, was to have her mother proofread the newsletter before it was sent out. Her mother was thrilled to help, and Martha benefited from a better product. Most importantly, it allowed them to have an even deeper connection through the joy of working together. "Because I listened to my Sage and my commitment to the principles of 'Everybody Gets a Prize,' 'Got Results?,' and 'How's the View from Your View?,' I ended up with a much closer relationship with my mother. The sharing that I was looking for was far deeper and more loving than I would have had if I had resisted her."

The afternoon sun angled lower, casting elongated shadows across the grass.

"So," Martha exclaimed, "there's a significant possibility here! You can be in resistance and feel like the victim, or you can move to acceptance and look at things differently. It really is a life-changing shift. And that brings us to the next principle that will help us thrive in business and in life."

Turning to a new page, Martha wrote:

Principle #6
So what's for lunch?

"What's for lunch?" Paula gasped with a laugh.

"Exactly," Martha laughed with her. "It goes like this: 'It is what it is. My resistance does not help me. It's a waste of time to keep resisting. So I need to diminish its importance, let it go, and focus on something else like 'what's for lunch?' As you can see, each of the principles is designed to be a memory trigger, instantly giving you a context."

She looked over at Dan. "Your perception is that the company should follow a different course. You have presented your ideas, but other managers don't agree. There is no consensus, and so that status quo remains for now."

"It is what it is. 'So What's for Lunch?'" he grinned. "I get it. By dropping my resistance and accepting it, I have a better chance of finding a workable solution by building consensus rather than fighting the war."

Martha turned toward Sarah. "The next time your in-laws come over and you perceive them nitpicking over everything…"

"I know, I need to let it go and focus on what's for lunch!" she interrupted with a laugh. "It even feels good to say that."

"The more we practice these principles, the more they become part of our mindset and vocabulary, and the more they will influence our behaviors and actions. That's the importance of practice, whether it's a principle, a behavior, or a musical instrument."

Martha cracked a broad smile. "You all must remember the old joke about practice?" Seeing the curiosity in their eyes, she shared:

"One day a young man was walking through Manhattan with a tourist map in his hand. He stopped an older gentleman for directions. 'Excuse me, sir,' he said, 'but can you tell me how to get to Carnegie Hall?' The old man nodded. 'Practice, practice, practice.'"

With that, she gave them their instructions for the evening: Dinner would be served a little earlier, at six o'clock, and then they would reconvene in the Great Room at seven-thirty. "We still have a lot to cover in the time remaining," she told them. "Between now and dinner, think about what you can change in your life by following the Acceptance Cycle. She wrote on the flip chart:

1) Let go of your Resistance. Suspend judgment.
   Accept that what "is" is.

2) Ask yourself "What is the experience I want to have?"

3) Stay fully in the Present moment.

4) Interpret the situation differently. Get creative

"Let's see what happens when you shift from resistance to acceptance. I bet this will make for some good dinner conversation."

As they picked up their things and began walking back to toward the lodge, Martha called Alex and Sarah aside. "I'd like to spend some time alone with both of you," she invited.

She and Sarah would meet for an herbal tea after dinner, around six forty-five, at Martha's cottage, which was just a short ways down the path. Sarah beamed at the invitation.

Martha turned toward Alex. "Would you be willing to take a short walk with me now?"

"Of course," he replied, eagerly.

She would meet him in the Great Room in ten minutes.

❖ Chapter Ten

Declaring Commitment

Alex stood by the fireplace in the Great Room looking out the window toward the pond where the afternoon session had been held. He wanted to commit every detail to memory so he could tell Ann about it when he called her that evening.

Martha approached slowly, a sweater over her shoulders. Together, they headed out the front door of the lodge. The sun was disappearing behind the hill, taking with it the warmth of the day and reminding them of the changing seasons. Martha accepted Alex's arm for steadiness as they walked together along a neatly tended gravel path toward a flower garden where the last of the marigolds bloomed beside yellow and white chrysanthemums. They reached a small stone table with two chairs in a charming corner of the garden.

Although the shadows were lengthening, the chairs were still warm from the late afternoon sun. Looking around her, Martha broke the silence. "I love the way the air smells this time of year." Breathing in deeply, she savored the earthy smell of the ground warmed by the sun and the distant scent of pine. She absorbed the feeling in the air when summer slips away on nature's flow and gracefully blends into fall. "This is a nurturing place," she said at last.

Alex scanned the grounds. "Yes, it is. I'd like to come back here sometime with my wife Ann. I think she'd enjoy seeing it."

Martha turned to him and smiled. "You know, you can come back to a spot like this any time you want. All you have to do is picture a beautiful place in nature, either in the country or in the city, a place of quiet and repose where you can be replenished, where you are alone with your thoughts—and your feelings."

Alex nodded, but silently wondered if he could ever recreate the experience of this place in his mind.

"You can trust your heart to nature, Alex. Nature allows you to open up to the feelings inside, the ones you have been hiding so long that you didn't even know they were there. Do you know what I'm talking about?"

"Yeah, I do." Alex leaned forward, his arms resting on the table. "Sometimes I don't know what I feel. Sure, I know when I'm angry or I'm happy. But there are times when I don't feel anything."

She inquired if he ever had a "gut reaction" to something: perhaps a physical shift inside his body such as his stomach churning, his muscles tightening, his heart pounding. Those bodily reactions can often be translated into a feeling. Whether or not he could label it didn't matter. "Just know that it may be a feeling and acknowledge it. Then you'll begin to see that you are feeling many things."

"I know that I'm feeling a lot more today than I have in years—maybe ever," Alex admitted.

When Martha asked him what he was feeling, Alex thought for a moment. "Happy. Content." He paused. "Anxious."

"Anxious?"

"I'm afraid that when I leave this place, I'll forget everything and go right back to the way I was before."

"And what was that like, Alex?"

"Just like you said: a stimulus-response machine. When I was a kid they called me 'The Robot.' It never made sense to me before, but now I get it. I was a machine that went through the motions, computed the data, and came up with the answer. I was all brain and no heart," Alex said.

"And now?" Martha asked.

"I feel like I'm opening up." He looked around. "It's as if I've spent a lifetime damming up my feelings with the logs, rocks, and whatever debris I could find inside of me. Now the blockage has been breached, and the water can finally run free."

"What's that water like?"

"Murky from being stagnant for so long. It's deep and dark, and slow moving." Alex closed his eyes. "But the more it runs, the clearer the water gets. The broken pieces of what's left over from the past are being flushed out, and all that's left is a pure spring."

Martha smiled at the imagery. "And what is the source of that spring?"

Alex looked at her. "The present moment."

Martha patted his arm gently. "You are a wellspring of many things, Alex: thoughts, ideas, creativity, emotions. You are reconnecting with what you have always known. You are coming alive and beginning to thrive."

Returning to the lodge, Alex found Dan, Sarah, and Paula talking together in the Great Room. When dinner was served, they sat at a round table in a small dining room, sharing observations about the course and what they had learned thus far.

Sarah listened intently to the conversation, aware of how hungry she was for intellectual and emotional connection with others. As the time drew closer for her meeting with Martha, she felt only happy anticipation. She stole glances at her watch until it was five minutes to their appointed time and then excused herself.

Walking down the path, Sarah was struck by the soft darkness that enveloped the pond and meadow and the warm light that was emitted through the windows of Martha's cottage. A few frogs croaked in the distance. At 6:45 P.M., precisely on time, Sarah walked up the three well-worn wooden steps and onto the porch. She knocked on the door.

Martha pleasantly invited her inside the pine-paneled cottage, furnished with overstuffed chairs and a rocking chair with a colorful cushion. A low fire crackled in the fireplace and, in the corner, tucked away in a cozy nook, was a table with upholstered high-backed benches and colorful pillows. Sarah's eyes took in every detail from the chintz curtains at the windows to the small bouquet of flowers on the table beside a teapot.

"Oh, Martha, this is so lovely," she gushed, as Martha poured steaming hot water into her cup. Sarah helped herself to blackberry tea. "I have to admit that when Bernie first asked me to come to this course I was nervous, but everything has been just wonderful. I can't tell you how much it's meant to me to be here with you and the others."

Martha was pleased to see Sarah's smiling face. "I'm happy to hear that you're turning this into a positive experience for yourself. I'm glad that you've chosen to grow and that you're learning from the others as well."

Sipping their tea, they talked briefly about the cottage and the beautiful natural setting before they moved on.

"So, Sarah," Martha said, "shall we talk about your resentment?"

Sarah set her cup back down on the saucer. "I don't think that's a problem anymore."

"Let's talk as if it is. You see, resentment eats away at a person's soul, and you've not always been a good protector of your own spirit. So I think it would be a good idea to look at this a little more deeply."

Sarah agreed reluctantly, unfolding herself from the comfortable position in her chair.

"Resentment comes from the French verb, *resentir*, which means to feel over and over again," Martha explained.

With resentment, instead of outwardly expressing the feelings of anger, frustration, and irritation, a person internalizes them. Emotions that are not constructively released are sealed within one's self. The problem, however, is that emotions are energy, and energy cannot be destroyed; thus the negative emotions remain sealed up inside and will cause a physical reaction. The body perceives this angry energy as a threat to its survival and immediately emits hundreds of chemicals as if it were fighting off a virus or an enemy. Physiologically one's body changes; for example, it releases coagulants to stop bleeding, adrenaline for super energy, and strength to either run from or fight the perceived threat. Muscles tighten, body temperature rises, heart pounds, and blood moves away from outer extremities to go to the heart, brain, and muscles to help the person survive.

"Unlike our prehistoric ancestors who needed this 'fight or flight' response for their very survival and to keep from being killed or eaten, today most people of privilege are not faced with such external dangers," Martha continued. "Rather, it's our own emotions that are triggering this survival response."

"I've heard about this," Sarah agreed. "It's as if someone is preparing to go into battle when all they're doing is sitting in their car, angry they they're stuck in traffic."

"Yes, and we need to realize that this response can also trigger some very real health risks."

Chemicals that aren't used for their intended purposes can end up hurting one's body. When clotting agents are running rampant throughout the body with no real wound to heal, they can influence strokes and heart attacks. "Scientists are even linking specific emotions with specific diseases," Martha added. "For example, it is suspected that autoimmune diseases could be linked to resentment. It's a known fact that stress can not only cause but also compound, many health conditions."

Sarah looked down at her own body and felt the bulk around

her middle. "When I'm stressed, I eat. I try to comfort myself with food—sugar, chocolate, carbs. Once I start eating, it's hard to stop, just like some sort of addiction. Instead of feeling better, though, I feel lousy afterwards, and I hate myself."

Martha reached for a paper napkin to draw a diagram: a vertical line with two short horizontal marks at each end. "Imagine this line is a ruler," Martha explained. She marked off a short section. "Let's say that the first two inches on the ruler represent short-term pleasure and payoff. The remaining ten inches, though, is long-term pain and price."

Martha drew a second line and marked it off in the same fashion. "On this ruler, the first two inches are short-term pain and price. The remaining ten are long-term pleasure and payoff."

PRICES and PAYOFFS

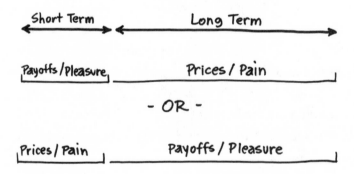

"There are two alternatives, Sarah," Martha explained. "Cookies may make you feel better for a little while when you're depressed, but in the long term there is a price to be paid in your health and your comfort with your own body. When you say 'no' to the cookies, you may feel like you're being deprived in the short term, but over the long term you will have the payoff and the pleasure of a trim figure. You're going to pay a price one way or the other. The question is whether you want it to be short-term or long-term."

"I know," Sarah agreed. "I've bought a million diet books and tapes over the years. I've tried every fad diet, but it all comes down to the same thing: I must permanently change my pattern of eating—eat less, significantly reduce empty sugars and saturated fats, balance my carbs and protein, and exercise more. That's how you lose weight."

"That, combined with keeping your commitment, is what works, Sarah. Short-term you won't have the pleasure, but long-term you'll have higher self-esteem." Martha paused. "You might want to pay close attention as we discuss Principle #7 tonight."

Sarah nodded. "And you know what, Martha? My Sage has always known this. Quick fixes don't work, and hating myself for being overweight doesn't help. I know that when I feel badly about myself, I'm a victim, and then I'm not motivated to diet. In fact, to try to feel better, I eat."

"Self-love and self-esteem are far more effective in keeping you motivated to take care of yourself than beating yourself up," Martha replied gently.

"You know, Martha," Sarah continued, "what really bugs me about Charlotte Coletti isn't that she calls me to handle her personal stuff. What really gets me mad is that she's so pretty and thin. She takes good care of herself, and she doesn't look her age even though I know she's five years older than I am!"

Martha sipped her tea, savoring the fruity taste and aroma. "This resentment that you feel didn't start with Charlotte, did it, Sarah? I'll bet it all goes back to when you were a child. What did you learn about anger back then?"

Sarah recalled the lessons that had been deeply engrained in her upbringing: showing anger wasn't allowed. If she did, the consequence was getting punishment.

"So the voices in your head tell you: 'Anger is bad. Bad equals negative. You can't be nice if you are negative.' Then you take that belief and expand it into a strategy, and because 'no' is a negative word, it's not okay to say no to people. Sarah, this may have helped you to survive in your childhood but I'm here to tell you, that is not the Capital-T Truth," Martha replied. "That's just a belief you formed, and it can be very unhealthy. To thrive, you'll need to form a different relationship with anger and disconnect the wiring you have in your head that links assertiveness with negativity. You need to truthfully confront rather than avoid your reaction, including your discomfort with your feelings and your own behaviors. Then you can learn to deal with them constructively. It's okay to say no sometimes. In fact, it is frequently the healthy thing to do."

Sarah admitted she had a long way to go, but quickly added she wanted to continue. Martha assured her that, for now, it was important to realize that negativity was neither bad nor good. Rather, it was just "what is." "Perhaps you should stop judging your feelings, pushing down your resentment, and trying to cover it up like it's not there."

Their teacups empty, it was time for Sarah to head back to the lodge before the evening session resumed.

"Thank you, Martha," Sarah said, blinking back tears. She fumbled in her pocket for a tissue and blew her nose. Martha gave her a gentle hug and told her how proud she was of the work she was doing.

Sarah opened the door. "I can't believe that tomorrow afternoon we'll all be headed home. It seems a little unreal."

"I understand, but for now just keep your focus on being here for the time we have left and on how you are progressing each day." Martha reached for a small cream-colored envelope on a table by the door. She handed Sarah the envelope and told her that the message within was just for her. Closing the door, Sarah stood on the front porch. A pair of loons called to each other in the darkness, and a moth fluttered around the porch light. Opening the envelope, she almost laughed as the rush of feelings of anxiety and anticipation came to her. The note inside read: "Resentment is like drinking poison and waiting for the other person to die–Carrie Fisher."

Reaching over, she held the porch railing and read the words again. Sarah gathered herself and walked slowly down the wooden steps to the path back to the lodge.

The evening session was held in the Great Room where the sofas and chairs were drawn in a circle in front of the fireplace. Chatting casually with each other, the group settled into their chairs. When Martha took her seat, their attention shifted to what they were about to learn.

"Look how far we've come in just two days," Martha began. "There are still two more principles, one that you'll learn tonight and one more in tomorrow morning's session. Thinking back on these past two days, I've heard you say that you're going to make changes. You're going to be different. You'll never do this or that again. These are strong statements to be sure, but I want you to know that you will go off track. You will forget, and you will revert to some old and ineffective behaviors. When that happens, the one thing that will get you back on track will be your commitment. You must stop and ask yourself, 'What am I committed to?' Remember, you are always committed to something, whether it's the old behavior of being right, or new ways of thinking such as 'Everybody Gets a Prize' and doing what works. So tonight, I'd like to talk to you about commitment."

The word echoed in Sarah's brain, remembering her conversation with Martha in the cottage. "Keeping your commitment is the only thing that works."

"Commitment is what I resolutely set my will to. Whatever you are committed to will show in your results. Commitments are statements of intention, not 'commandments' of what you're supposed to do. A commandment is put upon you by someone else as a parent would speak to a child. A commitment comes from within you, your free will. It starts with the word 'I' instead of the word 'you.'" Martha smiled at Sarah. "Before discussing this further, I'd like to share with you two stories about some unique and very different individuals whose deep levels of commitment were reflected in their results."

She told the story of Julie Moss, a competitor in the Ironwoman Triathlon. Martha recalled for them an image that some of them had seen on television: Julie crawling across the finish line, completely wasted. "That was back in 1982, and yet you remember her, but not because she won the triathlon. She actually lost to a good friend who passed her in the last minutes. You remember her because of her results: that she was committed to finish, against all odds."

Martha related the story of twenty-three-year-old Moss who competed in the Kona Ironwoman Triathlon in Hawaii, swimming 2.4 miles, then biking 112 miles, and finally running a 26.2-mile marathon. The heat was intense and dehydration was a real danger. Julie knew she was in trouble for the last several miles, but still she pushed on. She was way out in front of her nearest competitor, her friend Kathleen McCartney. Then in the last seconds of the race—a mere 20 yards from the finish line—Julie collapsed. Her body had shut down.

Martha imitated the animated commentary of the sports announcers. "'She's down! She's only 20 yards from the finish line! Can she get up? Will she make it across? Can she win this race?' People who were waiting at the finish line reached out, instinctively wanting to help her., but Julie couldn't move. Sitting there, dazed, she poured water over her head, trying to muster the strength to make it the last 20 yards."

Julie Moss crawled those 20 yards, across the hot asphalt, dragging her unresponsive body behind her. Sitting in the middle of the road only a few yards from the finish line, she tried to gather whatever was left in her. Her nearest competitor, Kathleen, rounded the corner and headed toward victory. The crowd tried to encourage Julie, screaming for her to get up. 'You can do it!' they yelled. The cameras showed Julie looking up as Kathleen passed right by her to win the race. Then, reaching into some unknown place within her, Julie forced herself to crawl the last few feet to finish. She lost by only 29 seconds after an 11-hour race.

"Clearly, Julie Moss was committed to finishing that race. Her results show that. Her mental determination and commitment were brilliantly demonstrated as she crossed that line. But was she committed to winning it?" Martha asked, then continued the story.

In 2003, at age forty-five, Julie Moss returned to the Kona Ironman Triathlon with two specific commitments. One was to beat Kathleen McCartney, who was also competing. The second was to post the same time or better than she did at age twenty-three. On the strength and clarity of those commitments, she did. With a time of 10 hours and 57 minutes, Julie Moss beat her own time and was about an hour and a half ahead of McCartney. This time, she was committed to more than just finishing, and her results show that.

"Wow," Sarah said admiringly. "I feel exhausted, just listening."

"Keep in mind that Julie Moss's results—first at age twenty-three and then at age forty-five—are a direct result of her commitments," Martha went on.

The second story was about Mother Teresa, who was best known for her work in India with the sick, the dying, and the destitute. In 1982, however, she became personally involved in the plight of thirty-seven children trapped in a hospital on the frontlines of fighting in Beirut. Martha recalled seeing a documentary of this tiny, frail-looking woman as she was being told by all the local authorities that if she went into the war zone, she could be killed. Despite the very real danger, Mother Teresa remained committed to rescuing those children.

"Nothing, absolutely nothing, would deter her from her commitment to those children. What's particularly interesting is how her commitment played out: She was so clear about what she was going to do, she single-handedly convinced the Israeli army and the Palestinian forces to adopt a ceasefire long enough for her to rescue thirty-seven children," Martha told them.

"Amazing," Paula murmured. "And then there was Lance Armstrong who was committed to beating cancer and returned to win the Tour de France more times than any human in history."

While these examples may seem larger-than-life, Martha urged them to focus on the lessons they contain: not one of these people allowed the thought of quitting to overtake them. Quitting was, quite simply, not an option. She pointed out that every choice they make in life and every action they take is determined by their commitments. The results—whether it's what they accomplish or don't accomplish, what they choose or don't choose—are all related directly to their commitments.

In addition, each person's commitments have energy, she continued. A person who is strongly committed is not going to allow anything to get in the way. Their commitments shift the energy around them, changing what manifests in their lives. There are choices, circumstances, and encounters with people that they will no longer allow into their lives while, instead, they attract the people and events that are aligned with their commitments.

Dan shifted forward on the sofa. "Okay, I get that what I'm committed to directly impacts my results. If I'm committed to meeting a sales goal, I will. If I'm committed to running a marathon, I will. But how can my commitment magically make everybody else line up with me?"

"You can't commit for someone else, but you can have great influence. There's nothing 'magic' about it, Dan," Martha replied. "It's energetic, as explained to us by science. We know that everything on the planet is made up of energy, molecules that are constantly in motion, constantly vibrating. You, me, these walls, that chair, the rocks and trees outside. The energy from everything—most especially from people—is emitting vibrations, much like a radio tower that emits radio waves. Our emotions, thoughts, and feelings have vibrational energy, too. Depression, for example, is a heavy, negative emotion. If someone is depressed, they usually move very slowly. People will even talk about someone's 'heavy' energy and how they are putting out 'bad vibes.' On the other hand, when you are experiencing a positive emotion, like being in love, you feel light as if you're 'walking on air.' That's physiological and emotional energy in action."

"Okay, I see that," Dan agreed.

"Just as these vibrations are being emitted like a radio tower transmits radio waves, they are also being picked up by others who act like radio receivers. People who vibrate with the same energy, or situations that have the same energy, will be in sync with what's being transmitted, like a radio tuned to a particular station. When the frequency is the same, the reception is clear. If not, there may be static or no reception at all. Now, when you broadcast your commitment to others, you are putting out a message into the world that will be picked up by people and situations that vibrate with that same energy, and they will become attracted to you. Those who aren't tuned to that frequency will not receive that message."

COMMUNICATION / LAW OF ATTRACTION

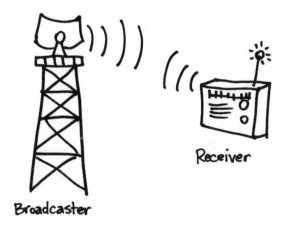

Receiver

Broadcaster

"Like when you're feeling good and you naturally attract people who are also happy," Paula added. "And when you're down, you'll attract other negative people and turn off anybody who is happy."

"Yes," Martha said. "Another consideration is amplitude," and she went on to explain that the height of a radio tower and the strength of a broadcast signal determines how far the radio waves can be transmitted. Using this analogy, the stronger one's commitment, the farther it will carry. When people are very clear and committed—when they speak it, write it, and visualize it—their transmissions become stronger. The farther their transmissions reach, the more they will draw to them what they need to for success to occur.

Martha turned to each of them in the circle. "When there is something that you wish to change in your life, a behavior, a situation, a feeling, or emotion, ask yourself, 'What am I committed to?' Then visualize it. Talk about it. Take actions that are consistent with it. Stay on course and trust that you will be supported. The support that you need will come to you. It never fails. Your job is to accept the support when it appears, no matter what it looks like. And frequently it doesn't look like you think it should."

"What happens if there are obstacles?" Alex asked.

"There will be," Martha told him. "But when you are committed, you need to be like water flowing downhill. When water encounters a barrier, it will go around it, over it, or even under it. They say water takes the path of least resistance. Perhaps another way of looking at it is that water takes the path of acceptance, flowing where it can, unattached to being right about how the path to get there should look. Water will make its way downhill even if it has to evaporate. It has no ego, no attachment to even being a liquid! People, on the other hand, don't tend to act that way. When they are met with obstacles and barriers that make it difficult, they frequently stop or give up. All of which proves water is smarter than people."

They all laughed.

Martha grinned. "Truly, it is commitment that distinguishes us from nature. A seed becomes a flower through automatic reaction to its genetics and produces more seeds to perpetuate the species. Commitment isn't necessary. You and I become fully human through the power of conscious choice and our commitment to that choice."

While a higher consciousness would be needed to remain committed, Martha reminded them there are abundant lessons available in nature that reflect these truths. She asked them to imagine a bear just coming out of hibernation in the spring—hungry and out looking for food. Turning over one log, the bear finds some grubs and gobbles them quickly. His hunger still not satisfied, he turns over a second log and finds more grubs. Then he turns over a third log: no grubs.

"Does the bear sit down and complain that this action ceased to work? Does he complain about the unfairness of it all? Does he become a victim and feel sorry for himself because there are no grubs under the third log? Does he blame himself for being a failure? Does he punish himself and send himself back to his cave? Does he let the circumstance of no grubs under one log stop him from reaching his goal of finding food? Does he quit?"

Their grins became low chuckles as they listened to Martha's list of questions.

"No! He moves on to another log, finds some berries, or lumbers his way down to the stream to catch a fish. He intends to find food, and so he will continue until he finds it—even if he must overcome initial disappointment, change plans or direction, navigate obstacles, or travel great distances. He is not ego-invested in the way he thinks the food should appear. He's simply invested in getting results."

"The bear gets creative and finds another way," Paula observed, nodding.

"When you stray off the path, which you will, stop and ask yourself, 'What am I committed to?' Then align your actions with your commitment. None of this is possible, however, without courage," Martha continued. "Courage is the capacity to move ahead in one's life in spite of failure, fear, or despair. It comes from the French word *coeur*, meaning heart. How often have we heard that someone overcame all odds because they had 'heart'?"

Too frequently, she told them, people have associated courage with physical strength and the ability to fight and conquer. Those who physically didn't meet the challenge were considered cowards. Gang wars in the inner cities are a sad example of how courage can be connected with violence. But that is not the only example: People from all walks of life link courage with the romantic notion of the Wild West. They figuratively march off to war in their homes and the marketplace and then literally kill each other on the battlefield. People use power to overpower. They create separation and disconnection.

"I think we're all familiar with this," she commented, "It's on the news every night." They nodded in somber agreement.

In an evolved society, Martha envisioned, each person embraces another kind of courage and exercises a different set of muscles. For this to happen, people must have the courage to develop their hearts, their sensitivity, their empathy, and their values, and to relate to the wants and needs of others in the same way as they do their own. They must learn to collaborate and cooperate and to think of others as much as they think of themselves. They must use their power to empower, thereby generating connection and unity.

"To be committed, one must have courage and be prepared to face the biggest obstacle to success, quitting, which is based in the fear that their ego will not survive," she said.

She explained that for the two or three million years that humans have walked on the planet, they spent most of their time being fearful of imminent death due to external threats: predators, starvation, the elements, and so forth. Today, however, most of people's fears are based on the survival of their egos—not their physical survival. "The saber-toothed tigers we face now are the people around us with their judgments. We want to look good in the eyes of others. We want to be accepted," Martha explained. "We want to be loved. We want to fit in. Therefore, we fear making mistakes, losing control, failing; we fear that we're not enough or that we're too much. All those fears could lead to rejection. Given a few million years of conditioning, during which rejection from the tribe literally meant death, we now subconsciously equate these ego fears with death." To move past this, she continued, requires each person to operate differently with courage and commitment. "When the board of directors, the managers, employees, and shareholders align behind common goals and objectives; when husbands, wives, and children respect each others' wants and needs; when neighborhoods work together, and when countries and continents build mutual respect for each others' cultures and autonomy; we build a different world, a world with a social and moral consciousness. 'Everybody Wins' and 'Everybody Gets a Prize.'" Martha paused. "And that brings us to the seventh principle."

Turning the page on the flip chart, she wrote:

Principle #7
Stick. Don't quit

"Face your fears and move through them," she shared, "and align all of your thoughts and actions with your clear intentions."

Martha handed out sheets of paper and gave them instructions to write down:

1) What they are committed to

2) The obstacles that will likely get in the way

3) How they will handle those barriers when they encounter them.

She advised them to think about what they were consciously and clearly committed to.

Dan's first commitment was at the top of his mind: He wrote, "I am committed to being promoted." The obstacles, however, were harder to face. They weren't his boss, people not appreciating him, or others being jealous of what he accomplished. The biggest obstacle was himself. He wrote down: "My own ego and my limited belief that I have to do everything myself, working over people and against people, rather than with people. That's what stands in my way of getting promoted."

He contemplated how he would confront that obstacle. "I will empower my team with training, experience, and greater accountability. I will mentor others and delegate appropriately. I will listen to the ideas of others," he wrote.

These were good intentions, he told himself, but did he have the mental discipline to carry them out? He added, "I will also get coaching to help me stay on course with my commitment to be a better leader and team player."

Dan moved on to his next commitment: "To have a healthy, loving relationship with Donna and to be a loving, involved parent in my children's lives." The enormity of that statement startled him for a moment, wondering if he could really accomplish it. He pushed the doubts aside and moved to the next step, obstacles: "My fear of not measuring up and letting my family down." He recalled his conversation with Martha at the pond. "My fear of true intimacy with others." There was only one way to handle these barriers. "I will go to marriage counseling with Donna. I will stop using my work as an escape from my family life." And reflecting on his own childhood, he noted: "I will play ball with my kids at least once a week."

Sarah wrote down a long list of commitments, and then scratched off all but the two most important ones. Her top commitment wasn't about losing weight; she had discarded that one as she was beginning to realize it was a symptom of a bigger problem. Rather, the top goal was "to engage in a self-respecting, supportive, and honest relationship with myself." Her second commitment was "to set healthy boundaries that will enable me to have a more honest and loving relationship with myself and others."

Looking over her commitments, Sarah knew the obstacles were the same for each: "My old limited beliefs that tell me I'm not important and that I'm only valuable when I'm doing for others." What could she do when the Martyr voice spoke up? She touched the note in her pocket. "Make copies of the self-esteem and resentment quotes and post them everywhere!"

Paula wrote down the word Commitments and stared at it for a long time. Now understanding the difference between a true commitment and a half-hearted promise, she felt the gravity of the step she was taking. If she loaded herself up with too many commitments, she ran the risk of failing. Instead she identified the most important one for her life right then: "I am committed to realizing my full potential." She met her first obstacle the minute she wrote down those words. A nagging, negative voice of self-doubt chided her: She would screw this up like she did everything else she tried. Who was she kidding? She couldn't even turn in a simple project on time.

Paula turned immediately to the steps she would take to counteract the internal barriers, which she knew would manifest themselves as external obstacles. "Get positive help and support! Sign up for time-management course! Get coaching!" The fear inside her eased its grip.

Alex wrote his commitments in the neat, square letters of the engineer he was by training, but in the new language of feeling and emotion that he had just learned. "I am committed to being more sensitive and showing that to other people. I am committed to a loving relationship with Ann. I will share my emotions and be more flexible." Pressing on, Alex continued writing. "I am committed to become a true leader, to empower others, to listen to their ideas, and to respect their viewpoints when they are different than mine."

Inspired by what he had written, Alex quickly identified the obstacles: For his feelings, the biggest barriers would be his own brain and the limited belief that his intelligence was the only thing that defined him. At work, the biggest barriers would be his survival strategies of excessive perfectionism and always having to be right and proving others wrong.

Analyzing what he wrote, Alex came up with a plan to tackle these obstacles. To honor his feelings, he would need the support of his wife, who he knew would encourage him to voice his emotions more. Wasn't that what she had been asking him the other day when she wanted to know how he felt about her? He wrote down, "Talk to Ann when I'm stuck in my head." He smiled and added, "Use my inner wisdom instead of just my brain." At work, Alex knew the best remedy would be to establish real team meetings where ideas could be openly shared and discussed. He would call one immediately, right after he met with Frank.

When they finished writing, Martha asked them how they felt about what they had written down. They admitted to feeling eager and excited but also a little scared.

"When something is written, we sometimes say it has been 'committed to paper.' Or when we concentrate on something we 'commit it to memory.' So what you've done here is 'commit to your commitments.' If that feels a little sobering, that's why," Martha explained. "Now remember, you're always committed to something and there are different levels of commitment. I'm sure you've all experienced times in your life when you had a weak commitment to something, like the New Year's resolution you forgot about long before January was over. Then again, there are probably things that you are deeply committed to."

Martha drew a vertical line and marked it off like a number line with zero in the middle and extending down to –7 and up to +7. She labeled –7 as "I quit" and +7 as "It's a done deal. I make it happen."

Levels of Commitment to a Personal Goal

+7 - It's a done deal! I make it happen!

+6 - I align all my thoughts and behaviors behind it
I'm willing to do whatever it takes, nothing will stop me

+5 - I am 100% committed to actively make it happen

+4 - It's my top priority

+3 - I'll try to make it happen

+2 - I wish, want and hope it'll happen

+1 - I'm not sure if it'll happen

0 - I don't care either way

-1 - I don't think it will happen

-2 - There are too many obstacles

-3 - It's not worth the effort

-4 - Other things are more important

-5 - I'm not going to do it

-6 - I actively sabotage it

-7 - I quit!

"At any time, you can be somewhere along this scale," she explained. "If you want to know where you are, all you have to do is look at your results."

"'Got Results?'" Dan offered.

Martha set the marker down on the tray in front of the flip chart. "So, how about having a little fun tonight? It's Friday night. You've all worked hard. Are you ready to let loose for a little while?"

As if on cue, the four of them threw down their pencils. "Sure," Alex called out, as he raised his fist with awkward playfulness.

"Bring it on!"

"Over the past two days you've been exploring the ways in which you have operated in the world based on your limited beliefs and survival strategies. You've explored the ways that you sabotage yourself and get in your own way of becoming an empowered, self-actualized person. Therefore, I'd like you to imagine what kind of character would embody those beliefs and behaviors. Then I want you to find some props and come back here 'in character' as your old way of thinking and behaving. Really lay it on thick. Exaggerate your act. You're on in twenty minutes!"

Dan chuckled. "This should be some show."

The hallways of the lodge echoed with voices as they hurried around, gathering all their props. They returned to the Great Room, laughing as they appraised each other's bundles.

"Okay, everyone," Martha announced. "In character! Let's see your acts. Who's up first?"

"Go, Dan!" Paula yelled, and the others clapped.

Wearing a hooded sweatshirt with a towel around his neck, Dan shadow-boxed, making exaggerated punches and ducking imaginary blows. "Hey, Plant!" he yelled at a green and leafy potted plant. "What are you doing just sitting there and doing nothing? Get to work!" He kept punching and pretended to take a blow to the jaw, shook his head, and came back swinging.

He looked at Paula, Sarah, Alex, and Martha. "So you're my new team. There are a few things we need to get straight right from the start: I'm the boss. We do things MY way, and if you have any ideas, that's fine, but they have to agree with mine, understand?"

He turned to the fireplace, "What are you doing, stuck in that wall? Move it! Get out of my way! I'm the leader around here, and I say what goes!" He pushed with all his might against the stone fireplace, with grunts, groans, and an exaggerated grimace. He finished by sagging to the floor. "I may be down, but I'm not out!" he shouted as he continued to punch the air.

Everyone laughed and applauded.

Sarah jumped to her feet. In the kitchen, she had found an apron and a big box of raisins. "Oh dear, oh me, oh my! Looks like somebody could use a raisin!" She filled up a huge serving spoon with raisins and tried to feed them to Dan. "Come on. Take them, they're good for you!" He grimaced and put up his hands to protect himself as she lunged toward his mouth.

She abruptly left him and scurried over to Paula. "Oh, don't tell me you don't like raisins!" she continued in a singsong voice. "Everybody loves raisins! Here sweetie, have some." She tried to force-feed her, too.

"Ew, raisins. I hate raisins!" Paula played along, curling up into a ball to fend her off. Sarah dumped a huge handful in Paula's lap anyway.

"And YOU!" Sarah rushed over to Alex. "You look like a man who is just dying for a raisin. Here, I'll feed them to you!" She thrust the spoon into his face. Alex couldn't help but laugh out loud as she propelled herself toward him. "Come on, open up! They're yummy." Alex thrust his hand out in the "Halt!" position.

"Well, then, I'll just have to eat them myself!" She sat in her chair and jammed as many as she could into her mouth while making loud crunching and smacking noises. Everyone laughed hysterically at her chipmunk cheeks stuffed with raisins. The ones that couldn't fit in her mouth fell in her lap and to the floor all around her.

Paula was up next. She had gathered a hefty stack of newspapers and magazines, and jogging between their chairs, she struggled with them while pretending to talk into the cell phone squeezed between her head and her shoulder. As she passed Dan she handed a few pieces of paper to him, saying out of the side of her mouth, "Here's that report you wanted," and promptly dropped them on the floor.

"This isn't the report I wanted," Dan called out, picking up the papers.

"Huh?" She took the phone away from her ear. "Oh, well, maybe next time."

"And then what did she say?" Paula returned to her phone, jogging over to Sarah. "Sure. Hey, let's do lunch!"

"I'd love to!" Sarah replied.

Paula looked at her and pretended to be confused. "No, not you." Then she held up the phone in front of her face. "Or maybe not. I don't know. I probably won't show up anyway." She flipped it shut.

Still in motion, she circled Alex, digging through the papers that were precariously balanced between her free arm and her body. "Let's see, somewhere in here I think I have something for you." She peered down at him. "Uh, what's your name again? Here, take the stack." She dumped the pile on Alex, staggered back to her chair and collapsed while everyone hooted and gave her a hand.

Sobering quickly, Alex stood up straight and took his time to calmly stack the magazines neatly on the floor. Then he fit a saucepan over his head like a hat. In one hand, he held a pair of tongs and in the other a spatula. He slid his feet across the floor with a series of jerking motions. "Unit Alex reporting for duty," he said mechanically, staring perfectly blank-faced at Sarah. He snapped the tongs three times. "Unit Alex waiting for directions."

"Go do your work," Sarah sputtered, chuckling. "Get on your computer."

"That does not compute. There is an error in your programming. You have made an error."

Stiffly turning to Dan, he asked: "What is the square root of 4,562,117?"

"Uh, 47," Dan replied.

"Incorrect! There is an error in your programming. You are inferior! You should be replaced."

With short, jerky movements, he turned toward Paula, who was laughing so hard she could barely catch her breath. "Hey, Unit Alex, love your hat. Can I borrow it?"

"That would be impossible," he replied. "The genius cap can only be worn by Unit Alex, not inferior life forms. I must reprogram all of you."

He turned toward Martha, who by this time had tears of glee running down her face. "Unit Alex senses an internal problem." Blinking his eyes rapidly, he jerked his arms and legs uncontrollably. "Must be short circuit! Unit Alex is not perfect! Must be reprogrammed."

He sank in a heap in his chair, the saucepan sliding over his eyes.

Martha cheered and clapped. "Oh, I wish I had a video camera. You were all great. And I've got to say, you really know yourselves." Laughing and wiping her eyes, she looked at each of them as she spoke. "The robot man with a saucepan on his head, the pushy mother hen, the scattered employee, and the boxer fighting a fireplace! It'll be a long time before I forget these images!"

Martha caught her breath. "You know, if we can't laugh at ourselves, how can we possibly learn anything? To grow, we have to be able to see and accept ourselves as we are, and, if you ever doubted that we're all nerds, remember this moment. Now tell me, isn't it more fun to play like this than to walk around pretending that you're slick and cool and that you've got all the answers? I'm not saying that you should go to work on Monday dressed like this. But once in a while, it wouldn't hurt to poke a little fun at yourselves, particularly when you find yourself falling back into your old traps. You'll be surprised at how people respond to you."

It was nearly midnight, the end of what had been an intense, but exciting day. Martha wrapped up the session, with instructions to reconvene at seven the next morning beside the pond. She asked them to arrive in complete silence and just to be aware of the environment around them.

Martha left them, and although it was late, Paula suggested they meet on the patio. As she and Dan went into the kitchen looking for refreshments, Sarah was already outside, breathing in the cool night air. Then she heard music, a piano being played.

Following the sound, she went back inside, through the Great Room and around the corner into what once had been a parlor. Alex was sitting at a baby grand, his head bowed over the keys as he played. Standing in the doorway, she listened to the delicate classical piece. A moment later, Dan and Paula came down the hall carrying plates of fruit and cheese and some bottled water. They stood beside her listening.

From classical, Alex segued into jazz. He looked up, smiling broadly, and kept playing. They tiptoed into the room, setting the food and drink down on a coffee table, clearly showing their admiration, and joined their friend around the piano. Alex paused, his fingers hovering over the keys until they finally began to play a little ragtime. Starting at the highest octaves, he danced down the entire keyboard, finishing with the deep, foggy bass notes. His audience laughed and clapped as he hammed it up. He paused again, and the music became dreamy and soulful. And then he stopped abruptly. "It's been a long time," he said quietly and closed the lid over the keys.

"Don't stop!" Sarah cried.

"What was that last piece you played?" Dan asked.

Alex shrugged. "Just something I was making up."

Paula grinned at him. "You've been holding out on us, Alex. We had no idea."

"Yeah, well, it's something I haven't done in a while," Alex admitted.

"One more song?" Paula asked.

"I dunno. I'm kind of rusty."

"Please?" Paula teased.

Outside, a crescent moon cast a faint light in the darkness and billions of stars filled the sky. Night animals, the possums and raccoons, went busily on their way, and a fox trotted silently across a field. The birds tucked their heads under their wings as they roosted in the bushes and trees. Only one room was lighted in the lodge, and from it flowed the most beautiful sounds. The music and the merriment went on and on…

❖ Chapter Eleven

Breaking Through the Barriers

Fog lifted from the meadow as they gathered by the pond early Saturday morning. They wore sweaters and light jackets to fend off the lingering coolness, but the warmth of the sun promised another beautiful day. They stood in companionable silence at the edge of the pond, each absorbed in their own experience of the beauty around them. Blankets and floor pillows had been spread on the dewy grass, facing the sun that was rising over the tops of the trees. The silence instilled a sense of reverent connection with the simple yet magnificent natural environment. It would have been almost sacrilegious to talk. Gratitude filled their hearts. They had come a long way in just a couple of days.

When the time was right, Martha spoke. "Each new day brings a fresh promise of possibility and the choice to become whoever you choose to be and to do whatever you choose to do. Yesterday is just a memory. Tomorrow is but a dream. All we have is today and the present moment. Each day you are presented with the same opportunity to interpret and respond to life in any way you choose. It's a time to begin again."

They settled onto the blankets and cushions, and Martha suggested they sit with their backs straight, but not stiff, then led them through a series of breathing exercises: breathing in deeply, holding their breath for several seconds, and exhaling completely in a smooth and continuous cycle.

"As you breathe, become aware of the sounds around you: the call of a bird, the wind in the trees, a little animal rustling in the grass, the water as it laps on the shore... Notice how easily we block out these gentle sounds." She paused. "Also notice what noise we normally let into our filters instead."

Taking in a deep breath, Martha asked them to take in the smells of nature: the sweet grass, the dampness of the wood, and the fresh clean air of fading summer.

"Our breathing is a stimulus-response reaction, a reflex that we respond to without thinking—awake or asleep, conscious or unconscious. But if you think about it, breathing is more than that. Literally and metaphorically, it is receiving and giving back, a cycle that reflects the balance of nature. The air that you are breathing in right now contains oxygen that is produced by plants and trees. The air that you are breathing out contains carbon dioxide, which the plants need in order to survive. Breathing in.... breathing out... receiving ... giving back... It's all the same cycle, of which you are a part each time you breathe, each day of your life."

With each breath, she told them, they partake of the abundance of oxygen on this planet, given freely without conditions. Whenever they exhale, they give back generously, without question. "You don't choose which plant you'll give to; you give to all without judgment. You don't say to the plants, 'I'll give you carbon dioxide if you give me oxygen. Rather, you unconditionally pour out into the same flow of life that sustains you. Indeed, everyone gets a prize."

A sudden gust of warm wind buffeted their faces, tossing their hair and ruffling their clothes.

"With every breath, you are part of an essential cycle of unspoken trust—a process of giving and receiving—that is fundamental to life itself. If we were to expand this activity into a concept, it would be I Win/You Win. I Win/You Win does not apply just to business or your interactions with other people; it is fundamental to the balance of nature and life itself.

"When you breathe in, do so with gratitude, thanksgiving, and joy. Say 'thank you,' whether to God, the Universe, Nature, or whatever concept is comfortable to you, for the gift of life in you and through you. And when you breathe out, do so with generosity, with unconditional love. Give... Give.... Give.... For to give is to live. Then breathe in again with thanksgiving and gratitude and replenish yourselves."

They were all with her, breathing her words in and out with that sweet late summer air.

Human beings with their egos and fear-driven need to win at any expense have the power to destroy the trees and plants, even though these are the very things that sustain life, she went on. The driving fear is that there is not enough for everyone. Afraid to lose, people play I Win/You Lose or I win the prize and you don't. "I've got to get mine," they tell themselves, "because if I don't, there might not be enough for me. In that case I'll lose, and then I'll die." Then the fight begins, or else they give up and play I Lose/You Win, seeing everything as hopeless. They quit and purposefully lose to avoid admitting what they have really lost.

Her voice brightened slowly as she continued, "To have everything work in the game of life, we must play I Win/You Win. One person gives to another, but does not deplete herself, because she knows that she must also receive. That person gives back, but does not deplete himself, because he also must receive. It is a cycle as natural as breathing."

But how often, she asked them, do they, like everyone, give until they're spent, never taking time off to relax, replenish, and renew themselves? Each of us think we lead such complicated lives, she observed, but all the busyness does is feed the ego, giving it a little game to play that distracts us. The ego creates dramas to feel important and to have something to do. Too much doing is like constantly breathing out without bothering to breathe in. If that happens, a person soon becomes depleted, completely spent, and, in the extreme, will die.

"Right now, you are doing nothing but breathing and being completely in the present. This is a quiet space that we must consciously create in our lives every day. This morning, in this space of pure possibility, as you breathe in with gratitude and breathe out with unconditional generosity, ask yourself: 'Who will I be today?' The gift of choice is yours. Will I be petty and small or courageous and committed? Will I choose to resist or to accept? Will I play I Win/You Lose, I Lose/You Win, or I Win/You Win? Will I choose to make someone else wrong, or will I see another point of view? Will I be truthful and honest, or will I make up excuses? Will I be a victim, or will I be accountable for my results? Will I choose to just survive, or will I thrive?"

Everyday, she told them, they have the choice to operate with integrity or with self-righteousness. They can give their word and keep it or shade the truth to fit their filters. Each day brings a choice, and each day they must be clear because there is one thing they can always count on: Life will test them.

Martha led them through one last breathing exercise and invited them to open their eyes. After a brief pause, she greeted them. "Good morning!" Smiling, she took her time to look at each one, noticing the calm expression on all of their faces.

"As you have become aware over the past few days, all the lessons we need are here, waiting for us." Martha extended her arms outward. "It's up to each of us to decide whether or not we are open to receive what's being offered and to realize that the world continually provides all manner of unexpected assistance for us to be the best we can be.

"When we grasp this concept, we are so filled with thanksgiving that we are moved to give back. When you unconditionally give to others and to the world, curiously enough you are really giving to yourself, because what you receive in return is deeper connection, abundance, joy, fulfillment, inner peace, and love. So given this awareness, how will you give back?"

"Contribute to others," Sarah said, "without depleting myself."

Dan straightened his back, feeling a pleasant loosening in his spine. "By being a leader who can serve my team, the people who work for me, and the people I work for, and by being a positive example."

"Yes, serving others is important, isn't it? We can choose to support and serve people with whom we are in relationship, just as we need to be supported and served by them," Martha continued. "We can choose to support our children, not by giving into them but by serving their best interests as well as our own. If we don't choose to serve our communities and instead hide on the sidelines or avoid confronting the injustice around us, we're accountable for the problems that persist. Live as you breathe: take in abundance and give back with generosity."

Martha lifted her chin, faced the sun and sighed deeply. "And what about in business? What happens when people don't give with generosity, when they become ensnared by fears of scarcity and the limited belief that there's 'not enough so I better get mine!' We know that's what awaits you beyond this little pond. What happens then?"

"Teams break down. There's no cooperation," Dan offered.

"Yes, indeed. This occurs a lot in businesses. Sometimes people withhold information or refuse to support others out of the fear that they will lose some of their power. Let's look at a situation in which you are competing for a promotion with someone who is undermining you. Many people would fight back in return, attempting to discredit their opponent. What if you decide not to act that way? Instead, you acknowledge the positive aspects of this other person and then go on to speak clearly and confidently of what you have to offer. Which person will come across as the one with integrity? Which one will people trust?"

"We should abolish smear campaigns—in politics, at the office, everywhere!" Paula said passionately.

"They would automatically disappear if enough people acted with generosity and gratitude," Martha continued. "That's the essence of operating with integrity, a journey that you've been learning to walk these past few days. If you choose the high road of honesty, you will be challenged and rewarded. You will be led to fulfillment, joy, satisfaction, and a life of significance and meaning. You will enjoy success and achieve your goals. We all know what it feels like to take the low road: doing anything to get ahead, making sure 'I get mine,' gossiping, lying, stealing, cheating, self-righteousness, making others wrong... These are all 'taking' behaviors. They drain energy and deplete others. Likewise, to refuse to let someone give to you is also a 'taking' behavior. By doing so, you deny another the benefit and joy of being generous, and you stop the flow of giving on the planet.

"Human beings are a work in process and, despite our best intentions, sometimes we trip and fall. The next time you face a dilemma listen to the Sage with whom you have reconnected this weekend. Your natural wisdom will direct you to what works. When your results or experiences are not what you want, when you get turned around, or when you feel insecure or scared, the eight principles will lead you back."

Martha turned to a clean page on the flip chart, held in place by two rocks: "Now, it's time for the last principle." She picked up her black marker:

Principle #8
Breathe.

"When you breathe, you are modeling the beliefs and behaviors of giving and receiving in a continual flow that sustains life itself. When you give and serve others with gratitude and generosity, and when you give and receive unconditional love, you are contributing, not taking from the world around you," she explained. "Please note that when I use the word 'love,' I don't limit it to intimate or romantic love. After all, there are some people we just don't like, but we can still operate with love when we interact with them. You may have heard of agape love, which is an altruistic love based in an unselfish concern for the welfare of others. This concept serves us well in this discussion. Agape love is demonstrated through compassion, kindness, respect, forgiveness, honesty, humility, and service to others. When we operate this way, we are loving, even if the feeling isn't there."

To illustrate, she shared a quote from Albert Schweitzer: "I don't know what your destiny will be, but one thing I do know: The only ones among you who will be truly happy are those who have sought and found how to serve."

"That sounds so simple," Alex said, "and very wise."

"Most great truths are. It's only our egos that want to complicate things," Martha said. "While you have been here, you have been giving and receiving, and it has not just been about the lessons of the eight principles. Just by being yourselves, with all your strengths and weaknesses, you have been unknowingly giving to and receiving from each other. The very things about someone else that have annoyed you have actually been gifts to you. They contain the lessons you most likely need to learn. I wonder if you were aware of these gifts that have been in front of you for these past three days or if you filtered them out?"

Heads turned and eyes met. From the way they looked at each other, Martha knew they saw each other differently, moving from conflict to camaraderie.

Just then a staff member from the lodge approached the group. He handed Martha a note. Opening it, she read it silently to herself and then out loud to the group. "Sarah, your husband called. Kyle fell out of his bunk bed and broke his arm. Everything's fine. Been to doctor and now home. No need to come back early. Kyle is in backyard getting his cast signed. No problems."

"Oh, my Lord! I have to go!" Sarah cried out as she struggled to her feet. "But Sarah, the note says that he is fine," Martha said. "It sounds like your son is doing okay, your husband has handled everything, and he wants you to stay and finish the course."

"But you don't understand. My son is hurt. I have to be there with him." She started gathering up her things.

"Sarah, let's slow down for a minute. You're being a stimulus-response machine right now. Let's think this through. If you need to call, then I will support you to do so. But we need to talk before you leave so abruptly. You have an agreement with the group to be here."

"Martha, are you kidding? This is not the time for that! My commitment to my son is bigger than my agreements here. I'm sorry everyone. It's been a good experience, but I need to go."

"Okay, Sarah. Obviously, I will not keep you from going, but I am asking you to stop for a couple of minutes before you decide to leave. We have all shared so much. Will you at least be willing to do that?"

"Martha, you're not going to talk me out of this."

"I'm not going to try to talk you out of leaving, Sarah. Leaving is your choice, not mine. However, I would like for you to reflect on what you're doing. Perhaps you could consider again that your husband has everything handled and that Kyle is doing fine. What did he say? Kyle is having his cast signed in the backyard. That sounds like things are okay, doesn't it? If you stay, you will be home in about four or five hours anyway. There is nothing you can do, nothing you can change by going home before the end of the course. You can call him right now to reassure yourself. That would be a responsible, loving thing to do. However, be aware that right now, you are at the crossroads I talked about. What choice will you make?"

Paula interrupted, "Martha, I think we should just leave her alone. I vote that she goes if she wants to."

"I don't," Dan said. He turned toward Sarah. "Last night we wrote down our commitments. Could you read yours to me?"

"I don't believe this," said Sarah, but she yanked open her notebook. A few papers dropped out, and Dan picked them up and gave them to her. One of them was her commitments. She read quickly: "To engage in a self-respecting, supportive, and honest relationship with myself; to establish healthy boundaries that will enable me to have a more honest and loving relationship with myself and others." She closed her notebook, pursed her lips, and stared at him.

"It sounds to me like you're letting some old beliefs and behaviors sneak back in," Dan observed. "This course is about you; it's for you. Sounds to me like you're back in your survival strategy of trying to take care of everyone else, and you're not following your commitment to keep boundaries for yourself."

"I'm his mother, Dan!"

"I know, but he also has a father, and it sounds like he's got everything covered. He told you not to come home."

Martha looked at Sarah. "If everything is under control and your son is fine, then you going home will send what kind of message to your husband? Who gets to be the strong one, who is the weak one?"

"Sarah," Alex joined in. "I want you to stay, too. Do you think if you called and talked to Kyle that you would feel better?"

"Yes!"

"Okay, Sarah," Martha said. "Why don't we all return to the lodge as a team and support Sarah in making her phone call."

They gathered their things and walked to the patio. Sarah went inside to call. The others sat silently around a table to wait for her. Above them two birds chased each other. By the meadow the leaves rustled in a little gust of wind, and a few fell to the ground as nature continued its own course, in spite of the drama that was unfolding.

Martha looked at Alex, Paula, and Dan. "I don't know if you realize it or not, but the entire course is happening here right now."

Sarah came out the door.

"What happened?" Paula quickly asked. "Did you talk to him?"

"Yes, he's fine. I guess it was a hairline fracture."

Alex spoke up. "Did your husband want you to stay and complete the course?"

"Yes. But I'm going."

"Sarah," Martha spoke up. "I'd like you to consider that the very reason you are leaving is the reason you need to stay here."

"Thank you, but I really do know what I'm doing." She rushed off, returning shortly with her suitcase.

"We're going to miss you, Sarah." Paula got up and gave her a hug. "We only have a few more hours to go. I know what I said before, but I really think you should stay. Will you please reconsider?"

"No. I know you're all trying to help and I thank you for everything we've shared. Thank you, too, Martha. I am sorry that it has to end like this, but I have to go home." With that, she walked down the stone path to her car. No one said a word. As she drove away, dust rose from the driveway and drifted into the meadow.

They all looked at each other. "Damn!" Dan said. "I've gotta tell you, I'm really pissed off. She's right back into her old ways. She almost had it and then she quit."

"Well, I feel sad," said Paula. "She's a nice lady, and she was doing so well. I'm going to miss her."

Leaning forward with his arms on his legs, Alex looked down at the ground and said, "I'm hoping she might turn around and come back, but I'm afraid she won't."

Martha responded, "Clearly a big part of our group is missing. Sarah doesn't realize what a valuable contribution she has been to all of us and what a big empty space she has left behind her. However, this is the time to apply what we have learned. Remember Principle #6 – 'So What's for Lunch?' It reminds us that 'it is what it is.' Accept and trust the process. There are some things we can change through our commitment and clear intention and others we must accept. Perhaps this is when we must become like water."

She explained that there is a tension between acceptance and the commitment to change that Martha called "The Dance of Life." Whether they realize it or not, people are always engaged in this dance, moving in one direction or another. Flowing with the currents around them, their movements are fluid, effortless. When they resist, the dance becomes rigid and lifeless. "This reminds me of my mother's favorite prayer. 'Lord, grant me the serenity to accept the things I cannot change, the courage to change the things I can, and the wisdom to know the difference.' Throughout your Dance of Life, you must be fully committed to the end result while at the same time letting go of the outcome. Know that what you want will happen but not necessarily the way you think it should. It may take longer than you think, or you may need to approach it differently."

Martha continued: "In this situation, I'm not sure if Sarah will return, but I trust that the ultimate outcome will be in balance with the Universal Truth that supercedes everything. Life is not what I think it is supposed to be. It is how it is. Our job is to interpret the outcome in a way that supports us to be effective and joyful human beings within that process. You cannot always change the circum-

226 ◆ *Your Survival Strategies are Killing You!*

stances, but the power to interpret those circumstances is entirely in your hands."

Alex looked up at her, closing one eye as he squinted a little from the sun. "So is that what you did with your arthritis?"

"Yes, it is. For as long as I saw this circumstance as my enemy, I remained a prisoner in my own jail, but I had the key—literally—right here in my hands." She held her gnarled hands out in front of her and pausing, looked at them. "Accept, accept, accept. It is how it is. No resistance. Interpret this disease differently and you will be free."

They sat quietly. So much had changed in just a few minutes. No one moved or spoke. They could hear the faint sound of dishes and silverware being set out as the staff prepared the buffet table inside.

Martha continued, "Here's what I have learned after many years of working with people. We all travel at our own rate of speed, and we move when we're ready and not one moment sooner. One way of interpreting Sarah's leaving is that she failed herself and her team. I prefer to think that maybe Sarah got all that she was ready to hear. I choose to trust the process and believe that Sarah will do exactly what she needs to do for her growth at this time. After all, remember Principle #3 'How's the View from Your View?' Who am I to say what is right for Sarah? I choose to release her with love and acceptance."

She asked them to examine their reactions to Sarah leaving. Dan got angry because he couldn't control. Alex became anxious and fearful because Sarah wasn't doing the right thing. In the beginning Paula was all for Sarah breaking her agreement by leaving, which was reminiscent of Paula's past pattern of being loose with agreements. "You have each taken issue with Sarah for returning to an old survival strategy, yet isn't the same true for all of you?" Martha asked them.

Silent, they looked at each other.

"Just like Sarah," Martha continued, "you're not bad or wrong, you just went off course. You resorted to your old, familiar, fear-based reactive behaviors. When this happens again—and it will—reconnect with agape love. This love, which is based in trust, can be felt for every living thing, including ourselves, although we lose touch with it from time to time. It means, 'I care about you and myself no matter what you know or don't know, say or don't say, and will continue to love always. I may not condone your behavior. I may even need to step in and stop an action that is illegal, immoral, or hurts another. However, I don't need to be angry at you or judge you because that only hurts me. Ultimately, it is a place of complete trust in the Universal Process and Universal Truth.'"

Martha looked at each of them and said, "Perhaps you should pay attention to your own emotional reactions around Sarah leaving. Your vibrational energy just may influence Sarah. Then trust the process. Keep your intention clear that you will all reconnect with Sarah in a meaningful way and don't get invested in how that looks. She might return; she might not. It will be how it will be. If we care about Sarah, then we need to let her go. Now I think it's time to ask 'what's for lunch?' I believe they have prepared something special for us today. I'll be joining you."

The weather couldn't have been more beautiful. They all sat on the patio chatting back and forth. No one spoke of Sarah, but when a vehicle came up the drive, they all stopped talking and strained to see who it was. When they saw it was a delivery truck, there was a drop in energy and a lull in the conversation. After lunch they had a little free time to relax. Alex and Paula walked out by the pond. Dan chose to lie in the chaise lounge.

Martha decided to reconvene on the patio for the remainder of the day. They had all just settled in their seats and were in the middle of sharing what they had learned when they heard a car coming up the drive.

"It's Sarah!" Paula exclaimed as she jumped up. She urgently motioned for Alex and Dan to get up, and together they left the patio and headed toward Sarah's car. Martha watched them go.

Sarah got out of the car, and Paula hugged her with a squeal of joy. Dan put his arm around her shoulder and squeezed her. Alex smiled and said, "I'm glad you're back, Sarah."

When they came up to the patio, their energy was high. Martha looked at her and said, "Welcome back, Sarah."

Everyone sat down except Sarah. "Okay, Principle #4 'Got Results?' I know I need to take full ownership and accountability for my choices while not blaming myself either. Still I do need to apologize for breaking my agreement, actually, agreements. I wasn't present, and I am late."

"Thank you, Sarah. I accept your apology," Martha responded. "Would you like to share your experience?"

"Well, I was about halfway home and, as much as I tried, I couldn't get Principle #7—'Stick. Don't Quit.'—out of my head. I realized that I was breaking my word, that my son was fine, and that I had allowed myself to get caught up in my old ways. I'm sorry to have caused this problem, but I do think it was a tremendous learning experience for me. I probably learned more in the last two hours than I have in most of my life."

Smiling, Martha invited Sarah to sit and asked, "So what was the one thing that brought you back, Sarah?"

"My commitment to operate with integrity by keeping my word. That triggered each one of the eight principles. For example, the first two principles: 'Tell the Truth. Period.' and 'Do What You Said You Would Do.' I needed to get honest with myself and acknowledge that Kyle was really okay and that I needed to keep my agreement with all of you. Then I started thinking about the third principle, 'How's the View from Your View?' I needed to reinterpret my belief that being a mother meant that I was the only one who could take good care of our children. Then there was number four, 'Got results?' I saw that I was totally accountable as to how I was going to respond to this situation, and I had a choice in my results. Being a martyr was not the only choice.

"Principle #5 'Everybody Gets a Prize' reminded me that I didn't have to lose the wonderful experience of completing this course with all of you. Then the sixth one, 'So What's for Lunch?' As soon as I accepted the situation exactly as it was, I could see the whole thing as an opportunity to grow and learn. Number seven, 'Stick. Don't Quit,' is, I guess, pretty self-explanatory," she said with a giggle. "And the eighth principle, 'Breathe.' I finally saw how my leaving was taking away from everybody including myself."

With a quirky little self-confident swagger and a huge smile, she summed it up. "So, I decided to come back!"

Martha nodded knowingly. "I acknowledge you for reclaiming your power and getting back on course by staying true to yourself. It reminds me of one more story I'd like to share with you.

"When my ex-husband asked for a divorce, we were living in Japan with our then three-year-old daughter. To make a long story short, I was devastated but could not change the outcome. His mind was made up. We finalized everything through Japanese court, and our daughter and I returned to our home in California. It was a week before Christmas. He flew back with us, and then the day after Christmas he left for Japan."

Martha recalled that day as the lowest in her life. Her arthritis was severe at that time. It took her a few minutes just to get out of a chair and walk across the room. Living on top of the Santa Cruz Mountains, she was twenty minutes from the nearest store. She had no job, very little money, no help, and a three-year-old running around the house. Seeing no way to handle this, she was deeply depressed and began plotting her suicide. At the time, she told them, she saw it as the only way out.

"At that moment, my daughter, Gabi, came running into the room with great exuberance and jumped into my lap. She wrapped her arms around me and spontaneously said, 'I love you, Mommy!' Something inside me snapped. I woke up to realize the implications of what I was planning. I remembered the first time she was placed in my arms at two days old as my adopted child, that I had made a silent vow to be the best mother I could possibly be to this precious new life. Recalling this commitment was a turning point for me, and at that moment, I realized that ending my life was simply not an option.

"I had given my word to this child, and I was going to keep it regardless of any circumstance or situation that interfered. With unrelenting conviction, I renewed that commitment and began a process of getting my mind, body, and life in alignment with my decision to live with joy, freedom, integrity, and love."

Martha paused for a moment. "So do you see why I'm so adamant about keeping agreements, Sarah? Doing so literally saved my life, and I dare say will figuratively save yours as well."

Moving seamlessly into the next topic of discussion, Martha drew a picture of an iceberg with only a small portion above the water and a far larger mass below.

COMMITMENT ICEBERG

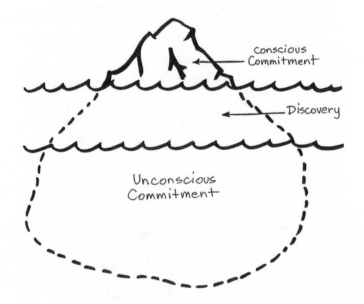

"It appears that the conscious commitments you made to yourself and to us," she pointed to the tip of the iceberg" were undermined by your unconscious commitment to be right about your old beliefs and survival strategies. Like the submerged part of the iceberg, that unconscious commitment dwarfed your conscious commitments. Fortunately, however, you stopped yourself and reconnected with the awareness you have gained in this course."

Martha drew a dotted line under the water. The space between this line and the water's surface is discovery. "When you bring to the surface the things you are unaware of, you become a more conscious person. The more of the iceberg mass you can expose, the more conscious awareness you have available to make constructive choices. It's what 'you don't know you don't know' that undermines your success."

Facing Dan she said, "Last night you wrote down that you have a commitment to being promoted. Has that been a conscious commitment for awhile?"

"Of course," he replied.

"Your results, however, indicate otherwise because underneath the water is your unconscious commitment to be right and make everyone else wrong. Up until this course, your unconscious commitment was about getting ahead at the expense of others. Would you agree, Dan?"

"Yeah, unfortunately." Dan blew out his cheeks. "I never thought about it this way before, but it's just like investing. We may believe we have put together the best portfolios and a winning approach to the market, but the reality is always in the results."

"Yes," Martha continued. "And just as those investment results speak volumes about the soundness of the portfolio, your own results will clearly indicate what you're committed to. For instance, Sarah's current results indicate that she is committed to maintaining her boundaries for herself on behalf of her own well-being, keeping her word with others, and trusting her husband. She had to tangle with a few things to get there, but she did it.

"Always build an honest relationship with your results. Results don't lie. They will tell you exactly what you're committed to. In your case, Dan, it seems that you have been more committed to being right than getting a promotion. It's that simple. Like I said two days ago, in life you'll always have one of two things." She wrote the words:

REASONS or RESULTS

"You will have the results you have been looking for or the reasons why not. Which one do you want?" Martha looked at each of them.

Alex spoke up. "I thought I was committed to our team working together and that Frank was the one in the way. Now I see that I was more committed to being right and making him wrong than having an aligned team that really works."

Paula looked over to him and nodded. "I have constantly undermined myself by making too many so-called 'commitments,' when they were all just empty promises. Even when I think I'm committed to doing great work—and I do—there is still a part of me that sabotages myself. I miss deadlines, some things are only ninety percent complete...I do it all the time, but I've never held myself accountable before. I've always had some reason or excuse."

"These are important things to be aware of," Martha continued. "Thanks to Sarah leaving and returning, we've had a chance to address them. What at first appeared to be a negative event has turned into a positive one. In fact, it's possible we have learned more than if she had never left. Trust the process, my friends. Our job is to stay on course and trust that our highest standards will be supported. They always will be, but not always as you expect.

"Albert Einstein once said that 'The most important question you could ever answer was: is this a friendly or an unfriendly world?' In the unfriendly world, you must fight to survive. The friendly world, however, gives you endless support to thrive."

She paused, meeting their eyes. "The choice is yours: which one will give you the results you want and the experience you are looking for? Neither one is right or wrong. They are just different ways of living, and each will produce its own experience. Now it's up to you to decide which one works for you. Which one is most closely aligned with your internal Sage, the source of your wisdom and natural knowing?"

"Well, I want to THRIVE!" declared Paula.

Martha smiled. "That is my choice, too, Paula. And I don't know about you, but for me, this choice frequently seems daunting. For those of you who choose this way, let me assure you, you will be challenged. As you leave here today and go back to your day-to-day lives of work, family, and friends, you will face life head-on. You will have setbacks and you will succumb to the temptation to revert to the old ways of operating. We've already had a good lesson in this today. The same will happen to the rest of you, too. I know because you sure look very human to me."

Martha reminded them that there will be times when each of them will get scared, uncertain, or turned around. They will want to whine, complain, and blame, and they will let their fears determine their actions. At times, she told them, we all face the temptation to gossip, judge, and win at any cost. But no matter what happens, she assured them, and thanks to Sarah's fine example, they now knew that they always have a choice about how to view and experience everything.

"With the eight principles, you now possess the tools to have your work and life be joyful, fulfilling, and successful experiences. I promise you that these principles will never fail you."

Martha put the cap back on the marker and set it down. She regarded each of them, their eyes meeting for a moment. "My friends, that's what is possible for you—a life of potential, possibility, freedom, choice, and unconditional love. You now have the eight principles as a guide for the rest of your life. Please remember that they are completely worthless without the Principle #1. It's critical to be truthful and honest in all of your actions, interactions, and communications with yourself and others. It is fundamental to all the rest.

"As a final thought I share with you one more thing. It has been my experience that when all is said and done, underneath all the fear, anger, hurt, and judgment, when one is completely truthful, there is one universal communication between all people. It is 'I love you and I want you to love me.'" She paused, taking a moment for a silent, heartfelt connection with each of them. Then she spoke: "After that there is nothing more to say..."

No one spoke or moved. No one reached for a cell phone or rushed off to pack. After a moment, they turned to each other. They spoke of their gratitude for each other, for Martha, and for the lessons they had learned. As they lingered in each other's company, a few tears were shed.

After phone numbers and emails were exchanged, they said their reluctant good-byes. Martha hugged each one, acknowledging the journey of the past three days and expressing what an honor it was to be their guide.

"As you leave, you'll be given a packet to help you remember what you've learned here. Inside, you'll find a sealed envelope with the same message to each of you. Please open the envelope at any time after you leave here."

Carrying their belongings, they walked out to the parking lot, exchanging one more embrace while saying goodbye. Then one by one, they pulled away from the lodge, the BMW, the Lexus SUV, the old Toyota Corolla, and the VW convertible, and began the journey home.

A few minutes later, one of the cars pulled off the road, into the parking lot of a diner that was closed. The driver put the car in park and reached for the sealed envelope. Inside was a cream-colored piece of paper, on which was written:

HOPI ELDERS SPEAK

You have been telling the people that this is the Eleventh Hour.
Now you must go back and tell the people that this is The Hour
There are things to be considered.

Where are you living?
What are you doing?
What are your relationships?
Where is your water?
Know your garden.
It is time to speak your Truth.
Create your community.
Be good to each other.
And do not look outside yourself for the leader.

This could be a good time!

There is a river flowing now very fast.
It is so great and swift that there are those who will be afraid.
They will try to hold onto the shore.
They will feel they are being torn apart, and they will suffer greatly.

Know the river has its destination.
The elders say we must let go of the shore, push off into the middle of
the river, keep our eyes open, and our heads above the water.

See who is in there with you and celebrate.

At this time in history, we are to take nothing personally.
Least of all, ourselves.
For the moment we do, our spiritual growth and journey comes to a halt.

The time of the lone wolf is over.
Gather yourselves!

Banish the word struggle from your attitude and vocabulary.

All that we do now must be done in a sacred manner and in
celebration.

We are the ones we've been waiting for.

(The Elders/Hopi Nation/Oraibi/Arizona/Date unknown.)

❖ Epilogue

Going Home

Windows down, Dan drove along the two-lane highway away from the lodge toward the interstate that would take him home. He took in the tranquility of rolling landscape, still the deep green of summer that was so markedly different from the constant activity of his days. He knew now that he used work to avoid his home life and used the pressure of his home life as an excuse to keep him at work. That was changing—had already changed—in his mind. It was time now to put it into action.

Dialing his home number, he spoke briefly to his son, Brian, who asked excitedly when he was coming home. Dan asked him to get out the baseball and gloves because, as soon as he was there, they were all going to the park. He laughed as Brian whooped excitedly into the phone and yelled for his sister.

"Put Mom on the line, okay? See you in a little bit."

Donna picked up the line a moment later. "What was that about?" she asked.

"I told Brian that I'm taking him and Brigitte to the park as soon as I get home."

"I'm sure they'll love that," Donna said softly.

A lump the size of a boulder lodged in Dan's throat. "I've been thinking a lot since our phone call the other day. I meant everything I said, Donna. I want things to be different. No, I am different, and I am committed to working with you to make our relationship different, right now."

He heard the catch in Donna's voice as she spoke. "I want it too, Dan, but I'm not... Listen, I can't talk now. The kids are here. I'll see you when you get home. Okay?"

"One more thing?" he asked. "Will you get a sitter for tonight?"

The restaurant was dimly lit and candles burned on every table. Dan looked at the woman across the table from him as if he were seeing her for the first time. "You look beautiful," he said.

Donna smiled nervously and looked away. "I..." She stopped herself. "Thank you. This is all very sudden. I mean, the kids had a great time playing ball at the park with you today. It's all Brigitte talked about, and now Brian wants to go back tomorrow. And we're here together but..."

"You're afraid," Dan said quietly.

Donna nodded. "Yes. I'm afraid that we'll wake up in a day or two, and whatever change you went through will have worn off, and we'll be back to the way we were."

Dan reached for her hand. Closing her eyes, Donna hesitantly extended her hand halfway across the table. Dan reached the rest of the way to take it firmly in his. "Will you marry me, Donna?"

Donna couldn't believe what she was hearing. Frowning slightly, she reminded him they had done that eleven years ago.

"I know, but that was in the past. A lot of things happened in the past, some of which I wish I could change, but I can't. What I can do is be accountable, learn from my mistakes, and move on from here."

He squeezed her hand and reached for the other one. "I want you for my wife, Donna. I want to be beside you for the rest of our lives. So, will you marry me?"

Donna looked at him, leveling her eyes, never straying from his. "Yes," she said. "I will."

Sarah drove straight through without calling home first. The kids were in the yard when she drove up, and her husband was puttering in the garage.

"Mom's home!" the kids yelled in unison, rushing over to the car before she got the door open.

Sarah opened her arms and Stevie rushed in first. Then she turned to Kyle. "Oh, my sweet boy. I'm so sorry you got hurt."

"It's okay, Mom. Look, I've already got eight autographs!" He showed her his cast.

She held his face and looked at him carefully. "Well, I have to say, you don't look bad."

Sarah reached for her daughter, Beth, and drew her in. Looking up she saw Stephen leaning against the open frame of the garage door with a big grin on his face. The kids were running and jumping around her, each wanting to talk. She told them she'd listen in a minute and made her way over to her husband and kissed him.

He gave her a hug and nodded toward the kids. "See, I did okay. One of them got banged up a little but none of them died!" he joked.

"Sweetheart, you did great," Sarah responded with a laugh.

"So, how was the course?"

"It was unbelievable. I have so much to tell you, but I have no idea where to start."

Stephen slipped his arm around her waist. "I can already tell that it was good for you. You look great, honey."

After the kids told their stories of the last few days, with Kyle's being the most dramatic, they ran around the backyard, chasing the dog and each other. She and Stephen sat on the deck watching them. Sarah closed her eyes a moment and recalled the goodbyes at the lodge and hoped that the others were having good homecomings as well. Turning to Stephen, she grinned mischievously. "So," she said, putting her feet up on the rail of the deck. "What's for dinner tonight?"

Later that evening when the kids were asleep, Sarah pulled on a warm sweater and handed Stephen his jacket. "Where are we going?" he asked, puzzled.

"Out to see the stars," she said, remembering how she had stood out on the patio at the lodge the night before.

Wistfully, she recalled the memory of Alex's music, went back in the house for the portable CD player, and looked through Steven's CDs. Returning to the deck, she popped in a disc and closed her eyes as the music filled the evening air.

"Since when did you like Oscar Peterson, Miss Country-and-Western?" Steven teased as he came out the sliding doors and joined her on the deck.

"Let's just say that last night we were treated to an impromptu concert."

"Hmm, sounds like that's a course I would enjoy," he joked. "You haven't said much about what happened."

"It was so much," Sarah began. "I think I'll be processing it for a long time. I have to keep strict confidentiality about what the others said and did, but I can tell you that I learned about myself, how I think and act. I understand that I'm a 'Supporter.' I give to other people, but I don't let myself receive from others, and then I turn into this big bundle of resentment." Her voice rose as she spoke, the words tumbling out faster. "I don't set boundaries for myself and respect them. Also I don't respect other people's boundaries, like when they don't want me to do things for them. When they say 'no,' I let my feelings get hurt, and then I get resentful over that! And I also learned to see myself, maybe for the first time, as being worthy of the same kind of care that I give to others!"

Sarah collected herself. "And I realized how much I love you and our family, and I want to change how I'm acting around here. I want the kids to learn to be more independent, and I want to get to know you again. I want to change how I act at work. I let everybody walk all over me, and I just seethe inside when they do. That's not helping me or anybody else." She turned toward him. "I feel like we've gotten lost as a couple lately..."

When she stopped speaking, Stephen didn't say anything for a while. "I'd like that," he said. "You were so busy taking care of everybody, you never had time for yourself or for us."

"Well," she giggled, reaching for his hand, "there's no time like the present."

Alex drove slowly past a florist just a few blocks from home, and then, on impulse, swung his car into a vacant parking space and walked into the shop. The fragrance of flowers took him back to the garden where he had sat with Martha, feeling his heart really open up for the first time. He stood for a few seconds, drinking in the memory.

"May I help you?" a woman behind the counter asked helpfully.

"I'd like to buy flowers for my wife," Alex began.

"You've come to the right place!" The woman smiled. "What does she like?"

Alex didn't have a clue. "I don't know what her favorite flower is," he admitted sheepishly. "I suppose roses, right? Or maybe something like that?" He pointed to a tall vase of carnations.

"How about a mixed bouquet? Very colorful and fragrant," the woman suggested.

Alex watched her put together a bouquet of red carnations, white roses, blue irises, bright orange day lilies, and a few pale pink miniature orchids with red markings. She put them in a glass vase with sprays of green and baby's breath.

"Do you need a card? Birthday? Anniversary?" The woman indicated a display.

Alex picked out a plain one on which he wrote: "I love you. Your husband, Alex." He thought for a moment and added: "P.S. I missed you."

The flowers were on the table in the dining room where Ann set out the plates and silverware. Alex brought in the platter of chicken they had barbecued on the tiny grill on their patio, laughing at the mess they were making as the sauce nearly caught fire. "I don't know how this will taste, but at least it's cooked," he said smiling.

"There's always takeout," Ann said.

As they ate, savoring the crispy chicken that was surprisingly good, Alex asked Ann what her plans were for the next weekend. "My plans? Nothing. I'm leaving next Tuesday for Detroit. I'll be there most of the week, meeting with a new client."

"So you think you can get next Monday off?" Alex asked.

"I suppose so. Why?"

"Because I was reading online that the London Symphony Orchestra is playing in Toronto that weekend. Flights are pretty reasonable, and I thought we could get away, go to a club or two..."

Ann's face brightened. "Really? Are you sure?"

"Uh-huh." Alex grinned slyly as he picked up a chicken leg. "I already made the reservations."

Paula flopped on the sofa, taking in the quiet of her apartment. Her cat sought her out immediately, jumping into her lap. "Hey, Maxie," she said affectionately. "Hungry?"

She carried the cat into the kitchen, grateful to see fresh water and food in his dishes. The rest of the kitchen, though, was a disaster: dirty dishes and unopened mail on the counter; clothes flung over the back of a chair. Walking into the bedroom, the scene was worse.

Putting on music, Paula started in the kitchen, stacking the dishwasher, wiping down the counter, throwing out the junk mail and putting the bills to be paid—a few of them marked "second notice"—in a pile for immediate attention. Her phone rang an hour later, just as she was pulling the sheets off her bed to change them.

"Hey! You're back!" Kelly squealed excitedly into the phone. "We're going out around nine, so will you meet us?"

Paula looked around the apartment, which she really needed to clean, and then thought about her friends she hadn't seen in a few days. Taking in a deep breath she centered herself. "Kelly, I'm staying in tonight. I'd like to get together with you sometime next week, but tonight I really have to take care of some things at home."

"Come on!" Kelly pleaded. "It's Saturday night. You can't stay in."

"Kelly, I'm beat, and I really need to be here. But I promise, I'll catch up with you later."

Paula hung up the phone, feeling Maxie's furry body against her ankles. "Don't worry," she laughed, picking up the cat and nuzzling him for a moment, before he squirmed to be put down again. "I'm staying put and taking care of business."

The apartment was cleaner and, although she still had a long way to go, she decided to take a break and get something to eat. Coming home from the Thai restaurant on the corner, where she'd ordered take-out, Paula groaned when her cell phone rang. It was another friend, asking her to come over. Again, Paula excused herself, saying she wanted to stay in and take care of things. Her friend sounded miffed when she hung up. Paula nearly called back but kept walking home.

She ate in the newly cleaned kitchen with music on the stereo and a cool breeze off the lake coming in the window. She'd get up early in the morning and run, Paula decided, as she rose from the table. If she and Dan were going to do the marathon next year, she'd better start training. The thought stirred the memory of her run up the hill... Paula looked at the phone. Dialing, she held her breath until someone answered.

"Hello, Mom? It's Paula," she began.

"Paula! This is a surprise. How are you?" Her mother's voice sounded warm, but cautious.

"Fine. Um, Mom, I know we haven't been talking a lot lately, but I just wanted to hear your voice."

"It's nice to hear your voice, too."

The silence on the line seemed to last for minutes, although it was only a second or two. "Okay, so this is difficult, but if you'll listen, I'll give you the short version. I was at a course for three days, for my company. And, while I was there I learned a bunch about myself. For instance, that I try to do too much stuff, and I don't finish anything that I start. Anyway, I learned all this, and I see how I haven't been on track in my life, and I just wanted to say that I know that."

"I'm glad, Paula. You know, you have a lot of potential, and you're not twenty-one any more."

Paula grimaced at the phone, but held her tongue. "I know, but I can't turn the clock back either. So, anyway, this isn't the time for a big discussion. Okay? But I'd like to come to see you and Dad sometime. Maybe in a few weeks."

"We'd like that," her mother replied. "I would like that very much."

Hanging up the phone, she washed her dishes and set them in the rack to dry. On her way to the living room, she passed the mirror in the hall. She stopped and looked closely at herself. Pointing at her reflection she said, "Tonight, I'm spending the evening with *you!*"

Monday morning came with a rush of activity, trains to catch and traffic to navigate. The Stellar Point Financial offices came alive early, as executives, managers, and staff people streamed in to start a new week.

Sarah brought flowers for her desk and a plastic container of salad for her lunch. At eight o'clock, the financial department was already busy when she arrived. She breezed through a small stack of messages and logged onto her computer.

"You're back!" Bernie Colletti said, stopping at her desk. "Let's see..." He stood back and looked her up and down. "You don't look like you've been brainwashed."

Sarah had expected this kind of reaction from him and reminded herself to keep centered. "Exactly, Bernie. I'd like to thank you for this experience. I have to say, this course far surpassed anything I could have imagined. I benefited so much from it."

Bernie's shoulders sagged. "Really? It wasn't some kind of mumbo-jumbo, get in touch with your woo-woo feelings thing?"

Sarah envisioned Martha's calm demeanor as she looked at him. Careful not to reveal too much about the program itself, she responded, "No, that wasn't my experience at all. Actually, it was very empowering for me. It helped me to see what I can do to make a difference in my life and in work and how I can be more effective in the future. I would love to talk with you more about what I learned about myself. I know that right now isn't a good time for either of us, but I would like to have about a half an hour of your time sometime today."

Bernie drew his eyebrows together in a quizzical expression. "Half an hour?" He hesitated. "Okay.... maybe late this afternoon."

"Good. I'll check with you later on to see when would be good. In the meantime, I'm sure that everything went smoothly while I was gone. Is there anything I have to take care of this morning?"

"No, everything is fine. We're crazy, of course, end of the third quarter coming up. But it's fine. Really good." He leaned over and lowered his voice. "Be honest with me. This thing, this course..."

"It was one of the most important things I've ever done in my life, and I'm so grateful that I was there. But right now isn't a good time to go into it, Bernie. I really want to talk with you more about it later. Will that work for you?"

"Okay," Bernie said cynically. "This is something I just gotta hear."

Paula arrived a half hour earlier than usual to go through her emails, carefully reading the comments and feedback from the other members of the marketing team. There was a note from Sylvia complimenting her on the design and wanting to discuss it with her.

Noticing Sylvia was in already, Paula walked over to her office and tapped lightly on the open door. "Got a minute?" she asked.

"Hi, Paula. Welcome back. So how was the course?"

"First of all, thank you. It was amazing. I'd like to tell you more about it, but first I have some other things to share with you."

"Please, I'm all yours."

Paula shut the door and took a seat opposite Sylvia's desk. "Again, I want to thank you for selecting me to go. It was very enlightening, to say the least. I learned more about myself in those three days than I have in twenty-eight years."

"Really? That's terrific. I'm glad it was valuable to you." Sylvia sat back in her chair and smiled.

"But that's not what I want to talk to you about," Paula continued. "I saw your note this morning. I'm glad you liked the design."

"Yes, I thought it was good. We'll have some changes, of course, but I thought it was a great start."

"It was almost a week late, Sylvia. We both know that. And as good as it was—and it was good—the truth is we both know that it could have been better, that I am capable of doing more. I have blown deadlines, done jobs halfway, cut corners, and made a lot of excuses. I've also ticked off more than a few people who have had to wait for me to get my act together so they could move ahead. I'm sorry for that."

Sylvia leaned forward, nodding slowly. "I appreciate that, Paula," she said quietly.

"I have a lot of potential, Sylvia, but I'm not utilizing it. I know how to get by, but that's not good enough anymore. I want to demonstrate to you—and to myself—just what I can do. This won't happen overnight, and I'm sure I'll be tempted to fall back into my old habits. But I am going to set strict deadlines for myself, and I am holding myself accountable. I'd like you to hold me accountable too."

"It will be my pleasure. You are very, very talented, Paula. I've always liked your work, you know that, and I do know that you're capable of more."

Paula grinned broadly. "Well, seeing is believing, and I am going to show you just what I can do."

Alex set his briefcase under his desk and logged onto his computer. A list of emails popped into his "inbox," but none of them seemed urgent. He started to type a response but quickly deleted it. Instead, he walked across the room to a cubicle where a man worked busily at the keyboard.

Alex cleared his throat. "Excuse me, Frank?"

Frank looked up, slightly surprised.

"Do you have a minute? I'd like to talk with you."

"I was just working on this program." He looked back at Alex.

"It's important, Frank. There's something I'd like to clear up with you if you could give me a few minutes."

Frank saved his work, stopped typing, and swiveled his chair around. "Okay," he said, bracing himself.

Alex wheeled a chair over from another cubicle and sat down facing Frank. "Listen, we've been at odds with each other for a while now," Alex began.

The look of caution on Frank's face was unmistakable. "Well, we've disagreed…"

"The truth is I haven't listened to you, Frank," Alex forged on. "I know you have a lot of ideas, and yes, they are sometimes different from mine. But different doesn't mean bad. I want to know more about your views, particularly for the database management programs. So I'd like to call a meeting of the tech team this afternoon. I want you and everybody to bring their thoughts on how we can improve."

"Sure, Alex. I mean, that's great."

"I want this to be a real team, not just a bunch of people doing their own thing." He imagined the alignment graphic in his head and reached for piece of paper on Frank's desk. "May I?" he asked, pointing to the paper. Frank nodded. Alex drew a rough diagram of a big wobbly arrow and one big straight arrow. He filled the wobbly one in with little arrows going in different directions and the straight one with little arrows aligned. "I want us to be here," he said, tapping the straight arrow with his pencil, "individual arrows all pointing in the same direction."

Frank looked at the simple picture. "That seems good to me."

Leaving Frank's cubicle, Alex saw Maureen in the doorway of her office, watching him. He walked over to her, meeting her gaze as he did. "So how are you?" she asked.

"Great," Alex said, following Maureen into her office. "I was just talking with Frank. I'm calling a team meeting for this afternoon to discuss the database management programs. Frank has a lot of ideas, and, well, I know I haven't really listened to him. But I want to put all the ideas out on the table. We'll look at them all and come up with the best solution."

Maureen nodded. "Sounds terrific. So tell me, what brought about this change? A few days ago you were complaining about Frank."

Alex suppressed a wince. "Yeah, I know. Let's just say I understand that one person can't have all the answers. I, uh, recently learned that."

"So the course was valuable?"

Alex scratched his head and raised his eyebrows. "In a word, yes. I'll admit I was skeptical. Actually, I was more than skeptical; I was downright critical. But I've really changed my outlook on things."

Maureen gave him a smile. "I'm glad for you, Alex. You deserve it."

Alex pointed out to the desks and cubicles behind him. "So do they."

Dan's first stop in the office was Tim's desk, where he was hunched over a report. "There's the man!" Dan called out.

Tim jumped a little at Dan's voice. "Well, you told me what to say..."

"No way. This was yours, Tim. I think it's great. In fact, I'd like you to take the lead on the Johnson account. You've established the relationship with them. I'll be glad to support you, but I know you can do this."

Tim's coworkers, their expressions ranging from dismay to pleasant surprise, glanced from one to the other. "We're having a meeting this morning," Dan called out, as they gathered around. "How about eleven? Does that work for everybody? Good. Bring your ideas. I want this to be a real brainstorming session."

Dan arrived at the conference room ten minutes ahead of time and purposefully took a seat in the middle of the table. As his team filed in one by one, they took places around the table. Tim was the last to arrive. He took the last seat at the head of the table.

"So, how's it going?" Dan asked.

No one spoke up. Tim looked around, then offered: "It's fine. Everything's okay."

Dan laughed. "What I mean is, how can we work together better as a team? Every person in this room is an intelligent and highly capable individual. I want to tap the talents and abilities of this team to really make a difference to our department and to this company. As you know I've been away at a course. I've come to realize how my leadership style was getting in the way of all of us operating as a team, and I am committed to change my ways and to empower you. So, I'm here to listen."

The mood in the room began to shift. Slowly, ideas were offered, opinions were shared. When a question was asked, all heads turned toward Dan. "I think..." he began, and then he stopped himself. Shrugging his shoulders he added, "You know I'm not sure. I want to hear what you think about this." The discussion continued, getting louder and livelier as each person added his or her views without any interruptions or corrections from Dan.

At twelve-thirty, with the team's agreement, Dan stepped out of the meeting and asked one of the assistants if he wouldn't mind ordering in lunch for them. They were on a roll, and he didn't want to interrupt the flow. On his way back into the meeting, Dan passed Peter in the hallway.

"Team meeting," Dan said.

"Good," Peter nodded.

"No, I mean a real team meeting, the kind where they talk and I listen."

Peter grinned. "That's even better."

When the meeting ended, Dan returned to his office, and there he found a FedEx package sitting on top of his desk. He looked at the return address; it was from his brother. Opening the box, Dan pulled out the note first.

"I was cleaning out the attic this weekend when I came across this. I saw your name on it; I thought you might like to have it."

Wrapped in brown paper was a baseball glove, the same glove he had used in high school. His name was written across the palm. Inside the glove was a baseball, old and worn, signed by all of his teammates. They had given it to him after he made the hit that drove in the winning run.

Dan slipped the glove on. It still fit.

Martha's phone rang a week later. She recognized the voice immediately. "Hello, Jack! I've been hoping to hear from you."

"You did it!" he exclaimed.

"No, Jack, not I. The four people you sent did it. They are out-standing individuals, committed to making changes in their lives. It was an honor to work with them."

"Everybody is buzzing about it. In fact, my VPs actually came up to me asking all kinds of questions about the course."

"I'm not surprised."

"I'd like my whole company to operate with those eight principles. Are you ready to take us on?"

"It will be my pleasure."

It was a cold evening in November when the first cars arrived at the lodge. The trees were bare, stripped of their leaves, and a strong wind rippled the grass in the meadow. A warm and welcoming fire crackled in the fireplace in the Great Room. There was no one in the lodge to greet them, but everything had been prearranged. On a table opposite the fireplace were five envelopes, with each person's name on them: Peter, Sylvia, Maureen, Bernie, and Jack. Inside was a key to their rooms and an invitation to help themselves to food and beverages in the kitchen. There was also a note with instructions for the evening. It said, "Your assignment for tonight is to DO nothing. Just BE…"

❖ Part II:

On the Playing Field

How Do the Eight Principles Show Up in Your Work Environment?

After reading the story of Dan, Paula, Sarah, and Alex and their experiences with the eight principles, in this section you will reflect on what you've learned through the fable and learn how to apply these insights in your work environment and in your life. As the story demonstrates, the eight principles provide a solid foundation for more aligned, empowered, and accountable teams of individuals. Very few teams, however, start out this way. As talented and experienced as team members and leaders may be, most people are operating with old, unconscious, and ineffective beliefs and behaviors that are based on survival thinking. In this section, you'll assess your team's (or company's) strengths as well as the areas that need further development.

Assessment I: My Team's Current Context

Every team is different. You might be part of a team within a large company, or part of a small business where your entire workforce is a team. Each has particular strengths as well as undermining behaviors. Although there are many conditions that lead to greater effectiveness, the basic attitudes of your team members are the most critical. *Your Survival Strategies Are Killing You!* emphasizes the importance of having solid, grounded, and empowering operating principles as the foundation of all human interaction.

Each person's operating principles (beliefs, attitudes, values, and priorities) lead to behaviors, and behaviors produce results. The following questions will serve as a valuable diagnostic tool for identifying the profile of your team's current context. The results will show how successfully your team is demonstrating the eight principles and will identify the areas in need of development as you support your team to continually raise the bar and thrive.

For leaders: Have every member of your team (including your-self) complete the following assessment. (If they read the book first, the questions will likely have more meaning.) After the results are calculated, you will have a good idea how your individual team members assess the behaviors and attitudes of the entire team. You will know which of the eight principles are working well within your team, department, and/or company, and which ones need to be reinforced.

Note: If assessments are kept anonymous, you will likely receive more honest feedback.

For individuals: After you tabulate your own assessment of the team's behaviors, identify the areas that need your support the most. Using the eight principles as your guide, identify what you want to change about your own behaviors so that you can be more effective when contributing and supporting others.

To the participant: It is important that you answer as truthfully as you can. Mark each statement as you think it really is on your team (not how you would wish, want, or hope it to be or how you'd like others to think it is). Do not belabor each question. Just trust your initial, "gut" response, the part of you that knows and tells the truth.

Mark each statement:

5 = Always
4 = Most of the time
3 = Sometimes
2 = Not very often
1 = Never

1) _____ Team members have a high degree of honesty. They can be trusted to be transparent and always tell the truth. They don't put a "spin" on things.

2) _____ Team members have a high degree of integrity. They do what they say they're going to do and keep their promises, agreements, commitments, and agreed upon goals.

3) _____ Team members view change as learning opportunities, and they readily adjust.

4) _____ Everyone holds each other accountable for achieving goals and keeping agreements.

5) _____ Team members consistently seek to understand the impact of decisions on all key people before acting.

6) _____ Team members are able to "go with the flow" even in very difficult, challenging situations.

7) _____ Team members stay on course even in the face of adversity, turmoil, problems, and breakdowns.

8) _____ Team members frequently acknowledge each other's success and regularly reinforce each other.

9) _____ This team can be counted on to share information honestly. There is no covering up or sense that anything is being withheld.

10) _____ Team members discuss their mistakes and weaknesses openly and freely with a clear intention to learn, grow, and act honorably.

11) _____ Team members actively invite input from others and listen with serious intent; they actively include others in key decisions and listen to differing views with genuine interest.

12) _____ On this team people don't hold grudges, blame others or complain.

13) _____ Team members cultivate open, trusting relationships with people at all levels throughout the organization, actively develop connections with other teams and departments, and look for ways to work together.

14) _____ When faced with obstacles and challenges, team members consistently find a way around them.

15) _____ Team members feel safe and openly and directly raise issues, even in uncomfortable situations, in pursuit of success of a goal.

16) _____ Team members show a great deal of sensitivity and care about one another's lives, feel affection and warmth toward one another, and actively support one another personally.

17) _____ On this team, if people don't understand something, they ask questions. They don't try to fake it and pretend they know.

18) _____ I have full confidence that my team members are always genuine in their commitment to decisions we make and that there will be good follow-through.

19) _____ Team members regularly accept honest communications and feedback in a constructive way and are willing to shift their thinking to support the overall goal.

20) _____Everyone regularly operates at a level of peak performance and carries their own weight; no one is just "gliding along."

21) _____Team members frequently experience a sense of unity (one for all and all for one) even if there are differences of opinion.

22) _____On this team people are willing to let go of the past and how things "used to be" and are open to new ways.

23) _____All team members are fully aligned with and loyal to this team. This is their primary team, and they don't split their allegiance with other teams.

24) _____Team members are willing to go beyond their personal approval needs to give constructive feedback that can support another person.

25) _____Team members are genuine in their intent to support others. There's no underlying agenda.

26) _____On this team people proactively keep each other informed if there are problems or delays achieving a goal.

27) _____On this team there are no power struggles. People don't take positions or build armies to be right.

28) _____On this team people don't take feedback personally or complain that people or life isn't fair; there are no victims.

29) _____On this team people take responsibility to set and keep personal boundaries; they let their needs be known by making respectful requests.

30) _____On this team people don't perpetuate problems; they actively look for solutions.

31) _____Team members regularly experiment, take risks, and "push the envelope" beyond the boundaries of current expectations.

32) _____Everyone communicates honestly, yet in ways that leave others feeling empowered and good about themselves.

33) _____Team members can be counted on not to participate in gossip or spread rumors.

34) _____On this team everyone pays attention to starting and ending meetings on time. Goals and projects are completed on time.

35) _____On this team individuals feel safe to express their reservations and opinions and to risk stepping "outside the box" with creative thinking.

36) _____Team members take full accountability for the success of the entire enterprise. Everyone recognizes their connection to organizational results.

37) _____This team looks out for each other and pays attention to the well-being of each team member. They willingly share ideas, information, support, resources, and credit for team and company accomplishment. There are no power "prima donnas."

38) _____On this team people are flexible, willing to adjust to change, and are genuinely happy and fulfilled.

39) _____On this team people are willing to do whatever it takes to get the desired results, even if it means major personal or organizational changes.

40) _____On this team people raise issues directly with the person with whom they have a problem. They don't complain, gossip, or talk about the person behind their back.

Scoring Assessment I: My Team's Current Context

Beside each number listed below, write in your assessment score for that corresponding question. For example, if you wrote "4" (most of the time) for statement #10, you would record a score as follows: 10) 4.

Principle #1	Principle #2	Principle #3	Principle #4
Tell the Truth. Period.	*Do What You Said...*	*How's the View?...*	*Got Results?*
1) _____	2) _____	3) _____	4) _____
9) _____	10) _____	11) _____	12) _____
17) _____	18) _____	19) _____	20) _____
25) _____	26) _____	27) _____	28) _____
33) _____	34) _____	35) _____	36) _____
Total_____	Total_____	Total_____	Total_____

Principle #5	Principle #6	Principle #7	Principle #8
Everybody Gets a Prize	*What's for Lunch?*	*Stick, Don't Quit*	*Breathe*
5) _____	6) _____	7) _____	8) _____
13) _____	14) _____	15) _____	16) _____
21) _____	22) _____	23) _____	24) _____
29) _____	30) _____	31) _____	32) _____
37) _____	38) _____	39) _____	40) _____
Total_____	Total_____	Total_____	Total_____

Now total all your scores for each column.

If you scored:

20 - 25	Your team likely does not have a problem with this principle.
17 - 19	Your team is doing fairly well with this principle and needs to be vigilant.
13 - 16	Your team needs definite improvement in this principle.
10 - 12	Your team needs to do a lot of work in this principle.
9 or less	What team?

For Leaders: Select the three principles that had the lowest score and identify the questions that correlate with that principle. Discuss each one with your team and brainstorm the best course of action for improvement.

For Individuals: Select the three principles that had the lowest score and ask yourself, "What do I need to change about myself in this area so that I can effectively contribute to team success?"

For more work on Principle #1 – *Tell the Truth. Period.*,
please refer to page 28.

For more work on Principle #2 – *Do What You Said You Would*,
please refer to page 34.

For more work on Principle #3 – *How's the View from Your View?*,
please refer to page 86.

For more work on Principle #4 – *Got Results?*
please refer to page 125.

For more work on Principle #5 – *Everybody Gets a Prize*,
please refer to page 153.

For more work on Principle #6 – *So, What's for Lunch?*,
please refer to page 184.

For more work on Principle #7 – *Stick, Don't Quit!*,
please refer to page 203.

For more work on Principle #8 – *Breathe*,
please refer to page 221.

Action Plan for Leaders
For a Principle-Driven Team

Enlightened leaders affirm and model a corporate culture that is proactive, empowering, and accountable. The implementation of any corporate strategy, however, is ultimately in the hands of your people. How your people conduct themselves is completely determined by the context of your culture. The moral, social, and behavioral norms of your organization, which are based on the principles (attitudes, beliefs, values, and priorities) of its members, will ultimately determine if your "best laid plans" go awry or fly!

The clear and empowered principles of your people lead to decisive action, bring alignment to teams, build collaboration, and help people to focus on what to do, how to do it, and what is important now. Your company will thrive when your people are principle-driven, united, focused, and possess an attitude of success.

As the leader, it is your responsibility to set and maintain the context of the organization's culture.

What to Do - Step One

- Starting with the Senior Executive Team, enroll all levels of leadership in on-site or off-site Culture Context workshops.
- Institute the eight principles as your corporate operating principles.

It is also the leader's role to integrate these eight principles throughout the organization and maintain an environment that continually supports them.

What to Do - Step Two

- Have all employees participate in Culture Context workshops so they are "enrolled in," not "sold on," the eight principles as their own operating principles. When they personally experience the eight principles at work, they are empowered to choose the paradigm shift themselves, and they will be more likely to choose to adopt, practice, and endorse them as their own.

- Have all employees read *Your Survival Strategies are Killing You!*

- Have HR distribute *Your Survival Strategies are Killing You!* as part of an orientation for new hires.

- Purchase the companion workbook, *Your Survival Strategies Are Killing You! Your Guidebook on How to THRIVE, Not Just Survive,* for all your employees. Use the *Guidebook* for discussion groups, team meetings, employee development, or "lunch and learn" programs.

How Do You Personally Score with the Eight Principles? Assessment II: My Personal Current Context

The eight principles which lead to more empowered and account-able teams at work, will also serve to enrich your personal life, es-pecially in areas that are most important to you. In this section, an assessment of your Personal Current Context (similar to the team assessment in the previous section) will help you assess your own strengths as well as your developmental needs.

To the participant: It is important that you answer as truthfully as you can. Mark each statement according to how you think you re-ally are or how you really think (not how you wish, want, or hope you are, or how you'd like others to think you are). Do not belabor each question. Just trust your initial, "gut" response, the part of you that knows and tells the truth.

Mark each statement:

5 = Frequently

3 = Sometimes

1 = Rarely

1) _____ I tend to twist or change the facts to protect myself from embarrassment or criticism.

2) _____ No matter how hard I try, I have difficulty being on time for appointments, meetings, and social engagements.

3) _____ When someone gives me critical feedback, I react defen-sively.

4) _____ When I am unhappy, I find myself thinking "if this person would just change" or "if only this situation was different," I would feel much better.

5) _____ Because I don't want to bother others, I won't ask for help even if I really need it.

6) _____ In my job and when I am with certain people, I feel as though I'm swimming upstream against the current.

7) _____ I have difficulty finishing projects I have started.

8) _____ I find myself keeping score with what I do for others and what they do for me.

9) _____ I'm an expert at covering up some of the facts, especially if it helps me get my own way.

10) _____ I have difficulty saying "no' to people even though I know I may not be able to get it done.

11) _____ I tend to play it safe.

12) _____ I often feel powerless to change my feelings and the situations around me.

13) _____ I think it's a dog-eat-dog world and you've got to do everything you can to win.

14) _____ I hold on to resentments for a long time.

15) _____ When I don't get the desired result, I often feel that it's because of circumstances beyond my control.

16) _____ When someone compliments me, I tend to reject it.

17) _____ I am timid and shy about expressing myself and keep a lot inside.

18) _____ When a project becomes tedious, repetitious, or too difficult, I let it go and find something else to do.

19) _____ People who know me would describe me as stubborn.

20) _____ I think a lot of negative things that have happened to me are a result of "bad luck."

21) _____ I'm very competitive, and I find myself frequently trying to be better than the next guy.

22) _____ I get frustrated when people keep doing what they shouldn't be doing and refuse to change their ways.

23) _____ I can easily get distracted and lose focus.

24) _____ Friends and colleagues would say that I need to give more compliments.

25) _____ I am good at using manipulation for getting what I want.

26) _____ Because I have trouble saying "no," I take on too much, become overwhelmed, and then don't fully deliver.

27) _____ When I see things that don't fit my paradigm, my immediate reaction is often judgment or rejection.

28) _____ I often feel upset, frustrated, used, or manipulated in my job.

29) _____ Friends and colleagues would describe me as someone who likes a good fight.

30) _____ My friends and colleagues would say that I am fairly critical.

31) _____ When faced with a challenge, I begin to doubt myself and start to see why it can't be done.

32) _____ If someone is rude to me, I am likely to be rude as well.

Scoring Assessment II: My Personal Current Context

Beside each number listed below, write in your assessment score for the corresponding question. For example, if you wrote "3" (sometimes) for statement #10, you would record a score as follows: 10) 3.

Principle #1	Principle #2	Principle #3	Principle #4
Tell the Truth.	*Do What*	*How's the*	*Got Results?*
Period.	*You Said...*	*View?...*	
1) ____	2) ____	3) ____	4) ____
9) ____	10) ____	11) ____	12) ____
17) ____	18) ____	19) ____	20) ____
25) ____	26) ____	27) ____	28) ____
Total____	Total____	Total____	Total____

Principle #5	Principle #6	Principle #7	Principle #8
Everybody	*What's for*	*Stick, Don't Quit*	*Breathe*
Gets a Prize	*Lunch?*		
5) ____	6) ____	7) ____	8) ____
13) ____	14) ____	15) ____	16) ____
21) ____	22) ____	23) ____	24) ____
29) ____	30) ____	31) ____	32) ____
Total____	Total____	Total____	Total____

Now total all of your scores for that column.

If you scored:

15 - 20　You need to take a long, hard look at yourself with this principle.

12 - 16　You need definite improvement on this principle.

8 - 11　You are doing fairly well with this principle and you need to be vigilant.

7 or less　You do not have a problem with this principle.

My Commitment to Myself

The following tool will help you stay on track by identifying and clarifying the specific areas of growth and support necessary to meet your goals. In this section you have the opportunity to take a stand for your future and state your commitment to yourself. By doing so you will be empowered to move beyond survival and truly thrive.

Complete the following statements:

The three main principles that I know I most need to work on are these:

The short-term payoffs (benefits to me) I get when I don't practice these principles:

The internal and external long-term prices that I (and others) pay when I don't practice these principles:

What I need to do differently:

The short-term prices (difficulties for me) will be as follows:

The long-term payoffs (benefits) to me (and others) will be these:

Using the Commitment Chart on p. 207, "My level of commitment to make these changes and actively practice these principles is a _____."

The reason why it is/isn't a +7:

How I might sabotage this commitment:

What I know I must do when I start to hear those self-sabotaging voices:

To gain a deeper understanding of yourself and for more tools to enhance your professional and personal life, see the companion workbook, *Your Survival Strategies Are Killing You! Guidebook on How to THRIVE.* (For more information on the *Guidebook* visit the web site at www.MarthaBorst.com).

Choose Your Culture Context

As we come to the end of our journey together, it is time to turn it all over to you. Your company's culture may fall into one (or more) of many structural forms: for example, start-up, relational, hierarchical, short-term or long-term, individual or community-focused. Regardless of the structure of the culture, when it comes to the context, you play an important role.

As a leader: You may have considerable authority and influence over the cultural norms of your organization. Consider your choices carefully.

As an individual: You may not have the authority to change the structure of a corporate culture; however, your behaviors and personal operating principles (beliefs, attitudes, values, and priorities) will always have a powerful influence on the context of your organization as well as on the environment around you.

The two personal and professional Cultural Contexts you have to choose from are "Collaboration/Thriving" and "Command and Control/Surviving:"

Collaboration/Thriving	Command and Control/Surviving
1) I operate from abundance. There is more than enough.	1) I operate from scarcity. There is not enough.
2) I operate with integrity and honesty. I do what I say I will, and I tell the truth as I know it.	2) I manipulate my agreements. I shade the truth and say and do whatever I want to suit my needs. I lie.
3) I accept things/people/events exactly as they are.	3) I am judgmental and think my judgments are the TRUTH.

4) I see things as being my perception only.

4) I believe I own the TRUTH.

5) I play "I Win/You Win." I look for solutions that work for everyone. I believe that at the core, we are all equal.

5) I play "I Win/You Lose" or "I Lose/You Win," Right/Wrong–Better/Less, Good/Bad–Superior/Inferior.

6) I take full accountability for the results around me without judgment—with no obligation, blame, or burden.

6) When things don't go my way, I blame others or outside circumstances, OR I become a victim of myself and I feel guilty.

7) I operate with courage and commitment.

7) I leave things up to chance and luck. I hope things will work out.

8) I am proactive. I think ahead.

8) I am reactive.

9) I am outwardly focused.

9) I am focused just on myself.

10) My actions generate connection, respect, and unity.

10) My actions generate separation.

11) I take a stand FOR something.

11) I maintain a position AGAINST something.

12) I am cooperative and a healthy competitor. I look for ways to work with others for mutual benefit.

12) I compete without rules or values. I look for ways to beat others, seeing it as their loss and my gain.

13) I am willing to take risks and trust the process.

13) I hold back and I am suspicious.

14) I have personal power. My choices direct my life.

14) I am powerless. My circumstances direct my life.

15) Agape LOVE and conscious TRUST drive my thoughts, choices, and actions.

15) FEAR and DISTRUST drive my thoughts, choices, and actions.

16) I choose the path of spiritual aliveness.

16) I choose the path of the self-righteous ego.

17) I/WE THRIVE

17) I/WE just SURVIVE.

Neither choice is right or wrong. They are just different ways of living life and conducting business. Each culture context can produce extraordinary monetary results. Each offers its own road to achievement. Now it's up to you to decide which paradigm works for you. Which one will give you the results you want and the experience you are looking for? Which one represents the kind of person you choose to be? One is the path of the Sage; the other is of the Survivor.

The choice is yours. It always has been.

A Different World

"We cannot, with integrity deny our responsibility for
stewardship of every part of the whole."
Scott Peck, author
The Road Less Traveled

Conscious members of society now realize that *"If we keep doing what we're doing in this world, we'll continue to have what we have."* Given the current state of human affairs and the condition of our fragile planet, that is concerning news. Operating with "kill or be killed—it's a jungle out there" as our current context, we are doomed to extinction. To create different results we must think and act differently. The time has come to fully utilize our God-given, inborn power of reason to elevate our thinking to a higher plane.

I ask you to carefully consider these questions:

If each of us embraced the eight principles and committed ourselves to live and express the beliefs and behaviors of honesty, integrity, accountability, win/win, acceptance, commitment, and agape love, would we have a different workplace? Would we operate differently within our families, neighborhoods, and communities and would that make a difference?

If we realized that commerce and a commitment to conscious awareness aren't mutually exclusive, would this affect our state, our country, our continent? If corporations, government leaders, and we, as individuals, took responsibility for our environmental footprint and the health and well-being of the community in which we live and work, is it possible that we could have a different world?

Can we afford to sit back and shake our heads at the state of affairs around us when we are capable of making great change?

Reflect on those who didn't. Think of Ghandi, Martin Luther King, Mother Teresa, just to name a few. Better yet, think about Rosa Parks who defied the rules of segregation and launched the civil right movement in America. Consider Candy Lightner who founded MADD when her thirteen-year-old daughter was killed by a hit-and-run driver. Bring to mind the heroes of Flight 93 whose courageous sacrifice likely saved the lives of countless numbers of people. Remember your favorite high school teacher or coach or someone in your personal past whom you admired and respected. World famous or not, they were all just people—like you and I. The reason they stand out, however, is because they played a bigger game. If you examine their lives carefully, you will see that their thoughts, actions, and deeds exemplified the eight principles.

If we are to truly survive as a species and thrive as a society, we must shift from a *Survival of the Fittest* context to one that supports *Survival of the Wisest,* because

Only the Wise Will Thrive

What Can You Do?

- Become active in your community, whether through a civic group, nonprofit organization, your religion, or other institutions.

- Choose a problem that resonates with you, something that you would like to change or improve. Take actions that reflect your commitment to influence the situation. Give of your time, talent, and resources in real ways.

- Write letters. Enroll others in the causes you champion.

- Vote. If you do not exercise your voice in the governing of your community, state, and country, you are giving tacit approval to the status quo. Be accountable yourself and expect accountability from your local, state, and national leaders.

- Make sure your actions—what you say and what you do—reflect the eight principles. Ask yourself truthfully: do I harbor negativity in my heart or am I a champion for positive interactions with others? (Aggression and isolation do not happen only some place else; they occur everywhere, from highways to hallways when we act negatively toward each other.) In your thoughts and attitudes ask yourself, do I see others who are different and think of them as being wrong or inferior? Or do I approach others with an open mind? Am I always honest, keeping my word no matter what, or do I shade the truth when I'm afraid of embarrassment or when it is more convenient for me?

- Change does not happen "out there." It begins "right here" with you.

"There can never be peace between nations until there is first known that true peace, which is within the souls of men."

– Black Elk, Native American Leader
(ca. 1863-1950)

About the Author

Photograph by Rick Tang

Martha Borst has enjoyed a highly successful twenty-eight-year career as a business owner, executive coach, corporate consultant, and facilitator working with close to 20,000 individuals. In her corporate workshops and personal development seminars, she has worked with CEOs and fast-track executives, entrepreneurs, writers, students, stay-at-home parents, and people in career transition.

Currently she is President of Avista Consulting Group Inc., a management-consulting firm that provides a systematic, integrated approach to organization effectiveness and culture change through professional consulting, executive coaching, and leadership/team development programs.

Martha's extensive organizational development and facilitation background is grounded in personal experience. Despite daunting challenges and significant physical limitations of crippling rheumatoid arthritis, she has started up and sold four successful companies. This experience gives her first-hand knowledge of human dynamics, the organizational challenges that every senior executive and manager faces, and the ability of all people to overcome any obstacle or circumstance to achieve success. Working with Fortune 100 companies as well as startup organizations, she knows the requirements, differences, and demands of a variety of corporate cultures.

Born and brought up on a farm in rural Massachusetts, where she learned to appreciate and respect nature, Martha has returned to the land she loves. She owns a small vineyard in the wine country of northern California where, on her days off, she enjoys sharing her time with close friends and family.

For more information on Martha Borst, her courses, and her books—including the companion workbook, *Your Survival Strategies Are Killing You! Guidebook on How to THRIVE*, visit her web site at www.MarthaBorst.com.

State of the Art Workshops

Experience Martha delivering the incredible *Your Survival Strategies Are Killing You!* **Workshop** and give your employees the tools they need to thrive! Also available are many other dynamic, fresh, new experiential workshops that give participants a practical, refreshing and empowering way to increase professional effectiveness. All workshops will be custom designed for your specific needs.

Executive Leadership Coaching

As your executive coach, Martha's primary concern will be to help you develop excellence in your world of influence. As your dedicated partner and mentor, she will assist you to find a new and more empowering way to look at things. Work personally with Martha and gain the guidance and coaching you need to make the skillful executive decisions that serve you and your organization.

Organizational Consulting

Working in partnership with her clients, Martha builds strong, vigorous leadership teams to have an aligned organizational vision, and designs dynamic cultures that thrive with a clear and compelling purpose grounded in personal responsibility. She specializes in culture design and transformation, change management, conflict resolution, leadership development, team building, self-mastery, and peak performance.

Public Speaking

Martha challenges existing paradigms, wakes people up, inspires them to raise the bar and opens new possibilities for effective change. Entertaining and fun, she combines a no-nonsense approach with humor, illustrative stories, interactive experiential exercises, exceptional and inspiring videos and time for audience interaction and questions.

Contact: martha@marthaborst.com   *Visit:* www.marthaborst.com

Coming Soon

The Guidebook on How To Thrive is a personal manual designed to help you deepen your understanding of yourself and your behaviors. It will support you to personally and professionally practice and live the Eight Principles so that you will *Thrive* not just survive in your life and workplace. It will also serve as a practical team building tool giving a multitude of tips and examples of ways to powerfully and positively interact in practical work related situations. It includes:

- Ecercises
- Questions to answer
- Quizes
- Personality and Behavior Characteristics Assessment
- Case studies showing workable and unworkable results
- And much, much more.

The Guidebook on How To Thrive is perfect for the leader who wants to develop his/her team and for individuals who are interested in taking themselves to their next level of growth.

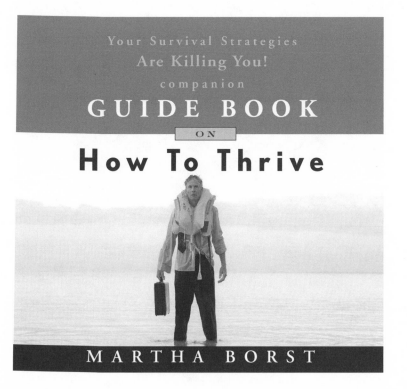

Your Survival Strategies
Are Killing You!
companion
GUIDE BOOK
ON
How To Thrive
MARTHA BORST